Reality

Reality

*From Metaphysics
to Metapolitics*

Wynand de Beer

RESOURCE *Publications* • Eugene, Oregon

REALITY
From Metaphysics to Metapolitics

Copyright © 2019 Wynand de Beer. All rights reserved. Except for brief quotations in critical publications or reviews, no part of this book may be reproduced in any manner without prior written permission from the publisher. Write: Permissions, Wipf and Stock Publishers, 199 W. 8th Ave., Suite 3, Eugene, OR 97401.

Resource Publications
An Imprint of Wipf and Stock Publishers
199 W. 8th Ave., Suite 3
Eugene, OR 97401

www.wipfandstock.com

PAPERBACK ISBN: 978-1-5326-8645-0
HARDCOVER ISBN: 978-1-5326-8646-7
EBOOK ISBN: 978-1-5326-8647-4

Manufactured in the U.S.A.   09/12/19

Dedicated to Ludmila

Contents

Foreword | ix
Abbreviations | xii

The Indo-European Background | 1
Being and Non-being | 9
Metaphysical and Physical | 23
Mind and Motion | 33
Intellect and Necessity | 44
Soul and Matter | 53
Levels of Being | 65
Well-being and Love | 73
Good and Evil | 81
Truth and Knowledge | 91
Time and Eternity | 108
Death and Immortality | 118
Consciousness | 135
Man and Woman | 164
Aristocracy and Democracy | 177
Freedom and Liberalism | 217

Bibliography | 241
Index | 247

Foreword

WHAT IS METAPHYSICS? THE term is derived from the Greek phrase *meta ta physika*, which means 'after the physics'. It first appeared as the title of a collection of writings by the Hellenic philosopher Aristotle, which followed upon his writings on physical phenomena.[1] Extrapolating therefrom, we could say that the metaphysical follows upon the physical. In other words, if the physical denotes the reality here and now, then the metaphysical indicates those realities beyond the here and now. The metaphysical therefore includes the invisible and intangible realities denoted by terms such as God, the One, Spirit, Intellect, the Logos, the Forms, and Soul.

What is metapolitics? In view of the previous paragraph, it makes sense to state that metapolitics stands in the same relation to politics as metaphysics stands in relation to physics. We could therefore say that from a metapolitical perspective one views the political world 'from above,' just as from a metaphysical perspective one views the physical world 'from above.' It should be self-evident that metapolitics has nothing to do with the ridiculous spectacle of party-politics, just as metaphysics has nothing to do with the futile practice of armchair philosophizing. On the contrary, both metaphysics and metapolitics are crucially important issues, dealing as they do with the nature of reality and how human societies should be ordered according to its precepts, respectively.

In the first part of the book, we draw a distinction between that which exists, or being, and that which does not exist, or non-being. Within the realm of being, we then differentiate between its various levels of reality. It may be asked whether an investigation is really needed to distinguish the

---

1. The term 'Hellenic' is more accurate than the customary 'ancient Greek,' since these people referred to themselves as Hellenes and to their culture as Hellenic. The term 'Greek' came to be applied to the Hellenes by their Roman conquerors, through whose Latin language it entered other European languages. However, for the sake of convention we will use 'Greek' when referring to the Hellenic language as well as to the Christian theologians writing in it.

real from the unreal and the more real from the less real. This question must be answered in the affirmative, given the preponderance of misconceptions among human beings.[2] For example, there are many who view the material world as the only reality, while it is actually the lowest level of reality. In addition, just as there are different levels of reality, so there are different levels of perception thereof. And since we are living in a world in which semantic confusion, conceptual obfuscation, and deliberate distortion of the truth are all-pervasive (especially at the hands of the mass media), we will also consider this issue pertaining to the knowledge of reality.[3]

In the second part, we touch upon various philosophical and theological themes in the light of the preceding metaphysical discussion on the nature of reality. As before, we discuss these issues from a combined Hellenic and Patristic perspective.[4] They include well-being and love, time and eternity, good and evil, truth and knowledge, and the most vital issue of all—the survival of the soul beyond bodily death, as the only kind of immortality that humans may attain.

In the third and final part, we subject some salient aspects of the Western socio-cultural phenomenon known as 'political correctness' to critical scrutiny. In the process, these ideologically driven and media-promoted 'isms' (including liberalism, feminism, and globalism) are contrasted with both Hellenic and Christian political philosophy (as presented by Plato, Aristotle, and St Augustine) and the penetrating writings of a range of traditionalist and/or anti-modernist thinkers from different parts of the world, including Friedrich Nietzsche, Oswald Spengler, Francis Parker Yockey, Alexander Dugin, and Nicolas Laos.[5]

---

2. Therefore, the scientific name for the human species, *Homo sapiens* (Latin, 'wise man'), ought to be viewed as one of the grandest misnomers in intellectual history.

3. A pertinent example of media-instigated semantic confusion is the label of 'homophobia,' which is applied by the enforcers of political correctness to those who are unwilling to support homosexual marriages. This term is derived from the Greek words *homos*, meaning 'one and the same,' and *phobos*, meaning 'fear' (LSJ, 488, 764). Homophobia therefore literally means 'fear of the same,' which is utterly nonsensical.

4. The term 'Patristic' denotes the Greek and Latin theologians of the early Christian era, most of whom employed insights from Hellenic philosophy in their writings. The teachings of these theologians, generically referred to as Church Fathers, have remained normative in the Orthodox and Catholic traditions to this day.

5. In this context, 'anti-modernist' involves a rejection of the humanist and rationalist assumptions that underlie modernism, which manifested ideologically in projects to promote 'freedom' and 'equality.' These in turn culminated in the 'hard' totalitarianisms of communism and fascism, as well as the 'soft' yet surreptitious totalitarianism of liberalism.

FOREWORD

It is our sincere hope that this publication will contribute, however modestly, to serving the interests of the eternal Kingdom of truth and justice—the same Kingdom that was proclaimed by the God-man from Galilee around 2000 years ago.

Abbreviations

Scripture

Gen	Genesis
Matt	Matthew
Rom	Romans
Cor	Corinthians
Eph	Ephesians
Col	Colossians
Jas	James
Rev	Revelation

Ancient, Patristic, and Medieval Sources

Aristotle

Cat	Categories
De An	On the Soul
De Gen et Corr	On Generation and Corruption
GA	Generation of Animals
Nic Eth	Nicomachean Ethics
Met	Metaphysics
PA	Parts of Animals
Phys	Physics
Pol	Politics

Augustine

Conf	Confessions
De civ Dei	On the City of God against the Pagans

Basil of Caesarea

Hex — Homilies on the Hexaemeron

Dionysius

CH — Celestial Hierarchy
DN — Divine Names
MT — Mystical Theology

Eriugena

Per — Periphyseon

Plato

Pol — Politeia
Sym — Symposium
Theaet — Theaetetus
Tim — Timaeus

Proclus

Elem Theol — Elements of Theology

General

A.D. — Anno Domini
B.C. — Before Christ

Reference works

LSJ — Liddell, H. G., R. Scott & H. S. Jones. *A Greek-English Lexicon.*
OSB — *The Oxford Study Bible. Revised English Bible with the Apocrypha.*

The Indo-European Background

A COMMON ORIGIN HAS been ascribed to Indo-European humanity, dating back to its sojourn in the southern parts of the vast land known since medieval times as Russia, the name of which is derived from *Rus'* in Old East Slavic. More precisely, this people lived in the Pontic-Caspian steppe, adjacent to the northern shores of the Black and Caspian Seas. This location of the *Urheimat*, or ancestral homeland, of the prehistoric Indo-Europeans has been demonstrated on the grounds of historical linguistics, archaeology, quantitative analysis, and archaeogenetics. Other possible locations of the Indo-European *Urheimat* advanced by scholars include Central or Northern Europe, Northern Mesopotamia, and even the Arctic regions. However, none of these are as convincing as the Southern Russian hypothesis.[1]

What kind of culture did these original Indo-Europeans possess? A leading scholar in this area, the archaeologist and anthropologist Marija Gimbutas, has enumerated some of the features of their Kurgan culture, named after its burial mounds (singular, *kurgan* in Russian). These features include a patriarchal society, a class system, the existence of small tribal units ruled by powerful chieftains, a predominantly pastoral economy including horse breeding and plant cultivation, small villages and massive hillforts, and religious elements including a Sky/Sun god and a Thunder god.[2] Evidently, the early Indo-Europeans valued patriarchy, social differentiation, leadership, agriculture, communal defense, and nature-based religion.

---

1. Quiles and López-Menchero, *Grammar*, 58–66; Haudry, *Indo-Europeans*, 104–111.
2. Haudry, *Indo-Europeans*, 105–106.

Migrations and Languages

From their ancestral homeland on the steppe the Indo-Europeans ventured forth in successive waves, first westwards into Europe from around 3000 B.C. and then southwards into the Near East and the Indian subcontinent from around 2000 B.C. Through these migrations new cultures arose, such as the Corded Ware culture in Northern Europe and the Vedic culture in the Indian subcontinent. The western branch of the Indo-Europeans developed into the Germanic, Slavic, Baltic, Celtic, Italic, and Hellenic peoples, while the eastern branch unfolded as the Indo-Aryans of Iran and India. An offshoot of the western branch migrated south between the Black Sea and the Caspian Sea, eventually settling in Asia Minor where they became known as the Hittites.[3]

Due to these extensive migrations, the Proto-Indo-European language (abbreviated as PIE) of the Kurgan culture developed into the numerous Indo-European languages spoken or studied today, of which Sanskrit, Classical Greek, and Latin are the most venerable ones. That the European languages only developed after the arrival of the Indo-Europeans is suggested by the fact that Europe is hydronymously uniform – that is to say, the names of watercourses from the Baltic to Spain occur in an identical form. To this observation, Jean Haudry adds that differentiation into Proto-Baltic, Proto-Germanic, and Proto-Celtic only occurred later, so that the languages diverge at the same time as the different peoples come into existence. Arguing along similar lines, Francis Parker Yockey remarks that language is no barrier to the formation of a people. This is suggested by the fact that all existing Western languages appeared after the formation of their respective peoples.[4]

By juxtaposing the Kurgan hypothesis in archaeology with the Three-Stage theory in linguistics, the Spanish scholars Carlos Quiles and Fernando López-Menchero found that the deployment of the Indo-Europeans and their languages occurred in the following stages:

i. Between around 3500 and 3000 B.C. the Late Indo-European language (LIE) became differentiated into at least two dialects, namely southern (or Graeco-Aryan) and northern.

---

3. Wikipedia: Indo-European migrations; Campbell, *Race and Religion*, 9; King, *Origins*, 28–33.
4. Haudry, *Indo-Europeans*, 107; Yockey, *Imperium*, 323.

ii. Between around 3000 and 2500 B.C. these dialectical communities began to migrate away from their *Urheimat*, so that the resultant Corded Ware culture eventually extended from the Volga to the Rhine.

iii. Then, between around 2500 and 2000 B.C., when the Bronze Age reached Central Europe, the southern LIE dialect had differentiated into Proto-Greek and Proto-Indo-Iranian.

iv. The invention of the chariot enabled the rapid spread of the Indo-Iranians over much of Central Asia, Northern India, and Iran during the next stage, dated between around 2000 and 1500 B.C. This stage also saw the break-up of Indo-Iranian into Indo-Aryan and Iranian, the differentiation of European proto-dialects from each other, and languages such as Hittite, Mitanni, and Mycenaean Greek being spoken or written down.

v. By between around 1500 and 1000 B.C., the European proto-dialects had evolved into Germanic, Celtic, Italic, Baltic, and Slavic, while Indo-Aryan became expressed in its sacred language Sanskrit, notably in the composition of the *Rig-Veda*.

vi. Finally, with Northern Europe entering the Iron Age between around 1000 and 500 B.C., the Greek and Old Italic alphabets appear in the south of the continent, and the Classical civilization flowers among the Hellenic peoples.[5]

Ethnicity

At this point we may well pause to consider if there is, or was, such an entity as an Indo-European race.[6] As remarked by Jean Haudry, "For more than a century, linguists have never tired of repeating that 'Indo-European' implies simply a linguistic, and not a racial homogeneity." However, despite this long-standing prejudice it is legitimate to speak of an Indo-European physical type, as is confirmed by the evidence from two sources: (a) anthropological study of human skeletal remains, and (b) ancient texts and

---

5. Quiles & López-Menchero, *Grammar*, 67, 75.

6. In the scientific sense, as used here, 'race' means a subspecies within a given species, since most animal and plant species consist of subspecies, or races. Consequently, there is no such entity as 'the human race,' as one often hears in political propaganda and media disinformation. Instead, the human species (*Homo sapiens*) consists of several races, or subspecies.

representations. Concerning the former category, skeletal remains found in the Kurgan sites display a predominance of tall, long-headed types with a straight aquiline nose, and a narrow face with much finer features than that of the massive Cro-Magnon skulls found in the Dnieper basin.[7]

Haudry also submits the following examples of texts and representations:

i. The Roman historian Tacitus (writing around A.D. 98) described the Germans as 'a separate nation, pure of all admixture'; they had 'wild blue eyes, bright blond hair, [and] large bodies' (*Germania*, 4); however, as Haudry notes, this depiction has been somewhat modified by modern anthropology;

ii. In Vedic India, we find the blond (Sanskrit, *hari*) god Indra granting the Aryan warriors victory over their dark-skinned adversaries, the *dasa*; here whiteness of skin reflects the whiteness of the day-sky, while black is the color of the night-sky and of Hell;

iii. The Hellenic poets, from Homer to Euripides, depict heroes who are blond and tall, while all statuary from Minoan to Hellenistic times represents gods and goddesses with golden hair and of tall stature; this physical type was idealized because it was that of the upper classes of the population, as is confirmed by the portraits of Hellenic nobles;

iv. When Pope Gregory the Great (reigned 590–604) received a number of Anglian prisoners, he was struck by their fair complexions and beautiful hair, which led him to remark that the name of their nation is appropriate for their angelic appearance.[8]

Francis Parker Yockey has remarked that the peoples which appeared in Europe under various names between around 500 B.C. and A.D. 1000 were all of similar stock, of which the physical characteristics correspond with the examples mentioned above. (It should be noted that Yockey rejected any rigid classification of races, arguing instead that race is something fluid due to the interaction between a population and the soil on which it lives; this mutability applies to humans, animals, and plants). These Indo-European peoples include the Celts, Franks, Angles, Goths, Saxons, Visigoths, Ostrogoths, Lombards, Belgae, Norsemen, Vikings, Danes, Varangians, Germani, Alemani, and Teutones. They eventually formed the

---

7. Haudry, *Indo-Europeans*, 112–113.
8. Haudry, *Indo-Europeans*, 112–113.

ruling strata in the countries now known as Spain, Italy, France, Germany, and England (with Scandinavia added to this list elsewhere in the same work), from which the Western Culture arose around A.D. 1000.[9]

Religion and Spiritual Philosophy

Having established this anthropological reality, let us consider the religion of these people. The evidence shows that the Sun, together with the Day-sky, was the highest god of Indo-European religion in its oldest form.[10] It has further been suggested that at an early stage, possibly before their migrations into Europe, the western branch of the Indo-Europeans became divided into northern and southern groups, called the Proto-Nordics and Proto-Mediterraneans, respectively. The religious beliefs of both groups were apparently based on the worship of a benign Father-god, with whom it was possible to be reunited in the afterlife. This paternal God was evidently conceived in two different though related aspects: while the Proto-Mediterraneans worshipped a Sun-god whose symbol was the Sun, the Proto-Nordics worshipped a Sky-god whose symbol was the thunderbolt. Regarding the former, it should be noted that it was probably not the physical Sun that was worshipped, but rather the Spirit that created the Sun with its heat and light, and of which the Sun was the physical symbol.[11]

Among the ancient Akkadians and Babylonians this Sun-god was called Bel, the memory of which has been preserved among some of the Celtic peoples in the annual fire-festival known as Beltane. This festival was mostly held on the first day of May, and used to be widely observed across Ireland, Scotland, and the Isle of Man. Also found among the Celts was a Druidic prayer in which God was entreated to grant his supplicants the love of the right, the love of all things, and the love of God.[12] This Indo-European notion of a benign, paternal Divinity is also encountered in a prayer ascribed by Plato to Socrates: "King Zeus, whether we pray or not, give us what is good for us; what is bad for us, give us not, however hard we pray for it" (*Second Alcibiades*, 143a). Such a prayer is evidence of a lofty spirituality indeed.

---

9. Yockey, *Imperium*, 276, 282, 289.
10. Haudry, *Indo-Europeans*, 63, 66.
11. Campbell, *Race and Religion*, 8, 13–14.
12. Wikipedia: Beltane; Campbell, *Race and Religion*, 8–10.

As the Indo-European cultures developed in their respective abodes, it was only a matter of time before intellectual reflection, i.e., philosophizing, began walking hand in hand with religious beliefs and practices. The spiritual-intellectual tradition (Sanskrit, *sanatana dharma*; Greek and Latin, *sophia perennis*, 'eternal wisdom') of the Indo-Europeans came to be expressed above all in classical Indian and Hellenic philosophy, the combination of which remains unsurpassed in the profundity of its thought and the brilliance of its exposition. However, this does not imply that metaphysical thought has been limited to the Indo-European worlds, since major contributions in this regard also came from ancient Egypt, Mesopotamia, and China. The eminent Traditionalist author Frithjof Schuon affirmed that this perennial wisdom is of Aryan (i.e., Indo-European) origin and is typologically close to the Celtic, Germanic, Iranian, and Brahmanic spiritual philosophies.[13]

Contrary to the prevailing rationalistic paradigm in Western academic circles, it must be emphasised that Indo-Hellenic thought is primarily rooted in spiritual experience. We could say that the mystical vision (Greek, *theōria*) of the Reality that surpasses and underlies the world of empirical phenomena preceded the philosophising of the Vedantic, Presocratic, and Platonic thinkers. This mystical vision of the One and all found its earliest literary expression in the Upanishads and the works of early Hellenic thinkers such as Heraclitus and Parmenides. It is therefore not surprising that the Hellenic metaphysical tradition of Orphism, Pythagoras, and Plato is akin to the mysticism of the Upanishads. In both traditions one encounters a shift of emphasis from the physical to the spiritual and from the temporal to the eternal. The salient dictum of this Indo-Hellenic mystical vision is the recognition that ultimate Reality (variously called Brahman, God, or the One) lies beyond sense perception.[14] In other words, reality is not limited to the physical world, contrary to the claims by those who reject transcendent reality, such as atheists and materialists.

Socio-political Organization

Having touched upon aspects of Indo-European religion and philosophy, let us briefly look at some socio-political aspects of these trailblazing people. In his informative book *The Indo-Europeans*, the French linguist Jean

---

13. Schuon, *Ancient Worlds*, 64.
14. Günther, *Religious attitudes*, 51; Marlow, "Hinduism and Buddhism," 39.

Haudry writes that the Indo-European people is identified by its name, as is the case with the individual. He adds, "We might even say that it [the people] identifies with its name, as is demonstrated by the formulaic parallelism of Latin *nomen Latinum*, 'the Latin people' and Vedic *aryam nama*, 'the Aryan people' and Indo-Iranian *aryaman*."[15]

Furthermore, the Indo-European people is not an undifferentiated mass of individuals, but a structured community articulated by functions. Accordingly, Aryan society was divided into three function-classes in both India and Iran, each class associated with a symbolic color (it is relevant to note that the Sanskrit word *Varna* means type, order, color or class). In India, a fourth class came to be added to accommodate the manual laborers (drawn from the native Dravidians). Arranged from highest to lowest, the Indo-Aryan function-classes and their symbolic colors were the following (with names in Sanskrit): *Brahmins*, i.e., priests (white); *Kshatriyas*, i.e., warriors and rulers (red); *Vaishyas*, i.e., artisans, merchants, and farmers (yellow); and *Shudras*, i.e., peasants and other laborers (black).[16]

The Traditionalist author Frithjof Schuon has remarked that these castes are related to fundamental tendencies of human nature, which are different ways of envisaging an empirical reality. Thus, for the *Brahmin*, it is the changeless and transcendent which is real; for the *Kshatriya*, it is action which is real; for the *Vaishya*, it is material values such as security and prosperity which are real; and for the *Shudra*, it is bodily things such as eating and drinking which are real. Interestingly, even the outcast, or *Chandala*, is related to a basic human tendency, namely an inclination to transgression due to a chaotic character. Psychologically speaking, a natural caste is a world, and people live in different worlds according to the reality on which they are centred. On the relation between caste and race, Schuon writes that race is a form [or formal reality] while caste is a spirit [or spiritual reality]. Therefore, caste takes precedence over race because spirit has priority over form.[17]

It has been pointed out by Hans Günther that the caste system in India corresponded to the universal order of life, as conceived by the Indo-Europeans. In this understanding, the whole cosmos, including divine rule and responsible human life, comprises a divine order. The Indians called it *rita*, of which the gods Mitra and Varuna (the latter called Ouranos, meaning

---

15. Haudry, *Indo-Europeans*, 38.
16. Haudry, *Indo-Europeans*, 38–39; Wikipedia: Caste system in India.
17. Schuon, *Castes*, 11–14, 33, 36.

Heaven, by the Hellenes) are the guardians. The meaning of *rita* in Sanskrit is order, rule, or truth. *Rita* is thus the principle of natural order which regulates and coordinates the operation of the universe and everything within it. Such a cosmic, ordering principle is also recognized in Hellenic philosophy (where it is called the *Logos*) and Chinese philosophy (where it is called the *Tao*). As Günther remarks about the Indian system, "The caste law was regarded as corresponding to the law of world order (Sanskrit, *dharma*), or the *ius divinum* as the Romans described it. Participation in the superior spiritual world of the Vedas, Brahmanas, and Upanishads originally determined the degree of caste. The higher the caste, the stricter was the sense of duty to lead a life corresponding to the world order."[18]

In a later chapter we will see how Plato appropriated this Indo-European social organization in his political philosophy. Now, when considering traditional Indo-European thought, we could say that Indian and Hellenic philosophy represent its Eastern and Western branches, respectively. Henceforth, we will focus on various themes encountered in Hellenic philosophy and their continuation (in a qualified manner) in traditional Christian theology, both Greek and Latin, as well as in socio-political thought, including forms of government.

---

18. Wikipedia: *Ṛita*; Günther, *Religious attitudes*, 33–34.

Being and Non-being

WHY IS THERE SOMETHING instead of nothing? This question may at first glance appear to be irrelevant or even foolish, but it is actually one of the most important of all questions. According to the Second Law of Thermodynamics, also called the Law of Entropy, the total entropy of an isolated system can never decrease over time. In other words, a net loss of energy is inevitably taking place within any closed system. And since the universe in which we live is a closed system (albeit an unimaginably vast one), it should be inexorably moving away from things that exist to a state of nothingness. But instead, we observe a plethora of new things arising all the time, from the birth of solar systems to new life-forms appearing through evolutionary processes.

Our initial question could also be cast in ontological terms: why are there beings at all instead of only non-being? Broadly speaking, 'being' denotes that which exists and 'non-being' indicates that which does not exist, or nothingness. The study of being has come to be known as ontology. The Greek word *ousia* means the being, substance, or essence of a thing, while 'ontology' is derived from the Greek *ta onta*, meaning the things which actually exist;[1] in other words, that which has being, or reality. Ontology is therefore an investigation into the nature of being. The purpose of such an undertaking is to distinguish that which is real from that which is unreal, and, since there are different levels of reality, also the more real from the less real. In other words, ontology deals with reality in the widest sense of the word.

The first Western thinker to distinguish between being and non-being was Parmenides (fifth century B.C.), who hailed from the Hellenic colony at Elea in southern Italy. It is not widely known that during the first millennium B.C. and continuing well into the Christian era, there was such a large Hellenic population in southern Italy, including Sicily, that the

---

1. LSJ, 491, 507.

Romans referred to these areas as Magna Graecia, meaning Great Greece. In an influential poem titled *On Nature* (the contents of which was revealed to him by an unnamed goddess), Parmenides wrote about "the one, that it is and that it is not possible for it not to be," and "the other, that it is not and that it is necessary for it not to be" (Fragment 2). An identical terminology is encountered in the Indian spiritual classic, the *Bhagavad Gita*: "What is non-Being is never known to have been, and what is Being is never known not to have been" (2:16).

The numerous and striking parallels between classical Indian and Hellenic philosophy have been explored by various authors. Hellenic thinkers mentioned in this regard include Thales, Anaximander, Heraclitus, Empedocles, and Plato. Concluding his informative survey of these parallels, A.N. Marlow suggests that Indian influence probably reached the Hellenic world through Iran as intermediary.[2] Without denying a flow of thought in either direction, we suggest that these parallels should be ascribed primarily to a common spiritual-intellectual inheritance. For instance, the Indo-European names for the supreme Deity (of which more later) certainly indicate a common origin.

The characteristics of being, as Parmenides understands it, have been summarized as follows: (i) It is without origin or cessation, since it could only arise from or return to non-being, which does not exist other than as an abstraction; (ii) it is an indivisible whole, which is to say a homogeneous continuity; (iii) it is motionless, since motion requires empty space, but that is non-being (which does not really exist); and (iv) it is perfect, since any lack therein would imply the existence of non-being, which is impossible.[3] Again, an identical ontology is presented in the *Bhagavad Gita*: "Know that to be imperishable whereby all this is pervaded. No one can destroy that immutable being" (2.17); "This is never born or ever dies, nor having been will ever not be any more; unborn, eternal, everlasting, ancient" (2.22); and "Perceivable neither by the senses nor by the mind, This is called unchangeable" (2.25). In summary: true being is eternal, continuous, motionless, immutable, and perfect.

The celebrated paradoxes of Zeno were written by a student of Parmenides to support this ontology. The paradox of Achilles and the tortoise is probably the most famous of these arguments, in this case directed against the concept of motion. The Hellenic hero Achilles and a tortoise compete

---

2. Marlow, "*Hinduism and Buddhism*," 45.
3. Dreyer, *Wysbegeerte*, 44–45.

in a race, with the tortoise given a hundred metres head-start. If Achilles runs ten times faster than the tortoise (which would make it a fast tortoise indeed), then by the time he reaches the tortoise's starting point the reptile would have ran ten metres. By the time Achilles reaches this hundred-and-ten metres mark from his starting point, the tortoise would have moved a further metre, and so the process continues *ad infinitum*. Therefore, Zeno concludes, Achilles will never overtake the tortoise.

Not surprisingly, Zeno's paradoxes have from the outset been opposed by a variety of thinkers, including Aristotle in his *Physics*. After all, everyday observation suggests that the physical world we live in is characterized very much by origin, cessation, motion, and imperfection. However, the reason for this apparent contradiction of Parmenides' ontology is that our living world is the realm of becoming and not the world of true being. The imperfect world of becoming, in which things (both living and inanimate) come to be and cease to be and are in motion, is therefore situated somewhere between true being and non-being. We could therefore postulate the following provisional hierarchy of reality, arranged from higher to lower: Being, becoming, and non-being.

The One beyond Being and Non-being

The differentiation between being and non-being, as encountered in both Hellenic and Indian philosophy, might at first sight suggest that the cosmos entails a duality of something and nothing. However, transcending both being and non-being there is the supreme Reality of the Godhead: "I will expound to thee that which is to be known and knowing which one enjoys immortality; it is the supreme Brahman which has no beginning, which is called neither Being nor non-Being" (*Bhagavad Gita*, 11.12). It actually precedes the differentiation between being and non-being: "There was then neither being nor non-being. Without breath breathed by its own power That One" (*Rig Veda* X.129).[4] This supreme Reality is called God (in Christianity), Brahman (in Hinduism), and the One (in Neoplatonism).

As could be expected, the greatest Western philosopher of all time, Plato, pondered the question of being and non-being.[5] The notion of di-

---

4. Quoted in Perry, *Treasury*, 26.

5. Plato founded the Academy in Athens that would function (intermittently) for over 900 years, thereby laying the foundations of the later Western university system. In his book *Process and Reality* (1929), the British mathematician and philosopher Alfred

vine transcendence was developed in his dialogue *Parmenides*, in which the One is described as indivisible, unlimited, and shapeless, neither at rest nor in motion, neither like nor unlike anything else, not partaking of time or being, and not an object of knowledge (137c–142a). Moreover, the One is beyond the duality of being and non-being, since it sometimes partakes of being and sometimes does not partake of being (155e). A similar stance is found in the Indian philosophical school known as Advaita Vedanta, where the concept of divine transcendence is encapsulated in the phrase *neti neti*, which means 'neither this, nor that' in Sanskrit. It negates all descriptions about the ultimate Reality, but not the Reality itself.[6]

In the cosmology of Plotinus, the One (*to hen*) is conceived as beyond all being (*Enneads*, V.5.6). He insists further that the One is nothing, i.e., no thing (*ouden*), not anything at all (*Enneads*, VI.9.3). Even the term 'One' contains only a denial of multiplicity (*Enneads*, V.5.6). Now, since the One is eternally beyond the manifested cosmos, Plotinus reasons, the metaphysical realm consists of Intellect (*Nous*, also translated as Mind) in its higher aspect and Soul (*Psychē*) in its lower aspect. To be more specific, the One is absolutely transcendent in respect of Intellect, Forms, and Being (*Enneads*, VI.8.15).[7] Nonetheless, as ultimate source of all Being (through the Intellect), the One provides the foundation (*archē*) and location (*topos*) of all things that exist (*Enneads*, VI.9.6). In this way the One is both nothing, being indistinct and pure unity, and everything, as the principle of all things.[8] Or, as stated by Krishna (an incarnation of the God Vishnu in human form): "Whatever is the seed of every being, O Arjuna, that am I; there is nothing, whether moving or fixed, that can be without Me" (*Bhagavad Gita*, 10.39).

The Hellenic and Indian affirmation of the transcendence of the Godhead beyond being and non-being implies that the One is essentially beyond thought and speech. We can have no opinion, thought, or knowledge of the One; it is beyond everything. This insistence on divine ineffability would

---

North Whitehead famously characterized the whole course of European philosophy as a series of footnotes to Plato. However, despite his intellectual brilliance, Plato did not lay claim to originality. In his dialogues he builds on cosmological and metaphysical insights by a number of his Hellenic predecessors. What Plato achieved, among others, is to provide this metaphysical tradition with a thoroughgoing theistic foundation, thus affirming God as the beginning and the end of all things.

6. Wikipedia: Neti neti.
7. Perl, *Theophany*, 12; Dillon and Gerson, *Neoplatonic Philosophy*, 174.
8. Moore, *Plotinus*; Camus, *Christian Metaphysics*, 94.

be elaborated by the Neoplatonist philosopher Plotinus and the Christian theologian Dionysius the Areopagite, among others.[9] Stating the same approach in Trinitarian terms, the German mystic Meister Eckhart writes of the Godhead that transcends the God of the three divine Persons, as "the absolutely simple One, without any mode or any property; He is not there in the sense of Father, Son or Holy Spirit, but He is nonetheless a Something which is neither this nor that"; adding that "all that is in the Deity is one, and of that Godhead there is no occasion to speak." And regarding activity, he writes that "God acts, the Godhead acts not at all. God and Godhead differ by acting and non-acting."[10]

However, if the One is beyond all being, how can it also be the ground or source of all being, as the metaphysical tradition asserts? According to this tradition, all that exists is established by the movement from the Principle into Manifestation, which is the flow of the One into the many. The foundation of all things in the supreme Reality, which is to say of the immanent in the transcendent, is affirmed in the *Bhagavad Gita*: "By Me [Brahman], unmanifest in form, this whole world is pervaded; all beings are in Me, I am not in them" (9.4). This world-view is sometimes called pan-en-theism, derived from the Greek *pan* (all), *en* (in) and *theos* (god); in other words, all things are in God, in the sense of receiving their being from the supreme Reality. This concept is not the same as pantheism, which is defined as the view that God is in everything, or that God and the universe are one.[11] In contrast, the ontological gap between the One and the many is preserved in pan-en-theism.

We read further in the *Bhagavad Gita*, "The state of all beings before birth is unmanifest; their middle state manifest; their state after death is again unmanifest" (2.28), and also, "But higher than the Unmanifest is another Unmanifest Being, everlasting, which perisheth not when all creatures perish" (8.20). And in the *Politeia* (usually translated as *Republic*), Plato employs the example of the Sun, which makes the things we see visible and also causes the processes of generation, growth, and nourishment, without itself being such a process. In the same way, the Good (which the Neoplatonists identify with the One) is the source of the intelligibility of the objects of knowledge, as well as of their being and reality, while in itself it is beyond that reality, being superior to it in dignity and power (*Pol*, 509b).

---

9. Lossky, *Orthodox Theology*, 24.
10. Quoted in Schuon, *Divine*, 21.
11. Blackburn, *Oxford Dictionary*, 266.

From these statements we learn that the One is beyond all manifestation, even though all existing things (i.e., the many) receive their being from it.

The Manifestation of Being

How and whence does Being (i.e., the totality of beings) arise? This question was pondered *per excellence* by the late Hellenic thinkers of the early Christian era, including Plotinus, Porphyry, Iamblichus, and Proclus. Since the eighteenth century they have been called Neoplatonists by Western scholars, although they viewed themselves as loyal Platonists. It has been convincingly argued that the modern distinction between Plato and Neoplatonism is utterly erroneous. The founders of modern philosophical hermeneutics rejected the Neoplatonist thesis of harmony between Plato and Aristotle, in the arrogant belief that they understood Plato better than his disciples of the late Classical era did.[12]

By drawing together the cosmologies of Plato, Aristotle, and the Stoics, and enriching it with his own penetrating insights, Plotinus presents an all-embracing cosmology in the *Enneads* (from the Greek *ennea*, 'nine'; the work consists of fifty-four treatises arranged in six groups of nine each). To begin with, Plotinus distinguishes between four modes of being: The One, the Intellect, the Soul, and matter. The first three modes of being are intelligible (i.e., accessible to the mind only) and named hypostases (*hypostaseis*, the plural of *hypostasis*), comprising a divine Trinity. The Greek term *hypostasis* translates as 'anything set under, or a support'; from which is derived the meanings of subsistence or substance.[13] For Plotinus, the primary hypostases are the fundamental realities underlying the cosmos. He explains: "There is the One beyond Being; next, there is Being and Intellect; and third, there is the nature of the Soul" (*Enneads*, V.1.10). This scheme is attributed to Plato, who understood that the Intellect comes from the Good (i.e., the One), and the Soul comes from the Intellect (*Enneads*, V.1.8).

According to Plato and the Neoplatonists, the universe is produced through the imposition of order onto pre-cosmic disorder. It is significant that the Greek word *kosmos* means order, ornament, and decoration, and ultimately the world or universe (Latin, *mundus*), from its perfect arrangement. Its opposite in Greek is *chaos*, which means the unformed mass and/

---

12. Uzdavinys, *Golden Chain*, xii.
13. Oosthuizen, *Plotinus*, 83; LSJ, 743.

or infinite space. This is posited by Hesiod as the initial state of existence.[14] We could say that the divine Creator fashions the world by transforming chaos into cosmos. Plato describes this creative activity in detail in his dialogue *Timaeus*, of which more later.

One of the most important Greek theologians, Basil of Caesarea (fourth century), wrote that God (Greek, *Theos*) created everything by drawing it out of nothing, or non-being. However, it has recently been commented that this 'nothingness' should not be confused with non-existence. Basil depicts this state as follows: "It appears, indeed, that even before this world an order of things existed of which our mind can form an idea, but of which we can say nothing ... The birth of the world was preceded by a condition of things suitable for the exercise of supernatural powers, outstripping the limits of time, eternal and infinite" (*Hex* I, 5). In other words, the 'nothing' out of which God creates is an imperceptible condition that precedes the creation of the observable universe. Thus, in the early Christian understanding the creation of the world entails a transition from the non-perceptive to the perceptible.[15]

According to the immensely influential Latin theologian Augustine (who served as Bishop of Hippo in North Africa from 395 until 430), God is the opposite of non-being. To begin with, God is the Supreme Being. Next, He gave being in various degrees to all things that He created 'from nothing' (Latin, *ex nihilo*). Augustine adds, "To that Nature which supremely is, therefore, and by Whom all else was made, no nature is contrary save that which is not; for that which is contrary to what is, is not-being. And so, there is no being contrary to God, the Supreme Being, and the Author of all beings of whatever kind" (*De civ Dei*, XII.2). In this theological understanding, God is the highest or ultimate Reality, as opposed to the unreality of non-being. And in one of his polemical works against the Manichaeans, the Latin theologian depicts Being in terms virtually identical to those of Parmenides: being is that which always exists in the same way; it is in every way like itself; it cannot be injured or changed; and it is not subject to time.[16]

Another influential figure in Christian thought is the mystical theologian writing under the pseudonym of Dionysius the Areopagite (one of St Paul's first converts in Athens; Acts 17:34). Perceptively utilizing Neoplatonic categories in his exposition of Christian doctrine, Dionysius

---

14. LSJ, 389, 777; Wheelock, *Latin*, 528.
15. Kalachanis et al., *Theory of Big Bang*, 36.
16. Perry, *Treasury*, 773–774.

writes in the *Divine Names* that the Good (i.e., the One) is the source of all that exists: archetypes, heavenly beings, souls, animals, plants, and inanimate matter (*DN*, 4:1, 2). This pre-existent Supreme Being is the cause and source of all eternity, all time, and every kind of being. Everything participates in this Being, which precedes the entities that participate in it (*DN*, 5:5). This includes souls, which receive their being and well-being from the pre-existent Being (*DN*, 5:8). Ultimately, Dionysius writes, just as every number participates in unity, so everything participates in the One. The One precedes oneness and multiplicity, whereas the latter only exists through participation in the One (*DN*, 13:2). In other words, in the relation between the One and the many, the latter receive their reality from the One, which is the ultimate Source of all that exists.

With his penetrating intellect, Maximus the Confessor (seventh century) developed a theistic cosmology which is formulated in Neoplatonic and Aristotelian terms. In his important work *Difficult Passages* (known as *Ambigua* in Latin), Maximus writes that God's creative activity establishes five concentric spheres of being. The first division is between uncreated nature (God) and created nature; the latter is divided into the intelligible universe and the sensible universe; the latter is divided into heaven and earth; the latter is divided into the inhabited earth and paradise; and finally, humankind is divided into male and female.[17] And since all these divisions are brought about by God, it implies that gender differentiation is the will of God and any subversion thereof is an offence against the cosmic order.

One of the most thoughtful investigations into being and non-being from a Platonist Christian perspective has been undertaken by the Irish philosopher John Scottus Eriugena, who achieved renown while working at the Carolingian court of the ninth century. In his *magnum opus*, the *Periphyseon* (subtitled *On the Division of Nature*), this enigmatic yet brilliant thinker presents an all-inclusive world-view in terms of being and non-being. Continuing the ontology of Parmenides, he declares the fundamental division of reality, or nature (Latin, *natura*), as between that which is and that which is not (*Per* I, 441). Eriugena was probably influenced herein also by Dionysius the Areopagite (whose complete writings he had earlier translated into Latin), who made a similar distinction between 'all things that are and that are not' (Greek, *panta ouk onta kai onta*) in his influential *Mystical Theology*.[18]

17. Lossky, *Mystical Theology*, 108.
18. Wheeler, *Latin*, 528; Moran, *Eriugena*, 217–218.

However, for Eriugena the division of reality into things that are and things that are not is not a static one, since it could be interpreted according to five different modes (*Per* I, 443–445): (i) All things that are intelligible or sensible (being) and all things that are beyond thought and sense-perception (non-being); (ii) affirmation of a level of being (being) and negation of a level of being (non-being); (iii) visible effects (being) and invisible causes (non-being); (iv) all things that are intelligible (being) and all things that are subject to becoming (non-being); and (v) restored human nature (being) and fallen human nature (non-being). In this way, instead of holding a substantive view of being and non-being, Eriugena presents a shifting, dynamic ontology according to which being is a question of perspective, and it should therefore be conceived in relative terms.[19] In other words, being and non-being are not absolute realities, but relative realities in which the perspective of the observer plays a decisive role. We will encounter scientific confirmation of this 'observer effect' in a later chapter.

From Non-being to Being

The transition from non-being into the realm of being has been investigated by Plato and the early Christian theologians. Plato describes a dialogue between Socrates and Diotima in the *Symposium*, in which poetry and all other crafts are presented as 'creating something out of nothing' (205c). Nicolas Laos comments that for Plato, authentic creation (*poiēsis*) involves a transition from non-being into being. For example, a sculpture is a creative act because it is a material manifestation of a specific form, so that its creation entails a passage from formlessness into form. However, there is a fundamental difference between human and divine creative activity: unlike God, man cannot create out of nothing. Nevertheless, "When man's creative activity imitates God, it is *poiēsis*, and, in this sense, it can be understood as the passage from non-being into being, since it produces a meaningful world from formless matter."[20]

In this regard, Nicolas Berdyaev draws a fundamental distinction between creation (whether divine or human) and procreation through birth. Unlike birth, which arises from nature, creation springs from freedom. Creation is thus out of nothing, for freedom is nothing, while birth is always from something. In this way, through creation there arises something

---

19. Moran, *Eriugena*, 218.
20. Laos, *Metaphysics*, 194–195.

perfectly new that has never existed before, i.e., 'nothing' becomes 'something.' Human creativity is therefore similar to God's, although God does not need any material for creation, while humans do. As the Russian philosopher concludes, "A creative act is therefore a continuation of world-creation and means participation in the work of God, man's answer to God's call. And this presupposes freedom which is prior to being."[21]

It is axiomatic in Patristic theology, both Greek and Latin, that God creates the entire realm of being out of nothing, thus effecting the transition from non-being to being. The first biblical mention of creation from nothing (Latin, *creatio ex nihilo*) is found in the apocryphal book of Second Maccabees. There it is declared that God created the heavens and the earth, as well as human beings, from what did not exist (2 Macc 7:28; *ek ouk onton* in the Greek text of the Septuagint).[22] This terminology is significant, for *ou* or *ouk* is more emphatic than the customary *mē* used for negation. Accordingly, *mē* expresses that one thinks a thing is not, while *ou* that it is not. This reasoning implies that nothing can exist 'before' creation or 'outside' God, for time and space are presupposed by the act of creation. Therefore, 'before' creation or 'outside' God there is only the nothingness out of which He creates.[23] The only occurrence of this doctrine in the New Testament is a passing reference by St Paul, namely that God 'calls those things which do not exist as though they did' (*kalountos ta mē onta hōs onta*) (Rom 4:17). In this way, a new entity is produced which is wholly other, removed from God not by place but by nature (Greek, *ou topō, alla physei*), in the words of John of Damascus. The created order is therefore not co-eternal with God, but moves from non-being to being.[24]

The essential nothingness of all beings created by God has been powerfully described by Meister Eckhart. All creatures are a mere nothing, for they are without being; they are not even small, but absolutely nothing. He adds, "Creatures have no real being, for their being consists in the presence of God. If God turned away for an instant, they would all perish." The German mystic remarks that even if someone had the whole world as well as God, he would have no more than God by himself. "Having all creatures

---

21. Berdyaev, *Destiny of Man*, 65–66.
22. OSB, 1244; Lossky, *Orthodox Theology*, 51.
23. LSJ, 442; Lossky, *Orthodox Theology*, 51–54.
24. Lossky, *Mystical Theology*, 92–93.

without God is no more than having one fly without God; just the same, no more nor less."[25]

For another German mystical theologian, Jakob Böhme, the nothingness out of which God creates is the *Ungrund*, the bottomless abyss which is neither light nor darkness and neither good nor evil. Commenting on this view, the Russian philosopher Nicolas Berdyaev sketches the deployment of the *Ungrund* as follows: being-less freedom ignites like a fire in the darkness, and light comes to be (which reminds one of the divine command at the commencement of the creative process in Genesis 1: 'Let there be light!'). Nothing becomes something, and out of bottomless freedom nature is born. The *Ungrund* is the Divinity of apophatic theology and simultaneously the no-thing that precedes God. No-thing is more fundamental than some-thing, darkness than light, and freedom than nature.[26]

The transition from non-being into being through the divine creative activity has been poetically depicted by more recent authors. Referring to the creation of the heavenly beings, which in the traditional Christian understanding preceded the creation of the physical universe, Alan Watts writes: "From beginningless time they were not. And then, by the sudden command of the Word, they appeared—circle upon circle, sphere upon sphere of lesser lights about the Light—points of substantialized nothingness, reflecting in a million ways the central radiance of the Trinity as if they had been great clouds of crystal fragments swirling about the sun." And in the words of Deirdre Carabine: "The paradox of creation is that the original darkness of God, which is no-thing, becomes light, becomes some-thing. God's fullness above being is the 'nothing' that is the negation of something, but through its becoming, it becomes the negation of the negation: the divine nature becomes 'other' than itself: God becomes not-God through the process of *ex-stasis*, literally, God's *going out from* God."[27] Thus, darkness becomes light, nothing becomes something, and non-being becomes being.

In the traditional Christian understanding, it is the creative activity of the Logos, or the divine Word, which brings the universe into being, including all its life-forms.[28] The following statement by Philaret of Mos-

---

25. Quoted in Perry, *Treasury*, 803.

26. Berdyaev, "*Being and Existence*," 374–375.

27. Watts, *Myth and Ritual*, 35–36; Carabine, *Eriugena*, 35.

28. See the author's book *From Logos to Bios. Evolutionary Theory in Light of Plato, Aristotle & Neoplatonism* (2018) for an extensive treatment hereof.

cow, a leading Orthodox theologian of the nineteenth century, has to be one of the most evocative depictions of the created order: "All creatures are balanced upon the creative word of God, as if upon a bridge of diamond; above them is the abyss of the divine infinitude, below them that of their own nothingness."[29] In other words, all created beings are suspended, so to speak, between the Beyond-being above them and the non-being below them. In their essences, the many (i.e., the world of phenomena) are indeed nothing—their only reality is derived from the One which is the uncreated Ground of all Being.

Being and Nature

One of the prominent metaphysical thinkers of the twentieth century, Martin Heidegger, opens his *Introduction to Metaphysics* with the following question: "Why are there beings at all instead of nothing?" This is presented by the German philosopher as the fundamental question of metaphysics, for it is the broadest, the deepest, and the most originary (i.e., causing existence) question. It is the broadest in scope, being limited only by what never is, i.e., non-being; it is the deepest question, aimed at establishing the ground from where beings come and to where beings go; and it is the most originary question, addressing not a particular being but beings as a whole.[30] The striving to answer this question underlies the enduring metaphysical quest.

The Greek noun *physis*, which means the nature or inborn quality of a person or thing, is related to the verb *phuō*, which means to bring forth, produce, or make to grow. Evidently, the early Hellenic thinkers conceived of 'nature' as a creative power rather than a material environment.[31] Heidegger suggests that the Hellenic thinkers did not first experience *physis* in the natural processes, but in poetry and thought *physis* disclosed itself to them. Thus, 'nature' meant the totality of heaven and earth, animals and plants, humans, and even the gods. This wider meaning of *physis* comprises "what emerges from itself (for example, the emergence, the blossoming, of a rose), the unfolding that opens itself up, the coming-into-appearance in such unfolding, and holding itself and persisting in appearance—in short, the emerging-abiding sway." Therefore, although *physis* can be experienced

---

29. Quoted in Lossky, *Mystical Theology*, 92.
30. Heidegger, *Introduction*, 1–4.
31. LSJ, 772; Coomaraswamy, *Civilization*, 83.

in the processes of nature, such as birth and growth, it is not synonymous with these. Instead, *physis* indicates Being-itself, through which beings appear.[32]

Heidegger contends further that by translating *physis* into Latin as *natura*, which means 'birth,' the realm of nature became reduced to the world of biological phenomena. This Latin term is therefore said to represent the beginning of the alienation of Western thought on nature from its original essence in Hellenic philosophy.[33] However, Plotinus recognized an etymological connection between the noun *physis* and the verb *ephy*; in other words, between 'nature' and 'was born' (*Enneads* VI, 8, 8).[34] In the light thereof, we could say that *natura* is not limited to *physis*, but that it is embraced by the latter (which also reaches beyond the biological realm).

The traditional Indo-European understanding of Being has been perceptively sketched by Heidegger through an etymological analysis: (i) The oldest stem word in this regard is *es*, which becomes the noun *asus* in Sanskrit, meaning 'life' or 'the living,' and the verb forms *esmi, esi, esti* and *asmi*. To these terms are related the Greek *eimi* and *einai* (both meaning 'to be'), and the corresponding Latin terms *esum* and *esse*. In this regard the Germanic verb *ist* is cognate to the Greek *estin* and the Latin *est*, meaning 'it is.' (ii) Another root is the Sanskrit *bhu* or *bheu* and related to the Greek *phuō*, which for Heidegger means "to emerge, to hold sway, to come to a stand from out of itself and to remain standing." This is in turn cognate to the Greek terms *physis* ('nature') and *phainesthai* ('to show itself'), so that nature is described by Heidegger as "that which emerges into the light, *phuein*, to illuminate, to shine forth and therefore to appear." The German verbs *bin* and *bist* ('am/are') are also derived from this Sanskrit stem. (iii) Finally, the stem *wes* appears in the Sanskrit *vasami* and the Germanic *we-san*, meaning 'to dwell, to abide, to sojourn,' which in turn becomes the German verbs *wesen* and *sein*, 'to be' and 'being.' From these three stems, Heidegger concludes, one derives the "vividly definite meanings of living, emerging, and abiding"—i.e., the domain of Being.[35]

This 'emergence and abiding of Being' has been outlined by the South African philosopher Danie Goosen, building on the notion of theurgy (from the Greek *theourgia*, literally 'divine-working') as developed by the

32. Heidegger, *Introduction*, 15–16.
33. Heidegger, *Introduction*, 14.
34. Dillon and Gerson, *Neoplatonic Philosophy*, 169.
35. Heidegger, *Introduction*, 75–76.

Neoplatonic thinkers Iamblichus and Proclus. In terms thereof, Reality expresses itself in and through the 'actors of being' serving as mediators between the infinity of being and the finitude of the world. These actors assume roles such as being and beings, *esse* and *essentia*, transcendent and immanent, other and self, giver and receiver, subject and object, sublime and beautiful, *erōs* and *agapē*, and substantive and accidental.[36] Through this dynamic interaction between the One and the many, the cosmos obtains the character of a differentiated unity, or a many-in-One.

---

36. Goosen, *Nihilisme*, 94, 103.

Metaphysical and Physical

THE MOST BASIC DIVISION within cosmic reality is that between the higher, metaphysical world and the lower, physical world. We contend that this is a more accurate view of reality than the more commonly found differentiation between spiritual and material, since this physical world in which we live is already a combination of the levels of soul and matter. It is therefore, strictly speaking, wrong to say that we live in a material world, because the matter that we can perceive through our senses is formed matter, i.e., matter formed by soul. In contrast, unformed matter can be mentally conceived but not perceived, since it requires the addition of form to become accessible to sense perception.

Plato outlines the metaphysical view of reality as follows: "As I see it, then, we must begin by making the following distinction: What is that which always is and has no becoming, and what is that which always becomes but never is? The former is grasped by understanding, which involves a reasoned account. It is unchanging. The latter is grasped by opinion, which involves unreasoning sense perception. It comes to be and passes away, but never really is" (*Tim*, 27d–28a). Later in the same work, Plato adds that the first kind neither receives into itself anything else nor enters into anything else. It is invisible and cannot be perceived by any of the senses. In contrast, the second kind is constantly borne along, now coming to be in a certain place and then perishing out of it (*Tim*, 52a). In the Platonic tradition these realms are usually denoted as the intelligible world (*to noēton*) and the sensible world (*to horaton*), respectively. The adjectives 'intelligible' and 'sensible' indicate the respective means by which these worlds may be known, namely rational thought and sense perception.

The metaphysical and physical worlds are also known as the realms of being and becoming, which are respectively related to eternity and time. Whereas being is eternal, unchanging, and perfect, becoming is temporal, ever-changing, and imperfect. Since the primary elements of earth, air, water, and fire change into each other (e.g., in the process of condensation) and thus possess no stability, Plato concludes that everything which has becoming is unstable. It is therefore better to say 'what is such' than 'this' or 'that' to describe physical objects (*Tim*, 49c–50a). Incidentally, this recognition of the fluidity and impermanence of everything in the sensible world rebuts the oft-repeated charge that Platonism entails a static world-view.

Martin Heidegger has remarked that the opposition between being and becoming stands at the inception of the ontological question. He adds: "What becomes, is not yet. What is, no longer needs to become. That which 'is' has left all becoming behind it, if indeed it ever became or could become. What 'is' in the authentic sense also stands up against every onslaught from becoming." The German philosopher concludes that Heraclitus, to whom the doctrine of becoming is ascribed, is therefore saying the same thing as Parmenides, who introduced the doctrine of being in his famous didactic poem.[1]

One of the the greatest Christian thinkers of all time, Meister Eckhart, relates the distinction between being and becoming to their origins. He writes: "The first point to be made is that becoming is from secondary causes, but the existence of everything, either natural or artificial, in that it is what is first and perfect, is immediately from God alone."[2] Here the German theologian appears to suggest two distinct realms: an eternal world ('first and perfect'), derived directly from God; and a temporal cosmos, produced by secondary causes. However, if one keeps in mind Eckhart's view that all things exist only through participation in God, then even temporal things (i.e., the realm of becoming) exist insofar as they are supra-temporal. As Wolfgang Smith comments, the difference between the temporal and the eternal orders thus lies not in a *kind* of being, but rather in a *lack* of being. We could say that temporal things had not yet fully attained their being, but are "striving to be," as is indeed suggested by the term 'becoming'. Moreover, nothing can 'become' unless in some way it 'is'. It could therefore be said in conclusion that temporal things both 'are' and 'are not', since they consist of both being and non-being.[3]

The term 'metaphysics' first appears in the writings of Aristotle, Plato's most famous student and founder of his own philosophical school at the Lyceum (an Athenian temple dedicated to Apollo, the god of light, truth,

---

1. Heidegger, *Introduction*, 100–101, 103.
2. Quoted in Smith, *Christian Gnosis*, 166.
3. Smith, *Christian Gnosis*, 167–168.

healing, and music). Aristotle's extant writings were collected and published in the first century B.C. by Andronicus of Rhodes. A major work therein was titled *ta meta ta physika*, which means 'after the physics'—i.e., following Aristotle's writings on physical phenomena. In it, Aristotle declares the theoretical science called metaphysics to be the first philosophy (*protē philosophia*). Its object of study is being as such and the attributes which belong to being (*Met* IV.1003a).[4] Since the Greek prefix *meta* also means 'over beyond,' Martin Heidegger points out that philosophizing about beings as such is precisely *meta ta physika*, or metaphysics.[5] Evidently, in the Aristotelian view metaphysics is practically indistinguishable from ontology.

Moreover, for Aristotle metaphysics is closely related to theology. This term is derived from the Greek *theologia*, which means discourse on the nature of God or the gods. Aristotle views theology as the first and highest science, since it deals with things which both exist separately and are immovable; in other words, theology deals with the realm of the divine (*Met* VI.1026a). Several centuries later, theology is similarly conceived by Proclus as a branch of theoretical philosophy.[6] This is particularly evident in his main works, *Elements of Theology* and *Platonic Theology*, which together contains the fullest extant exposition of Platonism.

It is important to note that the recognition of a fundamental differentiation between the metaphysical and physical realms does not imply an ontological dualism, since both these worlds obtain their reality from a transcendent Principle. As we have noted earlier, this Principle is variously referred to as God, Brahman, or the One. But an important distinction should be made regarding the origins of these worlds: whereas the intelligible realm arises directly from the Principle, the sensible world comes into being through the intelligible world. The cosmic chain of causality may therefore be stated as follows: Principle → metaphysical/intelligible world → physical/sensible world.

The relation between God, the intelligible world, and the sensible world has been elegantly described by Maximus the Confessor, who in his writings combined the Greek Christian theology of his predecessors with the Aristotelian theories of time, eternity, motion, and rest. He depicts a triadic universe of Being (*ousia*), Power (*dynamis*), and Act (*energeia*), which

---

4. Dreyer, *Wysbegeerte*, 128–129.
5. Heidegger, *Introduction*, 18.
6. Dillon and Gerson, *Neoplatonic Philosophy*, 264, 287.

he probably obtained from the Neoplatonist Porphyry. In terms thereof, a being is (*ousia*), has the capacity (*dynamis*) to do something, and does it (*energeia*). Maximus reasons further that God is the Bestower of being, the Creator of becoming, and the Prime Mover (the latter being Aristotle's term for God). In this way, He is the Efficient Cause (*archē*) of the eternal, intelligible world which starts from being; of the contingent, physical world which starts from becoming; and of that motion which, as mutability, is the means whereby the sensible world reaches its end. Thus, Maximus views being as the mode of existence of the intelligible world, while becoming is the mode of existence of the sensible world.[7]

Participation

How does the metaphysical and physical realms obtain their reality? In the case of both these worlds, their existence is obtained by means of participation (Greek *metechein*, Latin *participatio*) in a higher level of reality. The metaphysical realm participates directly in the Principle, while the physical world participates in the intelligible realm and thus indirectly in the Principle. In this way, a specific level of reality obtains its being from the level directly above it by means of participation: the physical world receives its being from the metaphysical world, while the latter receives its being from the Principle, which is therefore the ultimate source of all being, whether directly or indirectly.

According to Plato's celebrated Theory of Forms, particular things share in or participate of the forms, while each form provides a pattern (*paradeigma*) to which the particulars approximate.[8] The notion of Forms (also called Ideas) is defined by Socrates in the dialogue *Parmenides*: "These forms are like patterns set in nature, and other things resemble them and are likenesses; and this partaking of the forms is, for the other things, simply being modelled on them" (132d). Since Plato insists that the participation of immanent things in the transcendent reality of the Forms is what constitutes cosmic reality, it is erroneous to accuse the Athenian thinker of emphasizing transcendence at the cost of immanence. Contrary to this charge by Nietzsche, *inter alia*, the Platonic notion of participation entails 'a shining affirmation of immanence,' as poetically stated by a recent commentator. Through their participation in the transcendent reality, the immanent things

7. Sheldon-Williams, "*Greek Christian Platonist*," 492–496.
8. Lee, *Republic*, 261.

obtain an ontological weight and durability that would have been impossible without such participation. Consequently, the rejection of immanence cannot be attributed to Platonism, but rather to the Gnostic deviations from it and the modernist continuation of these deviations.[9]

The South African philosopher Petrus Dreyer has pointed out that for Plato the Forms are the only real being outside the domains of time and space. And since the Forms represent the limited (*peras*), they are the opposite of the unlimited (*apeiron*), which is represented by the non-being of empty space (*to kenon*). It could also be said that as the negation of being, empty space exists only as a possibility. Dreyer adds that in Plato's cosmology the world of phenomena is interposed between the extremes of that which is (*to on*) and that which is not (*to mē on*)—in other words, between true being and non-being. As Plato states in the dialogue *Politeia*, the sensible realm participates in both being and non-being (478d-e). The physical world is thus conceived as simultaneously real, through participating in the Forms, and unreal, through existing in non-being.[10] In this way Plato establishes an ontological hierarchy of first the intelligible world (true being), then the sensible world (relative being, or becoming), and finally the abstract realm of non-being.

Ultimately, Philip Sherrard writes, Plato conceives of all things as partaking to some degree of the divine (since the Forms receive their reality from the Good, i.e., the One). It is precisely this phenomenon of participation which links the spiritual (or intelligible) world to the sensible world, including even the formless and the irrational. As Plato states in one of his late dialogues, the *Timaeus* (at 92c), the world (*kosmos*) is a sensible God made in the image of the Intelligible (*eikon tou noētou theos aisthētos*).[11]

As was done by his Platonic predecessors, so also Proclus explains the relation between the One and the many through the notion of participation. In his seminal work *Elements of Theology*, Proclus distinguishes between that which participates, that which is participated in, and that which is unparticipated (Propositions 23 and 24). This threefold scheme of participation has been illustrated by means of the following example: (i) a large thing, (ii) the largeness in the large thing, and (iii) the entity that possesses largeness paradigmatically (i.e., the Form of largeness).[12]

---

9. Goosen, *Nihilisme*, 200–201.
10. Dreyer, *Wysbegeerte*, 100.
11. Sherrard, *Greek East*, 11.
12. Goosen, *Nihilisme*, 93; Gerson, *Aristotle*, 212.

The Platonic concept of participation was employed by outstanding Christian thinkers such as Dionysius the Areopagite in the Greek tradition and John Scottus Eriugena in the Latin tradition. As Plato explains in the *Phaedo*, that which is determined (the effect) participates in its determination (the cause), through which the effect obtains the nature or attribute of the cause. Eric Perl comments that only by understanding Platonic participation can we understand the relation between cause and effect in Neoplatonism, and thus the sense in which, for Dionysius, God is the cause of all things.[13] And Eriugena, within his profound synthesis of Greek and Latin Christian theology and Neoplatonic philosophy, presents participation as follows: the Creator (i.e., God as the beginning of all things) does not participate but is participated in; the primordial causes (i.e., the Forms, through which God creates the sensible world) participate in the Creator and is participated in; and the created effects participate in their primordial causes (*Per* III, 630). Only God as the end of all things neither participates nor is participated in.[14]

Continuing the Platonic and Patristic doctrine that the created world receives its being from God through participation, the Scholastic philosopher and theologian Thomas Aquinas opens his *Treatise on Creation* as follows: "All beings apart from God are not their own being, but are beings by participation." Commenting on this quote, Wolfgang Smith suggests both an exoteric and an esoteric interpretation. From an exoteric viewpoint, it means that all things in the created order derive their being from God. This ontological dependence is illustrated by the example of red-hot iron, which receives its heat from fire, to which heat belongs essentially. However, from an esoteric viewpoint the above statement means that creatures possess a mere semblance of being, which actually belongs to none but God. In reality, the cosmos is a self-manifestation of God, which implies that in its theological conception as an 'other than God' the cosmos is really a pure nothing (Latin, *purus nihil*), as Meister Eckhart held. In the light of this reasoning, Smith concludes that the dichotomy of 'Uncreated versus created,' which is fundamental in Christian theology, may exist from the human point of view, but not in the sense of absolute truth.[15]

---

13. Perl, *Theophany*, 19.
14. Carabine, *Eriugena*, 58.
15. Smith, *Christian Gnosis*, 157–158, 166.

However, due to the lower receiving its being from the higher, the sensible world displays at least a measure of intelligibility.[16] The Orthodox philosopher Philip Sherrard has remarked that the multiple Forms (or Ideas) are both transcendent in relation to the sensible objects determined by them, and immanent in these objects. As a result, he writes, "the creature possesses its own intelligible nature through actual participation in the creative cause which brought it into being."[17] We are able to discern harmony, proportion, and regularity in, for example: (a) the movements of the Sun, the Moon, and the planets, and therefore in the rhythms of day and night and of the seasons; (b) the life-cycles of organisms, from microbes through plants and animals to humans; and (c) the movements of sub-atomic particles as they interact to constitute material reality. Evidently, the physical world is not devoid of intelligibility, for example as order and harmony, even though it represents a lower reality than the metaphysical world.

By combining the concepts of being and non-being, as well the metaphysical and the physical, we arrive at the following hierarchy (arranged from most real to least real), which encompasses the totality of 'something and nothing':

i. Beyond-being (or God), which precedes the distinction between being and non-being;

ii. True being, which comprises the intelligible realm of unchanging Forms, at the apex of which is the universal Mind, or Intellect;

iii. Relative being (or becoming), which is the sensible world of ever-changing phenomena;

iv. Relative non-being, which is unformed matter;

v. Absolute non-being (or nothingness), which exists as an abstraction in human thought.

Relevance

Does this traditional ontology and metaphysics we have been discussing so far have any relevance to the physical world, including its sciences? The answer is a resounding 'Yes.' It has been argued, for example, that the standard model of quantum physics allows for the return of metaphysics in the

16. Dillon and Gerson, *Neoplatonic Philosophy*, xx.
17. Sherrard, *Greek East*, 6.

sense in which Aristotle conceived it, after its expulsion from philosophy by Immanuel Kant and from science by nineteenth century materialism. Not only did it bring Being back into the picture of theoretical physics, but also Mind, as experimentation followed theorizing.[18] Here are some quotes from eminent scientists:

a. Theoretical physicist Amit Goswami in *The Self-aware Universe* (1993): "From a fully idealist point of view, we say that a measurement always means an observation by a conscious observer in the presence of awareness"; and therefore "the universe exists as formless *potentia* [Latin, force or power][19] in myriad possible branches in the transcendent domain and becomes manifested only when observed by conscious beings."

b. Theoretical physicist Brian Greene in *The Fabric of the Cosmos* (2004) on the illusory nature of space and time: "Space and time may similarly dissolve when scrutinized with the most fundamental formulation of nature's laws."

c. Mathematician Roger Penrose in *The Road to Reality* (2004): "Any universe that can be observed must, as a logical necessity, be capable of supporting conscious mentality, since consciousness is precisely what plays the ultimate role of 'observer.' This fundamental requirement could well provide constraints of the universe's physical laws, or physical parameters, in order that conscious mentality can (and will) exist."

d. Astrophysicist Arthur Eddington in *Space, Time and Gravitation* (1920): "Where science has progressed the farthest, the mind has but regained from nature what the mind has put into nature."[20] That is to say, Mind precedes nature, and the metaphysical is prior to the physical.

More recently, a number of Greek and Serbian scholars have argued that the Big Bang Theory is eminently compatible with the early Christian teaching on the creation of the universe out of nothing. Both conceptions assert that the universe, space, and time have a beginning, so that there is nothing 'before' this initial point of cosmic origin. In addition, there is a

---

18. Geldard, *Anaxagoras*, 89–90.
19. https://latin-dictionary.net/definition/31066/potentia-potentiae
20. Geldard, *Anaxagoras*, 90–96.

Greek Patristic notion that the non-being out of which God creates is not pure nothingness, but rather indicates an imperceptible state beyond space and time. This view appears to find a reflection in the astrophysical concept of the false vacuum, which is not entirely stable (unlike a true vacuum) but may nevertheless last for a very long time.[21]

The transition of the natural sciences from the gross materialism of the nineteenth century to the more 'metaphysical' paradigms of the twentieth century has been outlined by Francis Parker Yockey in his *magnum opus*. To begin with, science (in its materialistic conception) served as the supreme religion of the nineteenth century, so that 'unscientific' became the term of damnation. This went hand in hand with the 'progress' ideology, with the latter understood not as more knowledge, but as more technique. Some examples thereof are mentioned by Yockey: the problem of poverty was to be solved with more machinery; the horrible conditions that had arisen out of a machine-civilization would be alleviated by more machines; the problem of old age was to be overcome with 'rejuvenation'; racial problems would be solved by 'eugenics'; the weather would be 'harnessed' and all natural forces brought under absolute control; international problems would vanish, since the world would become one huge scientific unit. In this manner, Yockey writes, all Life, all Death, and all Nature would be reduced to absolute order, in the custody of scientific theocrats.[22]

However, as Yockey points out, there were already signs that this lifeless, mechanical picture would not last. When the Theory of Entropy introduced the idea of irreversibility into the picture, science was on the road that was to culminate in physical relativity and the subjectivity of physical concepts. Next appeared the Theory of Radioactivity, which again contains strong subjective elements and requires the Calculus of Probabilities to describe its results. Because of these and related scientific theories, Yockey writes, concepts like mass, energy, electricity, heat, and radiation, merged into one another, and it became increasingly clear that was really under study was the human soul. In other words, physical science returned to its foundation in mind, or consciousness. Consequently, "Scientific theories reached the point where they signified nothing less that the complete collapse of science as a mental discipline." On the one extreme, that of the macrocosm, the cosmos is depicted as finite but unlimited, and boundless but bounded. On the other extreme, that of the microcosm, "the closer it is

---

21. Kalachanis, *Theory of Big Bang*, 31–32, 36–37; Wikipedia: False vacuum.
22. Yockey, *Imperium*, 99–101.

studied, the more spiritual it becomes, for the nucleus of the atom is a mere charge of electricity, having neither weight, volume, inertia nor any other classic properties of matter."[23]

"In its last great saga," Yockey continues, "science dissolved its own psychical foundations, and moved outside the world of the senses into the world of the soul. Absolute time was dissolved, and time became a function of position. Mass became spiritualized into energy. The idea of simultaneity was discarded, motion became relative, parallels cut one another, two distances could no longer be said absolutely equal to one another. The profound knowledge was realized through the very study of matter itself that matter is only the envelope of the soul . . . matter cannot be explained materialistically. Its whole significance derives from the soul." Ultimately, "Man possesses a *metaphysical sense* as the hall-mark of his humanity."[24] There can be no doubt that Pythagoras, Plato, Aristotle, Plotinus, and the whole of the metaphysical tradition would have agreed wholeheartedly with this assessment.

---

23. Yockey, *Imperium*, 102–104.
24. Yockey, *Imperium*, 104–105.

Mind and Motion

THE FIRST KNOWN PHILOSOPHER to teach in Athens, Anaxagoras (fifth century B.C.), introduced the perennially relevant notion of universal Mind, or Intellect, into Western thought. Both Mind and Intellect are translations of the Greek *nous*, which is the equivalent of the Latin *mens*.[1] In the newly established cultural center of the Hellenic world, Anaxagoras soon earned the admiration of such luminaries as the statesman Pericles and the poet Euripides. With his unequivocal insistence on the role of universal Mind in the cosmos, as exemplified in both his life and his teaching, Anaxagoras earned the epithet *Nous* from the Athenians.[2] His social standing notwithstanding, Anaxagoras would eventually be exiled from Athens on charges of impiety. According to the early Christian theologian Hippolytus (in his *Refutation of all Heresies*), Anaxagoras had taught, for instance, that the Sun, Moon, and stars are not gods but fiery rocks.[3] Not surprisingly, this naturalistic view arose the ire of the guardians of the Hellenic pantheon. Banished to Lampsacus near Troy, Anaxagoras once again enjoyed high esteem there for the remaining few years of his life.

The Activity of Mind

In Anaxagoras' prose work *On Nature* the cosmos is depicted as arising out of an undifferentiated mass (i.e., formless matter) through the action of Mind: "Mind is unlimited and self-ruled and is mixed with no thing, but is alone and by itself ... For it is the finest of all things and the purest, and it has all judgement about everything and the greatest power. And Mind rules all things that possess life—both the larger and the smaller. And Mind ruled the entire rotation, so that it rotated in the beginning ... And Mind

---

1. LSJ, 467; Wheeler, *Latin*, 527.
2. Geldard, *Anaxagoras*, 86.
3. McKirahan, *Philosophy*, 210.

knew all the things that are being mixed together and separated off and separated apart. And Mind set in order all things, whatever kinds of things were to be—whatever were and all that are now and whatever will be—and also this rotation in which are now rotating the stars and the sun and the moon ... All Mind is alike, both the larger and the smaller" (Fragment 12); and also, "Mind, which is always, is very much even now where all other things are too, in the surrounding multitude and in things that have come together in the process of separating and in things that have separated off" (Fragment 14).

It appears from these fragments that Anaxagoras conceived of the cosmos as arising from a rotary motion of Mind, thereby causing a separating effect in the unlimited mass out of which the cosmos finally arises.[4] In an alternative translation a section of Fragment 12 reads as follows: "Mind took command of the universal revolution, so as to make (things) revolve at the outset." This activity of Mind explains the existence of a conscious order in nature, based on the principle of rotation or circulation. Moreover, since Mind 'takes command of' and 'understands' all things for a certain end or purpose, Anaxagoras should be credited with introducing the concept of teleology into Western thought.[5] Teleology is the study of design and purpose (Greek, *telos*) in the cosmos, including the living kingdoms.

The omnipresence of Mind implies that it is unlimited (Greek, *apeiron*) in time and space. As commented by Richard McKirahan, "Mind's unlimited spatial extent, its extreme fineness, and its lack of mixture with other things suggest that Anaxagoras is striving towards the notion of immaterial existence." This implies that Mind is a metaphysical essence and not a physical one. In Anaxagoras' conception, Mind is so fine that it penetrates and permeates everything (outside Mind itself) and causes them to move by its presence.[6] The cosmological parallels between the universal Mind of Anaxagoras and the divine Logos of Heraclitus are notable, and could be attributed to Anaxagoras being familiar with the thought of his Ionian predecessor. Ultimately, since Mind is eternal and infinite, it brings order to the primordial chaos through the imposition of cosmic law.[7] Thus, by transforming pre-cosmic chaos into cosmic order, Mind produces the physical world.

4. Curd, *"Presocratic Philosophy."*
5. Geldard, *Anaxagoras*, 26.
6. McKirahan, *Philosophy*, 219–220.
7. Geldard, *Anaxagoras*, 8–9, 29.

In the light of these statements, we could say that Anaxagoras is the father of philosophical Idealism in the Western world. According to this doctrine, reality is fundamentally mental in nature. In the Asian metaphysical traditions, Idealism also made an early appearance in the Vedanta and in Yogacara Buddhism (although the latter instance is disputed by some commentators). This philosophical tradition would be continued by Plato, the Middle Platonists, and the Neoplatonists, as well as their successors over the ages. They include several prominent physicists since the early twentieth century, when the crude materialism of some earlier scientists became undermined by the theories of relativity and quantum mechanics. For example, the astrophysicist Arthur Eddington wrote about a cosmic 'mind-stuff' which underlies space and time, and which is therefore the primary thing of which we can have experience, with all else being remote inference. Another British astrophysicist, James Jeans, famously stated that the universe is beginning to look more like a great thought than a great machine.[8] It thus appears that philosophical Idealism harbours a more valid explanation of reality than does materialism and its corollary, mechanism.

In the Western world, philosophical Idealism found its most lucid and comprehensive expression in Neoplatonism. Its hierarchical view of reality rests on two interrelated principles: the simple precedes the complex, and the intelligible precedes the sensible. Accordingly, the complex is explained by the simple and the sensible is explained by the intelligible.[9] In terms of the 'top-down' metaphysics of Neoplatonism, the material is explained by the psychical, just as the latter is explained by the intellectual. In other words, the physical world is explained in the light of the metaphysical world. In this world-view, which is the precise opposite of a materialist one, "the material world can only be accounted for in terms of the non-material, the visible in terms of the invisible, the measurable in terms of the non-measurable." Thus, Lord Northbourne concludes, "the ultimate truth is enshrined in the latter and not in the former [of each pair]."[10]

The cosmology of Anaxagoras is also relevant to other aspects of modern physics. In contrast to the commonly held view of his time on the separate realms of the gods and the cosmos, Anaxagoras postulates a bringing-together of the various levels of reality. In terms thereof, Mind indwells the physical cosmos while remaining unmixed with it, due to Mind

8. Wikipedia: Idealism.
9. Gerson, *Aristotle*, 33.
10. Northbourne, *Progress*, 94.

being the finest and purest of all things. It has been remarked by a recent commentator that this world-view is reflected in modern physical theories such as the equivalence of energy and matter, and the substantial nature of the 'vacuum' of space.[11]

The teaching of Anaxagoras on Mind furthermore evokes a correlation between the macrocosm and the microcosm. Through his observations of the motions of the celestial bodies as well as his own mind/body interaction, Anaxagoras became convinced that the cosmos likewise consists of body and mind. Just as in the human being the mind activates the body and controls its motions, so does the universal Mind control the motions of the cosmos. Thus, "the role of mind in the control and function of the body and the principles of birth, growth, decay and death extend outward into the creation."[12] This concept of a correlation between the macrocosm and the microcosm would become axiomatic in both Hellenic and Christian thought in the centuries following Anaxagoras.

As was the case with other Pre-Socratic thinkers, Anaxagoras viewed the cosmos as alive. The source of the living cosmos is the Logos of Heraclitus, the realm of Being of Parmenides, and the Mind of Anaxagoras.[13] The notion of a living cosmos fashioned by the Demiurge (i.e., the personification of Intellect) would be elaborated by Plato in his dialogue *Timaeus*: "This, then, in keeping with our likely account, is how we must say divine providence brought our world into being as a truly living thing (*zoion*), endowed with soul and intelligence" (29e–30c), and "Since the god wanted nothing more than to make the world like the best of the intelligible things, complete in every way, he made it a single visible living thing, which contains within itself all the living things whose nature it is to share its kind" (30c–31a). The cosmos is therefore alive due to the activity of the universal Mind.

It is highly significant to an authentic philosophy of life that Anaxagoras disagreed with the prevailing Hellenic view (not to mention the modern humanistic view) that among mortal beings, Mind is limited to humans. In contrast, Anaxagoras recognized that each living thing has a share of Mind, including the lower animals and plants. As we read in Fragment 12, "And Mind rules all things that possess life—both the larger and the smaller." It is precisely due to the presence of Mind that plants and

---

11. Geldard, *Anaxagoras*, 78–79.
12. Geldard, *Anaxagoras*, 78, 87.
13. Geldard, *Anaxagoras*, 91.

animals possess sensation, thought, and feelings in varying degrees. And since all living things are sources of change and motion, for Anaxagoras these are due to the activity of Mind, which is the universal cosmic principle of change.[14] This admirable stance towards our fellow Earth-dwellers provides a further link between Anaxagoras and Indian philosophy, with its teaching that the individual self is identical with the World-Soul, or *Atman*. The latter is the life-principle which animates all organisms, just as the universal Mind does.[15]

For the sake of conceptual clarity, we must emphasize that Mind, or Intellect, should not be confused with reason, as any number of translators and commentators have done. In the Hellenic understanding, reason (*dianoia*) is an individual faculty limited to humans, whereas Intellect (*nous*) is universal and divine. This was understood by Meister Eckhart, who wrote that there is something in the human soul which is uncreated, and this is the Intellect. The two are yet related, Thomas Taylor noted, since reason is the power of the soul which derives the principles of its reasoning (*logismos*) from the Intellect.[16] However, in most of modern Western philosophy the concepts of Intellect and reason have become conflated.

Moreover, since Mind is the first cause of the cosmos arising from the relative non-being of formless matter, it implies that Mind provides the ultimate standard whereby things are measured and judged. Idealism is by its very nature opposed to the world-view of humanism, which holds mankind as such to be the final arbiter in all things—in other words, reality is viewed as man-centred instead of Mind-centred. In Western philosophy, the notion of humanism was first enunciated by Protagoras, an Athenian contemporary of Anaxagoras, who famously held that man (*ho anthrōpos*, which in Greek comprises male and female) is the measure (*metron*) of everything. As reported by Socrates, Protagoras said that "Man is the measure of all things: of the things which are, that they are, and of the things which are not, that they are not" (*Theaet*, 152a). This implies that truth is relative, and that different individuals will view it differently—the opposite of the stance taken in Idealism.

With his doctrine that Mind/Intellect is the ultimate cause of motion, Anaxagoras also became the first Western philosopher to clearly distinguish between the mover and the moved. In other words, all the motions

---

14. McKirahan, *Philosophy*, 221.
15. Geldard, *Anaxagoras*, 30.
16. Schuon, *Unity*, xxix–xxx; Taylor, *Introduction*, 104, 108.

of material things can be traced to the action of Mind. The basis of Mind's rule over all things is its power of causing them to move, not in a random fashion but in a way that sets them in order; the verb *diakosmein* (to set in order) is related to the noun *kosmos*, which means order.[17] That is to say, Intellect is the first cause of the orderly motion of the cosmos.

Given the wide-ranging relevance of Anaxagoras' thought, it is fitting that the American scholars Daniel Gersenshon and Daniel Greenberg declared Anaxagoras to be the first scientist, in the sense in which the latter term is used today (in their 1964 book *Anaxagoras and the Birth of Physics*). A few years earlier the celebrated physicist Erwin Schrödinger had already opposed the modernist dismissal of the Pre-Socratic natural philosophers in his treatise *Nature and the Greeks*. As recently commented, "This convergence of science and philosophy in Anaxagoras is significant and brings us to a consideration of Universal Mind as a property of physics as well as a subject of philosophy."[18]

According to Diogenes of Apollonia, a younger contemporary of Socrates, the entire world of physical phenomena arises from the intelligence (*noēsis*) underlying it. The term *noēsis* is cognate to *nous*, which (as we saw) is used by Anaxagoras for Mind. The following fragments from Diogenes' writing are relevant here: "In my opinion, to sum it all up, all things that are, are differentiated from the same thing and are the same thing. But all these things (earth, water, air, fire, and all the rest of the things in the cosmos), being differentiated out of the same thing, come to be different things at different times and return into the same thing" (Fragment 2); "For without intelligence (*noēsis*) it [i.e., the same thing] could not be distributed in such a way as to have the measures of all things—winter and summer, night and day, rains and winds and good weather" (Fragment 3); "Humans and animals live by means of air through breathing. And this (air) is both soul and intelligence for them, as will be displayed manifestly in this book. And if this departs, they die and their intelligence fails" (Fragment 4); "And in my opinion, that which possesses intelligence is what people call air, and all humans are governed by it and it rules all things. For in my opinion this very thing is god, and it reaches everything and arranges all things and is in everything. And there is no single thing which does not share in this. But no single thing shares in it in the same way as anything else, but there are many forms both of air itself and of intelligence. For it

17. McKirahan, *Philosophy*, 220.
18. Geldard, *Anaxagoras*, 17, 88.

is multiform. And the soul of all animals is the same thing. Now since the differentiation is multiform, also the animals are multiform and many and are like one another in neither shape nor way of life nor intelligence, on account of the large number of their differentiations. Nevertheless, all things live, see, and hear by means of the same thing, and all get the rest of their intelligence from the same thing" (Fragment 5).

It appears that for Diogenes all things in the cosmos arise as differentiations of Mind/Intellect and eventually return to it. And since everything arise through differentiation, the cosmos is multiform and not uniform in nature. Therefore, although humans and animals obtain their intelligence through breathing air (thus sharing in Mind), there is no question of a monistic reality for Diogenes. Instead, Diogenes continues the traditional metaphysics according to which cosmic reality comprises a differentiated unity—that is to say, a many-in-One.

Furthermore, for Diogenes the order in the universe is conceived as the result of intelligence, since if everything is arranged in the best possible way, it follows that the cause of that arrangement is intelligent.[19] In this way, as is the case with Anaxagoras, the world-view of Diogenes is teleological and not mechanistic in nature. This understanding of reality as entailing design (although not entirely so, as we will discuss) and purpose would be continued by Plato and Aristotle in the century after Anaxagoras and Diogenes.

Motion

The phenomenon of motion (Greek, *kinēsis*) has been investigated especially by Aristotle. Motion is defined by him as the fulfilment of what exists potentially, in so far as it exists potentially (*Phys*, III.201a). Motion is thus conceived by Aristotle as linked with *entelecheia*, which means fulfilment or completion. Motion is therefore purposeful, representing a transition from potentiality to actuality.[20] Aristotle enumerates six kinds of motion: generation and destruction (or coming to be and passing away), increase and diminution, alteration, and change of place or locomotion. The opposite of motion, broadly speaking, is rest (*Cat*, 14 & 15a–b). Moreover, and contrary to the modernist view of Aristotle as an anti-Platonist, it is affirmed in the *Metaphysics* that the good and the beautiful are the beginning

19. McKirahan, *Philosophy*, 346.
20. Dreyer, *Wysbegeerte*, 135.

(or cause) of the knowledge and of the motion of many things (V.1013a). Indeed, Plato could not have stated it better himself.

The factors involved in motion are listed by Aristotle as (a) that which directly causes motion, (b) that which is in motion, and (c) that in which motion takes place, namely time. Moreover, every motion proceeds from something and to something. For instance, 'perishing' entails change from being to non-being, whereas 'becoming' entails change from non-being to being (*Phys*, V.224a–b). In summary, it could be stated that three types of being are distinguished by Aristotle in terms of motion: that which is moved but does not move (primary matter); that which is moved and moves (all natural things); and that which causes motion without moving, namely God.[21] A kind of kinetic hierarchy is thus established with God at the summit, primary matter at the bottom, and the world of natural things in between.

Aristotle's discussion of motion culminates in his celebrated notion of the Prime Mover. Since motion is continuous, Aristotle reasons, there must be an ultimate first cause of all motion in the cosmos. As stated in the *Physics*, "Since there must always be motion without intermission, there must necessarily be something, one thing or it may be a plurality, that first imparts motion, and this first movent must be unmoved" (VIII.258b). The Prime Mover is then described as the unmoved mover which is one and eternal (VIII.259a).

In Book 12 of the *Metaphysics*, the Prime Mover is associated with God, with Aristotle writing as follows: "We say therefore that God is a living being, eternal, most good, so that life and duration continuous and eternal belong to God; for this is God"; and also, "The first mover, then, exists of necessity; and in so far as it exists by necessity, its mode of being is good, and it is in this sense a first principle. On such a principle, then, depend the heavens and the whole of nature" (XII.1072b). Thus, Aristotle recognizes the dependence of the cosmos on an extraneous first principle, the Prime Mover. And since the latter is the ultimate cause of all motion in the cosmos, we contend that the Prime Mover is the equivalent of the divine Intellect, or Mind, of Anaxagoras and Diogenes.

By combining the Aristotelian theory of motion with Neoplatonic metaphysical principles in his work *Elements of Physics*, Proclus arrives at the following hierarchy of motion, arranged from higher to lower levels of reality: (i) The unmoved movers (the Forms); (ii) the primary self-movers

---

21. Dreyer, *Wysbegeerte*, 136.

(souls) and the secondary self-movers (en-souled bodies); (iii) things moved by another and moving others (en-mattered forms); and (iv) things moved by another but not moving others (physical bodies). The third category, en-mattered forms, is sometimes equated by Proclus with Nature.[22] This category is therefore the realm in which the Forms act upon matter to produce physical objects, in turn representing the fourth and lowest category of motion.

The colossal importance of motion is illustrated by its role as cosmic link between space and time. In the traditional Indo-European understanding, time is the complement of space, just as energy is the complement of matter.[23] However, time can only be measured indirectly by means of relating it to space through the intermediary of movement. In other words, motion provides the link between space and time as far as measurement is concerned. In its turn, space constitutes the 'field' (Sanskrit, *kshetra*) within which bodily manifestation occurs. This 'space-time' interaction is depicted in physical and mathematical theories that treat of 'space-time' as a single and indivisible whole. As a matter of fact, time is only comparable to a fourth dimension in equations of movement, where time acts as a fourth co-ordinate added to the three dimensions of space.[24] The physical model of 'space-time' as a four-dimensional continuum, as postulated in the Theory of Special Relativity, is therefore also metaphysically valid, at least in terms of motion.

Furthermore, since time is the measurement of the changing positions of objects in space, it implies that before the beginning of the cosmos there was no time, just as in the beginning there were no objects in space. Therefore, Jonathan Black reasons, in the absence of matter, space, and time, the original cosmic event must have been a mental event. In theistic terms, this primal mental event was God reflecting on Himself, and in that reflection, He saw beings like Himself, possessing freedom, creativity, love, and intelligence. Therefore, matter emerged from the mind of God—it was created to provide the conditions in which the human mind (housed as it is in a physical body) would be possible. And since the human mind ultimately derives from the universal Mind, it is feasible that matter is moved by the

---

22. Martijn, Review of *Physics*, 44.
23. Schuon, *Divine*, 64.
24. Guénon, *Reign of Quantity*, 35, 40, 192, 193.

human mind in a similar way, albeit certainly not to the same extent, in which it is moved by the mind of God.[25]

Scientific Relevance

The famous paradox of Schrödinger's cat, formulated by the Austrian physicist Erwin Schrödinger in 1935, is noteworthy in this regard. In terms of this 'thought experiment' (as he called it), a cat in a sealed box containing a radio-active source could be either alive or dead, which can only be confirmed by an observer opening the box. This 'observer effect' was already implicit in the equally celebrated Uncertainty Principle, as formulated by the German physicist Werner Heisenberg in 1927. It states that the more precisely the position of a sub-atomic particle is determined, the less precisely its momentum can be known, and vice versa. Finally, after decades of disputation and contention, the observer effect was empirically verified by means of the double-slit experiment, as reported in 1998. This was conducted by scientists at the Weizmann Institute in Israel, revealing how a beam of electrons is affected by the act of observation. It thereby confirms a basic premise of quantum theory, namely that by the very act of watching, the observer affects the observed reality.[26]

According to the Western tradition of philosophical Idealism, from Pythagoras in the sixth century B.C. to Rudolf Steiner in the twentieth century, reality has been conceived as a series of thoughts emanating from the universal Mind. Jonathan Black explains that these thought-emanations occur in the following sequence: from pure mind to energy, to ethereal matter, to gas, to liquid, and to solids. In other words, the various states of matter are none other than energy becoming increasingly dense.[27] This process whereby physical reality emanates from the metaphysical realm has been described in detail by the Neoplatonists. We have already noted some of their contributions to cosmology and metaphysics, and more of their insights will follow in the chapters ahead.

A fascinating application of the notion of universal Mind is found in the biological work of Alfred Russel Wallace (1823–1913), the British naturalist and founder of the science of biogeography. Having done extensive fieldwork in Amazonia and Malaysia, Wallace conceived a theory of

---

25. Black, *Secret History*, 29, 32, 34.
26. https://www.sciencedaily.com/releases/1998/02/980227055013.htm
27. Black, *Secret History*, 37, 39.

evolution by means of natural selection independently of Charles Darwin and at the same time as his more famous colleague. However, in due course Wallace moved from a reliance on natural selection to a kind of natural theology that incorporated organic evolution. In 1869, Wallace wrote a review of the tenth edition of his friend Charles Lyell's famed *Principles of Geology*, in which he argued that human intelligence is too great to have been facilitated by natural selection. As a matter of fact, since natural selection is guided by the principle of utility, it would be an effective barrier to the development of such an order of intelligence. Therefore, Wallace concluded, another cause must be involved, which he called an Overruling Intelligence.[28] We suggest that this is none other than the Universal Mind of Anaxagoras and the divine Intellect of the Neoplatonists.

---

28. Flannery, *Intelligent Evolution*, 16–17.

Intellect and Necessity

IN THE NEOPLATONIC UNDERSTANDING, Intellect (or Mind, the Greek *nous*) is the second of the divine hypostases, obtaining its reality from the One. However, since the One is a hyper-cosmic reality, it could be stated that Intellect is the first principle of all things that exist. In other words, Intellect is the ontological storehouse of all potential beings (*Enneads*, V.2.1, V.9.5). To be more precise, Intellect contains all of the eternal and immutable Ideas, or Forms, through which the physical world comes into being. Plotinus employs the Stoic term *logoi spermatikoi*, or seminal reasons, to indicate the productive 'seeds' that become actualized as distinct from Intellect (*Enneads*, V.9.6-7). These 'rational seeds' contain the potentialities of all beings.[1] This reasoning implies that without Intellect, or the universal Mind of Anaxagoras, there would be no beings in existence.

In his brilliant study of the interaction between Neoplatonic philosophy and Christian theology, as represented by Plotinus and St Augustine respectively, the French philosopher Albert Camus sketches the intermediary role played by the Intellect as follows: "This Being that lies at the bottom of all things, that gives to the world its existence and its true meaning, draws all of its unity from its origin. And scattered in its intelligibles [i.e., the Forms] though being known as Intelligence, it is the ideal intermediary between the indefinable Good that we hope for and the Soul that breathes behind sensible appearances."[2] As intermediary between the One and Soul, Intellect receives its reality from the One and in turn bestows reality upon Soul, thereby becoming the foundation of all beings.

The creation of the cosmos is described in considerable detail by Plato in his late dialogue *Timaeus*, where Intellect is personified and called the Father, or more often the Demiurge (*ho demiourgos*, which has the meaning of a divine Craftsman). As Porphyry explains, with reference to Plotinus'

---

1. Moore, *Plotinus*.
2. Camus, *Christian Metaphysics*, 98.

teaching that the essence of the Godhead extends over three hypostases: "The highest god is the Good [i.e., the One], and after him and second there is the Demiurge, and third is the Soul of the Universe; for the divine realm proceeds as far as Soul" (*History of Philosophy*, Book 4). This reasoning confirms that Plato's Demiurge is a personification of the divine Intellect.

The concept of a creative Demiurge was not limited to Hellenism. The Greek Christian theologian Basil of Caesarea, although highly critical of Hellenic natural philosophy, referred to "the Creator and Demiurge of the universe" (*Hex I.5*). It has also been remarked that Plato's Demiurge is comparable to the Egyptian god Ptah, the divine intermediary between the creative idea and the physical product, and to Jesus Christ as the Logos through whom all things are created (as taught in Christian theology).[3]

Thesis: The Creation of the World by Intellect

Plato commences his account of cosmic creation by arguing that something which is visible and tangible, like our universe, had to have an origin instead of having always existed. The Athenian philosopher adds that to find the maker and father of this universe (Greek, *to pan*, literally 'the whole'; Latin, *omnis*, 'every or all')[4] is hard enough, and to declare him to everyone is impossible. At any rate, this world of ours was fashioned after an eternal model and is grasped by a rational account, i.e., by wisdom (*Tim*, 28b-29a). Interestingly, Plato's apophatic theology (of which more in a later chapter) was admired by the Greek Christian theologian Clement of Alexandria, who described Plato as a sincere friend of the truth, for recognizing that the mystery of the divine being cannot be expressed in words.[5]

In the Platonic understanding, goodness is an essential attribute of the divinity. The goodness of the Demiurge is moreover stated as the motive for creation: "He was good, and one who is good can never become jealous of anything. And so, being free of jealousy, he wanted everything to become as much like himself as was possible. The god wanted everything to be good and nothing to be bad so far as that was possible, and so he took over all that was visible—not at rest but in discordant and disorderly motion—and brought it from a state of disorder to one of order, because he believed that order was in every way better than disorder" (*Tim*, 29e-30a). Motivated by

3. Ferguson, *Pythagoras*, 130.
4. LSJ, 535; Wheeler, *Latin*, 529.
5. Alfeyev, *Mystery*, 27.

his goodness, the divine Intellect transforms the pre-cosmic disorder into cosmic order.

To the question as to why God created all things, Patristic theology gave the same answer as Plato: out of the abundance of his goodness. As John of Damascus writes, "Because the good and transcendently good God was not content to contemplate himself, but by a superabundance of goodness saw fit that there should be some things to benefit by and to participate in his goodness, he brings all things from nothing into being and created them."[6] However, in this passage we notice a divergence from the Platonic cosmology, namely that God creates the world from nothing, as opposed to forming it from primordial matter.

Plato continues his account as follows: "The god reasoned and concluded that in the realm of things naturally visible no unintelligent thing could as a whole be better than anything which does possess intelligence as a whole, and he further concluded that it is impossible for anything to come to possess intelligence apart from soul. Guided by this reasoning, he [the Demiurge] put intelligence in soul, and soul in body, and so he constructed the universe. This, then, in keeping with our likely account, is how we must say divine providence brought our world into being as a truly living thing, endowed with soul and intelligence" (*Tim*, 30b–c).

An identical causal schema to the foregoing is depicted in the ancient Hermetic writings, according to which the soul makes copies in the physical world of the things which Mind (*nous*) makes in the soul itself. In its turn, Mind makes copies in the soul of the things which the First Cause of all makes in Mind. Consequently, all the shapes and images which we can see with our bodily eyes in the sensible world of becoming are only semblances and copies of the eternal forms in the intelligible world of real being.[7]

In his *Platonic Theology*, the great Neoplatonist thinker Proclus credits Plato for advancing our understanding of theology beyond some earlier views, such as the identification of 'gods' with first principles in nature, or with the faculties of soul. "Only the divinely-inspired philosophy of Plato," writes Proclus, "asserts, as has been said, that Intellect is the father and causal principle of both bodies and souls, and that everything that exercises its life in conditions of progression and unfolding possesses its being and its actualization in dependence on Intellect. But, then, it advances to another

6. Quoted in Alfeyev, *Mystery*, 43–44.
7. Perry, *Treasury*, 672–673.

first principle, completely transcending Intellect, yet more incorporeal and ineffable than it, from which all ... must derive their existence" (Book I.3). This transcendent Principle is, of course, the One.

Since the physical world must have bodily form, Plato continues, it must be visible and tangible (*Tim*, 31b). The components of the world therefore must include fire and earth, and since these elements are solids, the Demiurge also created air and water as intermediates to combine them. Each of these four elements are composed of different geometrical solids.[8] The Demiurge made the sensible world from these four elements, bound together as a 'symphony of proportion' (*Tim*, 32b–c).

It should be noted that initially the four kinds (*genē*) of fire, air, water, and earth are without proportion and measure. They are 'thoroughly godforsaken' in their natural condition, and therefore the Demiurge must give these kinds their distinctive shapes, by means of forms (*eidesi*) and numbers (*arithmois*) (*Tim*, 53a–b). The Demiurge employs specific geometrical figures known as regular solids: the tetrahedron for fire, the octahedron for air, the icosahedron for water, and the cube for earth (*Tim*, 55e–56a). These 'shapes and numbers' used by the Demiurge to produce the cosmos out of chaos are the basic intelligible features of the world.[9]

Plato adds that the world was created spherical in shape: "He [the Demiurge] gave it a shape appropriate to the kind of thing it was. The appropriate shape for the living being that is to contain within itself all the living beings would be the one which embraces within itself all the shapes there are. Hence, he gave it a round shape, the form of a sphere, with its center equidistant from the extremes in all directions. This of all shapes is the most complete and like itself, which he gave to it because he believed that likeness is incalculably more excellent than unlikeness" (*Tim*, 33b). As a matter of fact, the sphere is the most uniform of all solid figures and the only one which can move without change of place, through rotating on its axis. For Plato, the rotation of the world with all its contents shows the penetration and rule of intelligence over the entire universe.[10]

As a further step in the creative process, the Demiurge sets soul in the center of the cosmos, so that soul is given priority to rule over the physical universe: "And he [the Demiurge] placed soul into the midst of it, and stretched it through the whole of it, and enveloped its body with it from

---

8. Cohen, "*Plato's Cosmology*."
9. Gerson, *Aristotle*, 219.
10. Cornford, *Plato's Cosmology*, 54, 57.

without" (*Tim*, 34b). The visible world is therefore a living creature, having soul (*psychē*) in its body and mind (*nous*) in its soul.

Four kinds of living beings were made by the Demiurge, corresponding to the four primary elements (*Tim*, 39e–40a). These are: (i) the heavenly gods, in which the element of fire is dominant; (ii) the flying creatures (air); (iii) the aquatic creatures (water); and (iv) the terrestrial creatures (earth). Interestingly, the Demiurge himself makes only the heavenly gods, while the remaining three classes of living beings were made by these gods. Plato's delegation of the rest of the creative work to the celestial gods may reflect a notion that the heavenly bodies, especially the Sun, actively generates life on Earth.[11] We also read in the *Politeia* that the Sun is the cause of coming to be, growth, and nourishment of things in the visible world, without itself coming to be (Book VI, 509b).

Aristotle likewise recognized the influence of the Sun in the generation of living beings, as we read in the *Physics*: "Man is begotten by man and by the sun as well" (II.194). He suggests elsewhere that the efficient cause of things coming to be and passing away is the movement of the Sun towards and away from the earth: "Thus we see that coming-to-be occurs as the sun approaches and decay as it retreats; and we see that the two processes occupy equal times" (*De Gen et Corr*, II.336b). In other words, for Aristotle the generation and destruction of substance is caused by the annual movement of the Sun in the ecliptic or zodiac cycle.[12]

Antithesis: The Role of Necessity

Unlike the Judaic and Christian doctrine on God as creator, the Platonic Intellect is not viewed as omnipotent (or all-powerful) in fashioning the physical world. The reason for this limitation is that Intellect is constrained by an opposing force, which is necessity (Greek, *anangkē*; also translated as force or restraint).[13] This view was already stated in mythical language by Parmenides, writing that Necessity is a goddess who governs all things. This includes the celestial bodies, which are led and shackled by necessity.[14] Plato describes the role of necessity in the establishment of the cosmos as follows: "For this ordered world was of mixed birth: it is the offspring of a

11. Cornford, *Plato's Cosmology*, 118, 141.
12. Cornford, *Plato's Cosmology*, 11.
13. LSJ, 58.
14. McKirahan, *Philosophy*, 177.

union of necessity and Intellect. Intellect prevailed over necessity by persuading it to direct most of the things that come to be towards what is best, and the result of this subjugation of necessity to wise persuasion was the initial formation of the universe" (*Tim*, 48a).

In the Platonic understanding, necessity is associated with disorder and random chance. Necessity means the indeterminate, the inconstant, the anomalous; it is a force that is irregular and unintelligible. In his informative commentary on the *Timaeus*, Francis Cornford writes further that necessity resides in the properties of the elements. For example, fire has a characteristic power (Greek, *dynamis*) to produce burning heat. Since necessity is constrained by its own nature, Plato calls it a wandering cause; in other words, a cause without purpose.[15]

Plato therefore mentions two types of causes, "distinguishing those which possess understanding and thus fashion what is beautiful and good, from those which, when deserted by intelligence, produce only haphazard and disorderly effects every time" (*Tim*, 46e). Nonetheless, the Demiurge uses these lower, auxiliary causes (*synaitia*) to produce the best result possible (*Tim*, 46c). The properties of these contributing structures are unalterable by the Demiurge, which is the reason why persuasion by Intellect is required for creation to take place.[16] Necessity is therefore a second principle (*archē*) in the origin of things (*Tim*, 48b), next to Intellect.

The phenomenon of necessity was naturally explored by such a keen observer of nature as Aristotle, who made a distinction between two kinds of necessity. On the one hand there is absolute necessity, which is manifested in eternal phenomena, and on the other hand there is hypothetical necessity, which is manifested in everything that is generated by nature and everything that is produced by art (*PA* I.639b). A conspicuous example of hypothetical necessity is animals requiring food to live (*PA* I.642a). An important instance of absolute necessity is circular motion, such as that of the sun which ensures the continuity of alternate generation and destruction (*De Gen et Corr*, II.338a). Many other natural phenomena are due to absolute necessity, flowing inevitably from the nature of the specific matter.[17] The effects of gravity would be a notable example of absolute necessity. Whereas Aristotle thus views absolute necessity as unrelated to final

---

15. Cornford, *Plato's Cosmology*, 160, 165, 171–172, 174.
16. Zeyl, "*Plato's Timaeus*."
17. Ross, *Aristotle*, 81.

causality (due to lacking purpose), the hypothetical necessity in nature provides the conditions for an explanation in terms of final causality.[18]

It was further reasoned by Aristotle that the formation of a person's eye serves a certain purpose in accordance with the reason (*logos*) of the individual, while the color of the eye is incidental and must 'of necessity' (*ex anangkēs*) be ascribed to its matter and moving cause (*GA*, 778a–b). Sometimes necessity even opposes purpose, as in the case of monstrous births that are due to defective matter (*GA*, 767b).[19] This reasoning implies that tragic conditions such as physical deformity and mental retardation are due to material imperfections that could not be overcome by the activity of Intellect.

Aristotle's well-known insistence on final causality, or teleology, enables him to indemnify the Prime Mover (which is his conception of the divine Intellect) from the imperfections in nature. Thus, imperfections in the structure of animals are ascribed to defective material, not a defective maker. This phenomenon is due to the fact that matter is sometimes not suitable for the purpose in hand, Aristotle suggested. In their turn, imperfections in individual organisms are due to the inherent variability of matter, since the latter is formed of an endless variety of combinations of the four elements.[20] Nevertheless, final causality cannot be ignored, he writes: "Both causes must be stated by the physicist, but especially the end; for that is the cause of the matter, not vice versa" (*Phys* II.200a). By recognising the role of both final causality and necessity in the physical world, Aristotle continues Plato's notion that the cosmos is the product of the interaction between the divine Intellect and irrational Necessity.

The phenomenon of physical deformity has been explained by Thomas Aquinas in terms of Aristotelian causality: "For if the matter is not disposed to receive the agent's imprint [i.e., the operation of the efficient cause] a defect will follow in the effect, as when monsters are born because of unprepared matter: the fact that it doesn't transform and actualize the indisposed matter can't be laid at the door of the agent, for agents have powers proportioned to their natures and their inability to go further can't be called deficiency in power; we can say that only when its power falls short of the measure laid down by nature" (*Summa contra Gentiles*, 3.10).

---

18. Gerson, *Aristotle*, 122.
19. Ross, *Aristotle*, 82.
20. Ross, *Aristotle*, 130.

Synthesis: The Combination of Intellect and Necessity

After describing the role of Necessity, Plato devotes the next part of the *Timaeus* to a discussion of the physical cosmos, which is presented as the offspring of the union of Intellect and Necessity. Stated the other way around, Intellect persuades Necessity to form the initial universe: "For the generation of this universe was a mixed result of the combination of Necessity and Intellect. Intellect overruled Necessity by persuading her to guide the greatest part of the things that become towards what is best; in that way and on that principle this universe was fashioned in the beginning by the victory of reasonable persuasion over Necessity" (*Tim*, 48a; Cornford's translation). As Plato concludes, "That is why we must distinguish two forms of cause, the divine and the necessary" (*Tim*, 68e).

However, the result of the restriction of the activity of Intellect by irrational Necessity is that the physical world displays both design and accident, is both purposeful and contingent, and harbours both good and bad. This statement should not be confused with Gnostic dualism, according to which the world is inherently evil due to its creation by an inferior deity. In the traditional understanding, evil is not self-existing but follows from a privation of goodness, just as darkness is due to an absence of light.

Within this context of the interaction between Intellect and Necessity, Plato situates the constitution of the human being and the causal principles of its being. Earlier, in Book IV of the *Republic,* the various elements, or parts, of the individual soul had been sketched: the highest is reason, the lowest is appetite, and in between is *thymos*. The latter term is translated as any vehement passion, anger, or wrath, and in the good sense as spirit or courage.[21] Now, in the *Timaeus*, Plato depicts the creation of the soul's elements, as at least being a likely account (72d). The highest element, reason, is the immortal part of the soul and is therefore situated in the head, which is "the most divine part of us, and the master of all our other parts" (44d). This is followed by the creation of the mortal parts of the soul: the spirited part which is situated in the chest, and the appetitive part which is placed in the lower abdomen (69c–71a).

As a reflection of the intelligible and sensible realms of the cosmos, Plato thus conceives of the human being as consisting of two main components that differ essentially. On the one hand, there is the soul which participates in the realm of Ideas, and which is immortal and the bearer of

---

21. Lee, *Republic*, 207–208; LSJ, 323.

Intellect. On the other hand, there is the body which is part of the sensible world, and which is mortal and represents the principle of Necessity in the human being.[22] This anthropology would exercise an immense influence on Christian thought, in both the Greek and Latin traditions.

It has often been stated that the human body is a marvel of design, and in the case of religious believers this design is attributed to God. Now, if one considers the immense complexity and intricacy of organs such as the brain, the heart, and the eye, then the human body does appear to be marvellously designed. If, on the other hand, one considers the extreme susceptibility of the human body to an almost infinite range of illnesses and injuries during the entire lifespan between conception and death, a rather different picture emerges. One only has to think of the plethora of childhood diseases and bone fractures, the debilitating conditions appearing later in life, such as multiple sclerosis, diabetes, and arthritis, and the horrors of a whole range of cancers, as well as Alzheimer's and Parkinson's diseases.

There are two possible explanations for this organic ambivalence: either the human body was designed by God, in which case He would have to be held responsible for the prevalence of disease and physical suffering among humans; or the human body is the product of the interaction between the divine Intellect and irrational Necessity, in which case there is no blame or responsibility involved in this matter. We contend that the latter alternative, as taught by Plato and Aristotle, is the more accurate one, and in fact the only explanation that does justice to both the existential reality and the divine Goodness. In contrast, the human soul is of divine origin—in particular, the rational dimension of the soul, which is also the seat of its immortality.

---

22. Dreyer, *Wysbegeerte*, 102.

Soul and Matter

IN THE TRADITIONAL INDO-EUROPEAN conception, each manifested being is a composite of form and matter (Greek, *eidos* and *hylē*), these terms being the equivalent of the Sanskrit *nāma* and *rūpa*. Such a composite being could therefore be described as an embodied form, or *nāma-rūpa*. In addition, since *nāma* means idea, archetype or form, it is the efficient cause of the individual as *nāma-rūpa*. In the case of living beings this composition appears as the two levels of formal manifestation, namely the psychic and the corporeal (Greek, *psychikos* and *somatikos*), or soul and body respectively. And since Spirit, which is associated with Intellect, can never be individual or corporeal, it is transcendent in relation to the combination of soul and body. Therefore, a human being cannot speak of 'his' or 'her' Spirit, as can indeed be predicated of the soul and body.[1]

Incidentally, this differentiation between Spirit and soul enables one to understand certain biblical passages that would otherwise be problematic. For instance, we read of Christ saying that only someone who hates his own soul (*eautou psychēn*) can become His disciple (Luke 14:26). This verse is usually translated as 'hates his own life,' which literally means the same, but it is evident from the context that the lower soul is meant. We also find a statement by St Paul in his letter to the Hebrews (4:12) that the word of God pierces even to the division of soul and spirit (*psychēs kai pneumatos*), of which the latter term refers to the higher power of the soul, which is really the Spirit as the 'royal guest' of the soul.[2]

---

1. Guénon, *Reign of Quantity*, 20–21, 337; Coomaraswamy, *Civilization*, 31; Guénon, "Spirit and Intellect," 2–3.
2. Coomaraswamy, *Civilization*, 63.

Plato

In the Platonic understanding, the World-soul and all individual souls partake of both being and becoming. The reason for this ambivalence is that Soul is like the Forms due to being eternal and of one substance, but unlike the Forms in that it is alive and intelligent.[3] Plato writes that "by our bodies and through perception we have dealings with coming-to-be, but we deal with real being by our souls and through reasoning" (*Sophist*, 248a). We notice in this passage that sense-perception is a function of the body (albeit operating in conjunction with the soul), while reasoning is a function of the soul—to be more precise, the highest level of the soul, the rational (Greek, *logikos*, or belonging to the reason).[4]

Since the World-soul obtains its reality from the Intellect, it is the bearer of the reason (Greek, *logos*) which works in on the whole cosmos. Due to this indwelling rationality, the cosmos is ordered and lawful. For Plato the World-soul precedes the existence of the corporeal world, just as it is itself preceded by the Demiurge (or Intellect). The World-soul is intermediate between the Forms and matter, and is thus the agency through which matter participates in the Forms.[5] Soul is invisible, Plato adds, and is the most excellent of all things begotten by the Demiurge (*Tim*, 36e–37a).

In the dialogue *Timaeus*, Plato introduces a 'third kind' (in addition to being and becoming) that pre-exists the cosmos: "The earlier two [kinds] sufficed for our previous account: one was proposed as a model, intelligible and always changeless, a second as an imitation of the model, something that possesses becoming and is visible. Now, however, it appears that our account compels us to attempt to illuminate in words a kind that is difficult and vague. What must we suppose it to do and to be? This above all: it is a receptacle (*hypodochē*) of all becoming—its wetnurse, as it were" (48e–49a). The three kinds are summarized as follows: "For the moment, we need to keep in mind three types of things: that which comes to be [i.e., sensible objects], that in which it comes to be [i.e., the receptacle], and that after which the thing coming to be is modelled, and which is the source of its coming to be [i.e., the Forms]. It is in fact appropriate to compare the receiving thing to a mother, the source to a father, and the nature between them to their offspring" (50c–d). Plato also describes this third

---

3. Cornford, *Plato's Cosmology*, 61–64.
4. LSJ, 416.
5. Dreyer, *Wysbegeerte*, 101.

kind as space, which provides a fixed state for all things that come to be (52a–b). It has been commented that since the created world is visible and tangible, Plato is required to postulate a three-dimensional 'field' in which the universe may subsist.[6] The receptacle of becoming fills this need, for the Greek prefix *hypo* means 'under,' so that the receptacle is that which underlies the world of becoming.

Plato then proceeds to sketch the nature of the receptacle: "This is why the thing that is to receive in itself all the elemental kinds must be totally devoid of any characteristics. In the same way, then, if the thing that is to receive repeatedly throughout its whole self the likeness of the intelligible objects, the things which always are—if it is to do so successfully, then it ought to be devoid of any inherent characteristics of its own. But if we speak of it as an invisible and characterless sort of thing, one that receives all things and shares in a most perplexing way in what is intelligible, a thing extremely difficult to comprehend, we shall not be misled" (*Tim*, 50b–51b).

This description affirms that Plato's receptacle of becoming is formless or pre-formed matter, out of which the physical world arises. It is therefore similar to the Aristotelian *hylē* and the Scholastic *materia*, which are not identical to the modern, reductionist view of matter, as René Guénon remarks, but are in fact related to the traditional Indo-European concept of universal substance (Sanskrit, *Prakriti*). As a universal principle the latter is pure potentiality, in which nothing is actualized and which underlies all physical manifestation. The Latin term for substance, *substantia*, is derived from *sub stare*, which means that which stand beneath (as is the case with the Greek *hypostasis*).[7] As universal substance, the receptacle of becoming gives rise to the world of phenomena through the various elements: "Earth, Water, Fire, Air, Ether, Mind, Reason, and Ego—thus eightfold is my *Prakriti* divided" (*Bhagavad Gita*, 7.4).

It has been commented that Plato's receptacle is not that 'out of which' things are made, but rather that 'in which' qualities appear. It is therefore these qualities, not the receptacle as such, which constitute the sensible world.[8] And in his *Commentary on Timaeus*, Proclus adds to Plato's account as follows: "Perhaps it is better to say that the term 'things that pass in and out' is applied not only to the qualities, but also to the forms immersed in matter; for these, not the qualities, are likenesses of the intelligible

---

6. Zeyl, "*Plato's Timaeus.*"
7. Guénon, *Reign of Quantity*, 25–26.
8. Cornford, *Plato's Cosmology*, 181.

things."⁹ In other words, the invisible receptacle of becoming receives the imprints of the Forms and thereby produces the visible qualities that we observe in the cosmos.

The Platonic cosmology, in terms of which God creates the world through the imposition of order onto pre-cosmic disorder, appears to be at least partially compatible with the biblical cosmology. Before the commencement of God's creative activity, "The Earth was without form, and void; and darkness was on the face of the deep. And the Spirit of God was hovering over the face of the waters" (Gen 1:2–3). As Alan Watts comments on this text, before He made anything else, God made matter (Latin, *materia*, which is cognate to *mater*, mother) as the maternal womb of the universe, for it is a general principle in mythology that matter is the feminine component and spirit the masculine, their respective symbols being water or earth and air or fire. Thus, "In the beginning the Spirit conceived, the waters gave birth, and the world which was born from their conjunction was the first material image of the Word, of God the Son, the Logos who was the ideal pattern after which the creation was modeled."[10]

The biblical depiction of the Earth as being formless and void suggests the formless pre-matter out of which the world was to be created, or its 'astonishing emptiness' in the words of Philaret of Moscow. As further explained by his countryman Hilarion Alfeyev, this pre-matter is "a chaotic primary substance containing the pledge of future beauty and cosmic harmony." The 'darkness' and 'deep' indicate the formlessness of matter, while 'water' suggests its plasticity. And the 'hovering' of the Spirit denotes its protection and animation of the material world, by breathing life into it.[11] This view of primordial chaos evokes Plato's description of the receptacle of becoming, while its animation by Spirit echoes the role of Intellect, which transforms pre-cosmic chaos into cosmic order.

Evidently, for Plato the sensible world is produced by the interaction between the principle of form and formless matter. As commented by Philip Sherrard, this does not entail an absolute duality, since the principle of form (the Demiurge) is not the absolute reality, but a determination of the transcendent Good (the One). Furthermore, in Plato's understanding, formless matter (which he also calls space, *chōra*) is not the substance out of which things are made, but it precedes substance as the receptacle in which

---

9. Cornford, *Plato's Cosmology*, 183.
10. Watts, *Myth and Ritual*, 46–47.
11. Alfeyev, *Mystery*, 50.

sensible things originate. Also, this formless matter (the receptacle) does not pre-exist the cosmos like Aristotle's matter (*hylē*), but originates and participates ('in a most obscure way,' Plato admits) in the pre-formal Reality from which the principle of form derives (*Tim*, 50c–51b). Thus, both Form and formless matter originate in the supreme Reality of the One.[12]

Plato held further that Soul is the only source of motion and thereby of the cosmic order. Therefore, motion is not caused by one or more of the four primary elements, as some earlier philosophers had taught (*Tim*, 46d). Soul is not only the source of motion, Plato writes elsewhere (in the *Laws*), but it is more specifically the first cause of the birth and destruction of all physical things (891e), the main cause of their alterations and transformations (892a), and the cause of all change in things (896a). Moreover, the physical world obtains its orderly arrangement (which is the meaning of the Greek noun *kosmos*) through the activity of Soul, for it is Soul that 'implants' the reason-principles (*logoi*) into matter.

We could say that the reality of Soul affirms the reality of both being and becoming, while also preventing a dichotomy between the intelligible and sensible realms. Plato argued that the true philosopher will reject both notions, namely that everything is at rest (the being of Parmenides) or that reality changes in every way (the becoming of Heraclitus). Instead, "He has to be like a child begging for 'both,' and say that that which is—everything—is both the unchanging and that which changes" (*Sophist*, 249c–d). In view of this clear statement, we should again note the error of the oft-repeated charge that Plato espoused a static cosmology and a dualistic metaphysics.

In the Platonic understanding, the human being is a (temporary) composite of a mortal body and an immortal soul. It thus involves a duality of substances, which is not the same thing as to assert an anthropological dualism. The difference between duality and dualism has been lucidly explained by René Guénon: "Dualism (of which the Cartesian conception of 'spirit' and 'matter' is among the best known examples) properly consists in regarding a duality as irreducible and in taking account of nothing beyond it, thereby denying the common principle from which the two terms of the duality really proceed by polarisation."[13] This reasoning also applies to the composite of an immortal soul and a mortal body, since both of these substances comprising the human being are derived from a single Principle.

---

12. Sherrard, *Greek East*, 6.
13. Guénon, *Reign of Quantity*, 354.

Aristotle

Building on the metaphysical concepts which he had learnt from Plato, while adding his own powerful analytical skills, Aristotle emphasizes that each existing substance consists of both form (*eidos*) and matter (*hylē*). While matter is the principle of concreteness and individuality, form expresses generality and determines the essence of a thing.[14] This argument is illustrated by means of a bronze statue: the matter is the bronze, the form is the shape or pattern, and the concrete whole (i.e., substance) is the statue. However, the form is prior both to the matter and the compound (*Met* VII.1029a). This affirmation by Aristotle that the form of sensible composites has more being than the matter or the composite itself is harmonious with Plato's notion that eternal substances have 'more being' (*mallon onta*) than sensible substances (*Met* VII.1028b).[15] Aristotle thus continues the Platonic dictum that the formal precedes the material in the constitution of cosmic reality.

In the Aristotelian conception, real matter is formed matter possessing limited possibilities. Nonetheless, there is a positive side to material limitations, namely that a specific matter has a natural inclination to assume certain forms. For example, stone and wood naturally incline to become a house. This implies that there is a natural purposefulness inherent in matter, such as the body of a child to become an adult human. Furthermore, for Aristotle matter is a purely relative term, being relative to form. Accordingly, in nature the elements are matter relative to their simple compounds, namely tissues; the latter is matter relative to the organs; and the latter is matter relative to the living body.[16] Ontologically speaking, as we have noted in an earlier chapter, matter represents the realm of relative being.

Furthermore, matter is associated with potency (or potentiality) and form with actuality, as Aristotle states: "Further, matter exists in a potential state, just because it may come to its form; and when it exists actually, then it is its form" (*Met* IX.1050a). Therefore, to actualize a possibility is the same as to give form to matter. A particular matter only contains certain possibilities, and therefore matter depends on form for its realization. The Aristotelian notion of the interaction between potency and actuality has been stated as follows: when a being has exceeded its state of potentiality

---

14. Dreyer, *Wysbegeerte*, 131.
15. Gerson, *Aristotle*, 195.
16. Dreyer, *Wysbegeerte*, 133, 135.

and attained to its highest goal, namely pure actuality, it can be viewed as a fully realized being.[17]

The priority of Soul in the physical realm applies particularly to living beings, naturally including humans. Aristotle declares the priority of soul in human beings as follows: "Further, since it is the soul by or with which primarily we live, perceive and think:—it follows that the soul must be a ratio or formulable essence, not a matter or subject" (*De An*, II.414a). In addition, although all living beings possess soul, the faculty of mind (*nous*) is found only among humans. For Aristotle, it is this rational faculty that distinguishes humans from all other earthly beings.[18]

However, given the pervasive reality of human ignorance and stupidity, we would add that among many humans the rational faculty remains a potentiality rather than an actuality. As Friedrich Nietzsche writes, humans have made their way from worm to man, but much in man is still worm; and once humans were apes, but even now man is more of an ape than any ape.[19] And as Albert Einstein famously remarked, only two things are infinite, namely the universe and human stupidity; although he was not so certain about the universe.[20]

The Neoplatonists

According to Plotinus, Soul (*psychē*) is the third hypostasis of the Divinity. Soul emanates from Intellect through the latter's contemplation of the One. In its turn, Soul contemplates Intellect, which brings forth the cosmos through emanation. But whereas Intellect becomes divided within itself through contemplation, Soul becomes divided outside of itself. This division of Soul constitutes the cosmos, which is therefore the self-expression of Soul and is also referred to as Nature.[21] The totality of Soul in the cosmos is referred to as the World-soul (*psychē tou pantos*), a concept derived from the Stoic philosophy.

Plotinus writes in Book III of the *Enneads* that since God (i.e., the One) is pure spirit, Soul (as second emanation from the One, after Intellect)

---

17. Dreyer, *Wysbegeerte*, 133; Goosen, *Nihilisme*, 202–203.

18. Dreyer, *Wysbegeerte*, 140.

19. Nietzsche, *Zarathustra*, 42; keeping in mind that Nietzsche appears to accept the Darwinian theory of human descent, which this author does not.

20. https://www.goodreads.com/author/quotes/9810.Albert_Einstein

21. Moore, *Neoplatonism*.

is the effect and image of pure spirit. Soul is super-sensuous and intelligible, and by contemplating the Ideas, or Forms, it forms the cosmos in the image of the Ideas. Thus, as generator of and ruler over the material world, Soul forms the material beings according to their prototypes in Intellect (these being the eternal Forms). Accordingly, Plotinus reasons, the World-soul contains the realm of nature (*physis*) as an emanation from the One via Intellect. Nature is in fact the level where Soul becomes fragmented into individual, embodied souls. The position of the individual soul is therefore intermediate between the World-soul and nature, so that it displays points of congruence with both realms.[22]

In the cosmology of Plotinus, beyond the confines of the circle of the Soul lies the material world, into which the Soul breathes life. In this way the world reflects the divine reality received from Intellect and Soul, including the manifestation of beauty.[23] Regarding the relation between Soul and physical nature, Plotinus follows Plato's example by using the term living being (*zōion*) for the composite of body and soul in an individual: "What we should say is that the living being is either a certain kind of body [living], or the sum [of body and soul], or some other third thing that arises from both of these" (*Enneads*, I.1.5). It appears that Plotinus views a living being as the product that arises from the combination of body and soul, and not the mere sum thereof.[24]

The process of emanation from the One via the Intellect and the Soul ends in matter (*hylē*). In Books II and III of the *Enneads*, matter is variously described by Plotinus as without magnitude, bodiless, invisible, without quality, impassable, unalterable, indestructible, unlimited, and indefinite (these terms remind us of Plato's description of the receptacle of becoming). Nonetheless, these negative aspects of matter are required in order to receive the Forms as images, and for matter to serve as principle of generation and change. Matter is in this way conceived by Plotinus as the principle of differentiation among existent things.[25] Matter could therefore be viewed as the antipode of the One, which is the principle of unification in the cosmos.

The dissolution of the World-soul into individual souls and their descent into matter, as conceived by Plotinus, has been vividly described by

22. Laos, *Metaphysics*, 32; Moore, *Plotinus*; Oosthuizen, *Plotinus*, 114, 121.
23. Alfeyev, *Mystery*, 7.
24. Dillon and Gerson, *Neoplatonic Philosophy*, 278.
25. Gerson, *Aristotle*, 107; Moore, *Plotinus*.

Albert Camus: "To sum up, the complete unity of souls [i.e., the World-soul] is a unity of convergence by which they all participate in the same living reality. Their multiplicity is . . . a loosening that brings to the fore the particularities of individual souls. Plunging into darkness little by little, these souls sink into matter. For Plotinus, the cause of this fall of the soul is both audacity and blindness. The soul is reflected in matter, and taking this reflecting for itself, it descends to become united with it, when it should, on the contrary, elevate itself in order to return to its origins."[26] Recognizing the causal link between the soul's blindness to the higher realities and its entrapment in matter became axiomatic in Neoplatonic cosmology and psychology.

Another major Neoplatonist, Iamblichus, affirms Plato's teaching on the soul occupying a middle position between those things that are really existent and those things that are subject to generation (*On the Mysteries*, II.2).[27] He thus continues Plato's notion that the soul is intermediate between the realms of being (the Forms) and becoming (material bodies). However, against any notion of a soul/body dualism, Iamblichus held that the soul becomes fully embodied in earthly, material reality. The soul's awareness of its embodied reality is moreover a prerequisite for its return journey to the One.[28]

In his turn, Proclus states that Soul has an intermediate existence between the rationality of Intellect and the irrationality of matter: whereas the highest part of Soul consorts with rationality, the lowest part declines towards sensation.[29] In other words, Soul is the mediator between Intellect and matter, or the link between Mind and matter. The psychic level of reality is thus situated between the intellectual level above and the material level below. It is therefore wrong, as is often done, to either equate the psychic with the intellectual or to reduce it to the material. These are three distinct levels of reality, with Intellect as the higher, matter as the lower, and Soul in between.

Since Soul proceeds from Intellect, Proclus reasons, the individual soul possesses the reflections (*emphaseis*) of the Forms, albeit in a secondary mode. Moreover, because soul participates in Intellect it can impart the reason-principles (*logoi*) of material things, thereby causing bodies to exist.

26. Camus, *Christian Metaphysics*, 100–101.
27. Dillon and Gerson, *Neoplatonic Philosophy*, 228.
28. Goosen, *Nihilisme*, 96–97.
29. Cornford, *Plato's Cosmology*, 65.

Also, against Plotinus' notion that a part of the individual soul remains above the sensible realm, Proclus argues in favour of full indwelling: "Every particular soul, when it descends into the realm of generation, descends completely; it is not a case that there is a part of it that remains above and a part that descends" (*Elem Theol*, Proposition 211).[30]

Furthermore, since the origin of Soul lies in the intelligible world, it implies that the physical world has a transcendent origin. In the words of Proclus: "Beyond all bodies is the essence of the soul; and beyond all souls is the intellectual nature; and beyond all intellectual substances, the One" (*Elem Theol*, Proposition 20). Elsewhere Proclus affirms that all of Nature is ultimately rooted in the One: "That, then, is the One the principle of all generation both for the manifold powers of nature, and for particular natures, and for all those things under the sway of nature" (*Commentary on Parmenides*, VI.1046). Even matter, which is a privation of goodness, proceeds from and participates in the Good (*Elem Theol*, Propositions 57 and 72). This leads Proclus to conclude that the Good (i.e., the One) is more universally productive than Being, since the One produces even formless matter, while Being produces objects insofar they have some form.[31]

Further Aspects

The interaction between Soul and matter is aptly illustrated by the model of the labyrinth, as encountered from Hellenic myth down to more recent maze gardens. This model harbours the additional benefit of accommodating the restriction of Intellect by Necessity, as discussed in the previous chapter. In Hellenic myth, the labyrinth of Knossos on Crete was designed by the famed craftsman Daedalus to imprison the fearsome Minotaur, which would ultimately be slain by the hero Theseus. The labyrinth was so elaborate that only with the help of Ariadne's thread could Theseus navigate his way through it.

Jonathan Black has provided a helpful commentary on this myth of Theseus and the Minotaur. He writes, "On one level the labyrinth is an image of the spirit [or, more precisely, the soul] in matter. The spirit works its way to the middle, completes its divinely appointed task, then works it way out again. Living in matter, we have a certain amount of free will, but it is limited. Every so often we can choose to go this way or that. We cannot see

---

30. Dillon and Gerson, *Neoplatonic Philosophy*, 279–280.
31. Perl, *Theophany*, 68–69.

the overall pattern and are in that sense largely working in the dark. According to idealism, matter prevents us from seeing the overall pattern so that we are free to make our own choices. More particularly, the labyrinth is a model of the brain. According to idealism, the brain is a very special species of matter. It filters out spirit, like all matter, but it is also designed to let certain spiritual elements through."[32] Black's reference to idealism pertains, of course, to the philosophical idealism of Plato and his followers.

Undoubtedly, in all living organisms the soul is primary in importance and the material body is secondary. As Francis Parker Yockey reasons, "the development of an organism is the unfolding of a soul. The matter is the mere envelope, the vehicle of the expression of the spirit [or, more precisely, the soul]. The events of a human life are the expressions of the soul of that human at its successive stages of unfolding." However, it is experienced differently by each human being, for "an experience is a relationship between a soul and an outer event. Thus, no two persons can have the same experience, because the identical event is quite different to each different soul."[33]

From the above brief survey, it is evident that the role of the psychic level (i.e., the level of Soul) is to form and animate the material level, which is the lowest level of reality. Without the presence of Intellect through the agency of Soul, matter is formless, indeterminate, and chaotic. For all practical purposes, formless matter is indistinguishable from non-being or nothingness. Those who proclaim matter to be the only reality are therefore nihilists, metaphysically speaking.[34] However, as Vladimir Lossky notes, matter should not be conceived as absolute nothingness (*ouk on*) but rather as relative non-being (*mē on*), as is done in Platonism. Through contemplation, matter obtains an illusory reality, so to speak, from the intelligible world.[35]

In view of the foregoing reasoning, the chain of cosmic causality may be now be refined to the following: Principle → Intellect → Soul + matter → physical world. In other words, Intellect receives its being from the Principle (i.e., the One); Soul receives its being from the Intellect; and Soul forms matter in order to produce the physical world.

---

32. Black, *Sacred History*, 80.

33. Yockey, *Imperium*, 39.

34. The terms 'nihilism' and 'nihilist' are derived from the Latin *nihil*, which means 'nothing.'

35. Lossky, *Orthodox Theology*, 52.

A momentous result of this ongoing interaction between form and matter is that reality is polymorphic in nature. In other words, reality comprises a multiplicity of forms on both the metaphysical and physical levels. On the metaphysical level there exists the multiplicity of eternal Forms, as contained within the universal Intellect. On the physical level there exists the multiplicity of temporal forms or shapes, reflecting the eternal Forms within space and time. Consequently, the whole of reality (intelligible and sensible) is polymorphic. This is strikingly evident throughout the living kingdoms on Earth, with plants and animals manifesting an astonishing variety of physical forms, as any nature lover could affirm.

Levels of Being

WITHIN THE PHYSICAL WORLD a distinction is made between the non-living, or inanimate, and the living. Unlike inanimate objects, such as a rock or a cloud, living beings are indwelt by a soul which is the source of their life. It is significant that the Greek noun *psychē* means breath, as the sign of life, and also means the soul as opposed to the body. The Latin equivalent hereof is *anima*, which means breath or soul.[1] In this understanding, it is impossible for anything to be alive without the presence of soul, since it is soul that animates a physical form. This reality applies to all living beings on Earth, whether plants, animals, or humans.

It is noteworthy that the word 'animal' is derived from the Latin *anima*. Interestingly, these Greek and Latin terms do not have a precise equivalent in Sanskrit, the closest being *nāma* as the name or form of a thing by which its identity is established. The rendering of the Sanskrit *ātman* by 'soul,' as is often done in English translations, is therefore incorrect. A more accurate translation of *ātman* would be essence (Latin, *essentia*). Moreover, since animals are also in possession of soul, it is by *nous* (mind) and not by soul as such that human beings are differentiated from other animals.[2]

Among living beings on Earth various levels of organization are encountered, ranging from less complex to more complex organisms.[3] At the lowest level there are plants (which in this context include micro-organisms), next animals, and then humans. On the physiological level humans are of course part of the animal kingdom, but culturally they have the potential to attain higher levels of being.

---

1. LSJ, 798; Wheeler, *Latin*, 519.

2. Coomaraswamy, *Civilization*, 31, 67–68.

3. Keeping in mind that even micro-organisms, such as bacteria, display an astonishing complexity in their cellular structures, which by extension applies to all living beings, consisting as they do of cells. 'More' and 'less' complex are therefore quite relative terms in this context.

Hellenic Views

In the philosophy of Aristotle a hierarchy of beings is encountered, in terms of the interaction between form and matter. This ontological hierarchy appears as follows, ranging from lowest to highest: (a) Primary matter, consisting of the contraries of warm/cold and dry/damp (although, strictly speaking, primary matter exists as an abstraction only, being devoid of form); (b) the simple elements of earth, water, air, and fire; these already possess some form, but matter predominates; (c) all other sublunary objects are composite mixtures of the four elements: inorganic objects, plants, animals, and humans; in these, form becomes increasingly prominent at the expense of matter; and (d) the heavenly beings, from the lowest intelligences (i.e., the Forms) to God; these consist of pure form without any matter.[4]

How are the various levels of living beings established? In the Hellenic understanding, there are different levels of soul animating matter, with each level comprising activities that are peculiar to itself. The powers of the soul are enumerated by Aristotle as follows: nutritive, appetitive, sensory, locomotive, and cognitive. Plants have nutritive power, while animals have that as well as appetitive, sensory, and locomotive powers. Humans have all these powers as well as the power of thinking, which is mind (*De An*, II.414a-b). Since the nutritive faculty is the most widely distributed power of soul, Aristotle contends, it exists in all living beings from birth until death. It manifests itself in the use of food and in the act of reproduction (*De An*, II.415a, III.434a). The next level of soul is the sensitive, which occurs in all animals but not in plants. Each of the five senses has the power of receiving into itself the sensible forms of things without the matter (*De An*, II.424a). The five (physical) senses are well known: sight, hearing, smell, taste, and touch. It is further known that not all animal species possess all these senses, since some are sightless.

The Orthodox philosopher Philip Sherrard has commented that Aristotle does not view the sensitive soul as superior to the sensible (i.e., physical) body. Consequently, for Aristotle sensible objects can act on the soul, while the latter can abstract its knowledge from these objects. However, this notion would be rejected by the Christian theologian Augustine of Hippo, who held (following Plato) that the soul is transcendent in respect

---

4. Dreyer, *Wysbegeerte*, 132.

of the body. Therefore, the soul possesses a sensation of its own distinct from that of the body.[5]

Aristotle reasons further that the rational function differs from the other powers of soul, since mind must be related to what is thinkable, as sense is to what is sensible. "The thinking part of the soul must therefore be . . . capable of receiving the form of an object." It is therefore correct to view the soul as the place of forms (*De An*, III.429a). Against the modern reductionist view that mind is a product of the brain, Aristotle argued that mind cannot reasonably be viewed as blended with the body, since it cannot acquire a quality such as hot or cold, or be an organ of sense-perception. Accordingly, "that in the soul which is called mind (whereby the soul thinks and judges) is, before it thinks, not actually any real [i.e., physical] thing" (*De An*, III.429a). Evidently, in the Aristotelian conception reason has no connection with matter and enters it from the outside, being divine in nature (*GA*, 736b).[6]

Clearly, in this ascending hierarchy the higher always contains the lower, form becomes more dominant, purposefulness and its realization become more prominent, and possibility recedes into actuality. It has been commented that the law of analogy holds in this regard: although each level possesses its own being, the lower is analogous to and displays similarities with the higher. For example, on the lowest level of nature there is an analogy between the inorganic and the plant, since the former also contains the phenomena of origin, growth, and passing away. And on the highest level there is an analogy between the reason and the unmoved mover (or God).[7]

One of the last and most important Hellenic thinkers, Proclus, sketches the presence of the Forms in the various grades of being by applying the Neoplatonic principle that 'All things are in all, but in a manner proper to the essence of each.' In the *Commentary on Parmenides*, Proclus writes that on the intelligible level the Forms exist primarily in and for themselves, and not as images of anything higher. Next, the forms in souls have their being in a secondary way, "and thus are likenesses of the intelligibles [i.e., the Forms]." On the third level, the forms in nature are likenesses of likenesses, "for it is through the forms in souls that the reason-principles [*logoi*] in nature come to be and are." Finally, the forms in sensible things are images

5. Sherrard, *Greek East*, 144.
6. Ross, *Aristotle*, 125.
7. Dreyer, *Wysbegeerte*, 140.

only, "for the forms end their procession at what is unknowable and indeterminate. There is nothing after them, for all the reason-principles reach their final term in sensible things."[8] In other words, on different levels of being the Forms are present first in themselves; then as likenesses; then as likenesses of likenesses; and finally, as images.

Christian Views

Such an outstanding thinker as Augustine of Hippo naturally touched upon the issue of levels of being. He writes in his *magnum opus*: "To good and evil men alike He gave being, in common with the stones; and he gave life capable of reproducing itself, in common with the trees; and sentient life, in common with the beasts; and intellectual life, in common with the angels alone" (*De civ Dei*, V.11). In this way an ascending hierarchy is established on Earth: being, life, sensation, and intellect.

Augustine insists that all these levels of being receive their existence from God. From Him comes every mode, every species, and every order; from Him comes measure, number, and weight; from Him comes everything which exists in nature, including the seeds of forms and the forms of seeds and their movements. To the flesh, God gave its origin, beauty, health, and fertility; to the irrational soul (animals), He gave memory, sensation, and appetite; and to the rational soul (humans), he gave in addition mind, intelligence, and will. The Latin theologian then poetically depicts the universal providence of God: "Neither heaven nor earth, neither angel nor man, not even the inward parts of the smallest and most inconsiderable animal, nor the feather of a bird, nor a tiny flower of a plant nor the leaf on the tree, has God left unprovided with a harmony and, as it were, a peace among its parts" (*De civ Dei*, V.11).

Ultimately, God is the Supreme Being, which also entails that He is the source of all beings. Augustine adds, "God gave being to the things that He created from nothing, then, but not a supreme being like His own. To some He gave being more fully, and to others He gave it in a more restricted way; and so he arranged natural entities according to their degrees of being" (*De civ Dei*, XII.3). In the same passage, Augustine correctly remarks that the Latin term for being, *essentia*, is the equivalent of the Greek term *ousia*.

In the *Divine Names*, Dionysius the Areopagite presents a hierarchy of being in which the divine processions, or 'names,' establish the various

---

8. Dillon and Gerson, *Neoplatonic Philosophy*, 299–300.

levels of being. He writes: "For the divine name of the *Good*, manifesting the whole processions of the cause of all things, is extended both to beings and to non-beings, and is above beings and above non-beings. That of *Being* is extended to all beings and is above all beings. That of *Life* is extended to all living things and is above living things. That of *Wisdom* is extended to all intellectual and rational and sensitive beings and is above all these things" (*DN*, V.1; italics ours).

As Eric Perl comments, in ordering the divine processions based on their universality, Dionysius is again closely following Proclus. In this schema, the order of the divine processions is a mirror image of the ranks of beings: Good, Being, Life, and Wisdom → cognitive living beings, living beings, mere beings, and non-beings.[9] Regarding the level of living beings, Dionysius writes in the same work that all animals and plants receive life and warmth from the divine Life (*DN*, 6:3). Furthermore, the benefits of divine Power reach out to humans, animals, plants, and all nature, including fire, water, air, and earth. This Power stirs the powers that give nourishment and growth to plants (*DN*, 8:5). The latter refers to the nutritive faculty of the soul, which is also found in animals and humans as a prerequisite for bodily existence.

It is further held in most the spiritual traditions that there are beings above the human level but below the divine level. These celestial beings are usually referred to as gods or angels. The word 'angel' is derived from the Greek *aggelos*, which means a messenger from God.[10] Interestingly, this word may be preceded by either the male (*ho*) or female (*he*) article, which serves as linguistic confirmation of the theological notion that angels are neither male nor female—in other words, angels are beyond gender. The opening verse of the Bible, 'In the beginning God created the heavens and the earth,' has traditionally been understood as indicating the origin of the spiritual and material worlds, respectively. In this context, the heavens do not refer to the visible sky but to the spiritual realms, or the Kingdom of God of the scriptures. Its creation preceded that of the material world and included the inhabitants of the spiritual world, the angels. In the Christian view, the angels are bodiless spirits who possess a rational and free nature, receiving the divine Light due to their proximity to it.[11]

---

9. Perl, *Theophany*, 66.
10. LSJ, 4.
11. Alfeyev, *Mystery*, 44.

In the *Celestial Hierarchy*, Dionysius the Areopagite provides the first comprehensive account of the various levels of celestial beings, or angels. To begin with, a hierarchy is defined as "a sacred order, a state of understanding and an activity approximating as closely as possible to the divine." Its purpose, or goal, is to enable beings to approach the divine likeness and to be united with God (*CH*, III.1, 2). Dionysius devotes the remainder of this work to an elaboration of the structure and functions of the celestial beings. There are nine designations for the heavenly beings, taken from the Bible and divided into three ranks. Each level receives its illuminations and powers from the level immediately above it. The highest level is closest to God, thus receiving its illumination directly from the divine light, and consists of thrones, cherubim, and seraphim. The second level is composed of authorities, dominions, and powers. The third level contains the archangels, angels, and principalities. Interestingly, just as each of these celestial ranks is uplifted towards God by the rank above it, so is the hierarchy of the Church uplifted by the third rank of angels (*CH*, Chapters V to X). In the Orthodox understanding, the angelic hierarchy finds its continuation in the ecclesiastical hierarchy of sacraments, clergy, and faithful. "Thus, the ecclesiastical hierarchy partakes of the divine mystery through the mediation of the celestial hierarchy."[12]

Another brilliant Christian thinker who employed Platonic and Aristotelian categories, John Scottus Eriugena, writes that God creates the cosmos through a five-fold process out of the pre-ontological nothingness (Latin, *nihil*), through the primordial causes which are contained in the Logos. This creative activity results in the establishment of various levels of being: (a) natural bodies (e.g., rocks) are created for existence only; (b) plants for existence as well as life; (c) non-human animals for existence, life, and sensation; (d) human beings for existence, life, sensation, and reason; and (e) finally, heavenly beings (e.g., angels) for existence, life, sensation, reason, and intellect (*Per* II, 580).[13] In this way, each level of being obtains its own characteristic activity, while also sharing in those below it.

The Aristotelian hierarchy of forms in nature has been related by Thomas Aquinas to the activities peculiar to those forms. Firstly, the activities of elemental forms (which are the closest to matter) do not transcend the physical-chemical level. Next come the forms of compounds, which in addition to elemental activities display behaviour specific to their own

---

12. Alfeyev, *Mystery*, 45.
13. Carabine, *Eriugena*, 56.

natures, such as the magnetic properties of iron. On the next level we find the souls of plants, which are also capable of moving themselves. Above them are the souls of lower animals, which possess not only self-movement but also knowledge, albeit of a material kind for which they require bodily organs. On the highest level (terrestrially speaking) there are the life-principles of human beings, which resemble the higher substances in their capacity for understanding also immaterial things. However, the Latin theologian remarks, human souls acquire immaterial, intellectual knowledge from the knowledge of material things through the senses, and therefore the human soul has to be united with a body in order to have a complete specific nature (*Quaestio Disputata de Anima*, 1). This unity of body and soul is emphasized in the traditional Christian anthropology, according to which the human being comprises a psycho-somatic unity during this earthly life.

Evolutionary Origins

We have touched upon the creation of the levels of being, which is viewed theologically as the creative activity of God. It is also possible to provide an evolutionary explanation of the cosmic hierarchy, as was done by Alfred Russell Wallace. In his book *The World of Life*, the British naturalist suggested that an organizing (universal) Mind need not be infinite in its attributes, as in the usual understanding of the Deity. However, he wrote, if an infinite God is postulated, "it seems only logical to assume that the vast, the infinite chasm between ourselves and the Deity is to some extent occupied by an almost infinite series of grades of beings, each successive grade having higher and higher powers in regard to the origination, the development, and the control of the universe."[14]

How did this cosmic hierarchy arise? In the cosmogony of Wallace, the supreme, infinite Being might impress upon the highest angels to create a primal universe of ether, containing the inherent properties and forces for what was to follow. The next step in the process of creation is cosmogenesis, or the birth of the universe: a subordinate grade of angels would act upon the ether to develop from it various elements of matter, which under the influence of forces such as gravitation, heat, and electricity, would begin to form galaxies and solar systems. Wallace continues: "Then we may imagine these hosts of angels, to whom a thousand years are as one day, watching

14. Flannery, *Intelligent Evolution*, 199.

the development of this vast system of suns and planets until one or more of them combined in itself all those conditions of size, of elementary constitution, of atmosphere, of mass of water and requisite distance from its source of heat, as to ensure a stability of constitution and uniformity of temperature for a given minimum of millions of years or of ages, as would be required for the full development of a life-world from Amoeba to Man."[15]

Having thus provided the prerequisites for the appearance of life on Earth, or biogenesis, the next step in the process of creation would be the initiation of life by 'spirit-workers,' once the waters cooled down sufficiently to infuse it with suitable life-centers, to commence the process of organization. Here we find Wallace postulating organizing spirits with the duty to influence myriads of cell-souls (a term borrowed from Ernst Haeckel) towards growth and division. He writes further: "At successive stages of development of the life-world, more and perhaps higher intelligences might be required to direct the main lines of variation in definite directions in accordance with the general design to be worked out." This is viewed by Wallace as more plausible than the notion of direct action by an infinite Deity in every living cell. In view of these arguments, the almost infinite variety of nature is not attributed to detailed design by God, but as a foreseen result of His constitution of the universe in its materials and conditions. The cosmos is thus a manifestation of divine power by the agency of ministering angels, through many descending degrees of intelligence and power.[16] This is indeed an elegant affirmation of God's creation of the cosmic hierarchy, without requiring direct intervention or detailed design by the Creator.

Wallace concludes that the universe contains infinite grades of power, knowledge, and influence. He writes: "Holding this opinion, I have suggested that this vast and wonderful universe, with its almost infinite variety of forms, motions, and reactions of part upon part, from suns and systems up to plant life, animal life, and the human living soul, has ever required and still requires the continuous co-ordinated agency of myriads of such intelligences."[17] In this way, the evolution of life on Earth has been guided by the universal Mind, which is the divine Logos acting through the multiple *logoi* indwelling the entire realm of manifestation, bestowing both being and intelligibility on the cosmos and its life-forms.

---

15. Flannery, *Intelligent Evolution*, 200–201.
16. Flannery, *Intelligent Evolution*, 201–202.
17. Flannery, *Intelligent Evolution*, 207.

Well-being and Love

IN HELLENIC PHILOSOPHY AN interesting distinction is made between being (*to einai*) and well-being (*to eu einai*). For Plato, sight is not only useful for locomotion, but together with hearing reveal the harmony of the world. These two senses are therefore necessary for well-being, whereas the other senses are necessary for existence.[1] In the *Timaeus*, Plato reasons that human knowledge begins with sight: "As it is, however, our ability to see the periods of day-and-night, of months and of years, of equinoxes and solstices, has led to the invention of number, and has given us the idea of time and opened the path to inquiry into the nature of the universe. These pursuits have given us philosophy, a gift from the gods to the mortal race whose value neither has been nor will ever be surpassed" (47a–b). In other words, knowledge began with visual observation, which led to mathematics and ultimately to philosophy. Plato's account of eyesight brings the reader to the point of contact between the knowing soul and the external world of visible bodies.[2] Likewise hearing is a gift from the gods, Plato writes, both to enable speech and guided by intelligence to perceive the harmony in music, which is not given for the sake of irrational pleasure (*Tim*, 47c–d).

Aristotle concurs that sight and hearing serve well-being rather than mere survival, although he also adds taste in this regard. Sight enables an animal to see through air or water, taste enables it to distinguish painful or pleasant qualities in its nutrition, and hearing enables communication with its fellows (*De An* III.434b, 435b). Aristotle reasons further that in the case of humans, sight and hearing also pertain to the life of thought, in that the hearing of speech is the main instrument of teaching and learning, while sight reveals differences in color, number, size, shape, and movement (*Met* I.980a-b).

---

1. Cornford, *Plato's Cosmology*, 151–152.
2. Cornford, *Plato's Cosmology*, 156

It is relevant to note that the Hellenic concept of well-being should be distinguished from the modern concept of happiness. For example, in Plato's late dialogue *Philebus* we find Socrates in a disputation about what constitutes the good in human life, whether it is knowledge or pleasure. Socrates argues that it is a third thing, a proper mixture of knowledge and pleasure, although knowledge stands much closer to it than pleasure.[3] And for Aristotle, the end or purpose (*telos*) of human life is *eudaimonia*, which means good fortune or prosperity. As pointed out by David Ross, the usual translation of this term as 'happiness' is unsuitable, for the latter means a state of feeling, whereas Aristotle insists that *eudaimonia* is a kind of activity. It is more than pleasure, although pleasure naturally accompanies it. Therefore, well-being is the proper translation of this term denoting the purpose of human life.[4]

The relation between being and well-being has been described by Proclus in terms of the love (*erōs*) which draws all things back to their divine Source. Proclus writes in his *Elements of Theology*: "But all things desire the Good, and each attains it through the mediation of its proximate cause; therefore, each has appetition of its own cause also. Through that which gives it being it attains its well-being; the source of its well-being is the source of its appetite; and the primary object of its appetite is that upon which it reverts."[5] For Proclus, the dynamic nature of the cosmos is due to the erotic love through which the multiplicity of things participate in their causes and ultimately in the One. This notion of a love relationship between beings and Being had earlier been evoked in poetic-mythical language by Plato in the dialogue *Phaedrus*, with the mind flying on wings like those of Eros towards the Good.[6]

Erotic Love and its Spiritualization

The Hellenic and Christian thinkers employed various terms for the concept of love. First, we encounter *erōs*, which means desire for a thing; so that the god of love is Eros, or in Latin, Amor.[7] Clearly, the adjectives 'erotic' and 'amorous' are derived from these Greek and Latin names. We could say

3. Cooper, *Plato*, 398.
4. LSJ, 280; Ross, *Aristotle*, 198.
5. Quoted in Goosen, *Nihilisme*, 94.
6. Goosen, *Nihilisme*, 42.
7. LSJ, 273; Wheeler, Latin, 519.

that *erōs* means erotic love, including sexual attraction. As taught in the Hermetic writings of the Egyptian-Hellenic wisdom tradition, the conjunction of the two sexes, or more accurately, their fusion into one, is rightly named Eros. This is nothing less than a sacrament of eternal reproduction bestowed by God, the Master of all generative power, upon all creatures. Moreover, it is accompanied by affection, joy, and gladness, and the heavenly love inherent in its being.[8]

Plato also held that the procreative union of man and woman is something divine, since conception and generation represent an immortal principle within a mortal being (*Sym*, 206c). And in his late dialogue *Laws*, Plato envisions a law which permits the sexual act only for its natural purpose, namely procreation. Such a natural law forbids a man both homosexual relations and fornication with women of lesser repute. It will moreover check the sexual instinct that often leads to adultery, and will inspire men with affection for their own wives (*Laws*, VIII.838-839b). The same reasoning would naturally apply to women.

Furthermore, Plato devoted his dialogue *Symposium* (which literally means 'drinking together,' set in the context of a social event in ancient Athens) to a discussion of erotic love (*erōs*). In it, Socrates reports a discourse on love he once heard from a wise woman named Diotima, who taught him that Love is a great spirit, and like everything spiritual is in between immortal god and mortal being. The function of spirits is to mediate between gods and men, Diotima explains, conveying prayer and sacrifice from men to gods, while to men they bring commands and gifts from the gods (202e). After discussing various attributes of Love with Socrates, Diotima reveals the final and highest mystery of Love by depicting the stages through which a lover should move. At first, it involves the love of beautiful bodies; then, the realization that the beauty of people's souls is more valuable than the beauty of their bodies; and finally, he or she will become a lover of the beauty of knowledge, "the great sea of beauty" from which is born beautiful ideas and theories, "in unstinting love of wisdom" (*philosophia*). In this way, Diotima depicts the ascent of love beginning with individual persons and ending with love for the Form of Beauty, which "always *is* and neither comes to be nor passes away, neither waxes nor wanes" (210a-211a).[9]

Plato thus 'spiritualizes' erotic love by elevating it from the physical level to the level of beauty, and ultimately to the Form of Beauty itself. Given

---

8. Perry, *Treasury*, 629.
9. Cooper, *Plato*, 457.

this Platonic affirmation of the link between love and beauty, we suggest that *erōs* also denotes creative love, such as that of an artist for his or her music, poetry, painting, or any other artistic form. And although reasoning from a somewhat different perspective, Friedrich Nietzsche agrees that a transition of love from the physical to the cultural is possible. He writes: "He who directs his passion to things (the sciences, the national good, cultural interests, the arts) takes much of the fire out of his passion for people (even when they represent those things, as statesmen, philosophers, and artists represent their creations)."[10]

Among major Christian thinkers who built upon Plato's spiritualized concept of love count Dionysius the Areopagite. In the *Divine Names*, God is presented as the Good and the Beautiful, as well as Love (*Erōs*). Dionysius writes: "The cause of all things, through excess of goodness, loves all things, makes all things, perfects all things, sustains all things, reverts all things; and the divine love is good, of good, through the good. For love, the very benefactor of beings, pre-existing in excess in the Good, did not permit it to remain unproductive in itself, but moved it to productive action, in the excess which is generative of all things" (*DN*, IV.10). As Eric Perl comments, "God is Love, then, in that he is 'excess,' i.e., is distributed to all things, making all things to be by being differently present in each."[11]

The Platonic spiritualizing of love has been situated within a traditional metaphysical context by Ananda Coomaraswamy. He writes with poetic passion: "What this means in actual tradition is that the beloved on earth is to be realised *there* not as she is in herself but as she is in God. The beauty of the Beloved there is no longer as it is here contingent and merely a participation or reflection, but that of the Supernal Wisdom, that of the One Madonna, that of the intrinsic being of the Bride, which 'rains down flames of fire' and as *claritas* illuminates and guides the pure intellect. In that last and hidden station, nature and essence . . . are one and indivisible, knowing nothing of a within or without, and that is their supreme felicity, and of every liberated consciousness."[12]

That erotic love is bound up not only with life but also with death, has been powerfully argued by Nicolas Berdyaev. While the human being remains a sexual being, he or she cannot live in peace and harmony due to the fierce struggle between man and woman. Since masculine and feminine

---

10. Nietzsche, *Human*, 223.
11. Perl, *Theophany*, 44.
12. Coomaraswamy, *Civilization*, 27–28.

psychology differ completely, mutual understanding is highly problematic. This divergence arises from the division of human nature into two sexes, resulting in disharmony, passionate longing, and dissatisfaction. Therefore, sex is the source of both life and death. Erotic love always brings death with it, as movingly depicted by Wagner in his opera *Tristan und Isolde*. However, sex may be overcome and sublimated to become a spiritual power. In this way, erotic love may be transformed into a force that creates values.[13] We conclude that erotic love should be spiritualized, if human beings wish to recover their wholeness and integrity.

Loving Friendship

Another kind of love is *philia*, which means loving friendship (in Latin, *amicitia*).[14] This affection is found, for example, between friends or family—thereby countering the enmity that so often manifests between parent and child or among siblings (hence the adage that one's friends are chosen but one's relatives are not). We would also mention the reciprocal love between an animal lover and a cat, dog, horse, or any other domestic animal, as well as the numerous cases of parental love in the animal kingdom, as clear instances of *philia*.

In Hellenic philosophy, the importance of friendship was already taught by Pythagoras and his school. In the *Golden Verses*, we read the following: "Honour likewise thy parents, and those most nearly related to thee. Of all the rest of mankind, make him thy friend who distinguishes himself by his virtue. Always give ear to his mild exhortations, and take example from his virtuous and useful actions. Avoid as much as possible hating thy friend for a slight fault" (4-7).

For his part, Aristotle devoted the whole of Books VIII and IX of the *Nicomachean Ethics* to a discussion of loving friendship. In this treatise, *philia* is depicted as loyalty to friends, family, and community, and it requires virtue, equality, and familiarity. Different levels of loving friendship are mentioned by Aristotle: friendships of utility, for the sake of economic interaction; friendships of pleasure, in which friends take a natural delight in the society of their fellows; and friendships of goodness, the highest level, in which friend helps friend to live the best life.[15]

---

13. Berdyaev, *Destiny of Man*, 64-65, 67.
14. LSJ, 758; Wheeler, *Latin*, 519.
15. Wikipedia: Greek words for love; Ross, *Aristotle*, 236.

However, as someone who valued friendship above all other human relations, Friedrich Nietzsche found the Hellenic inclusion of blood relatives in the concept of friendship (he clearly has *philia* in mind) somewhat perplexing. While crediting the ancient Greeks for "alone of all peoples having a deep, many-sided, and philosophical discussion of friendship," they also called *relatives* by a term that is the superlative of the word 'friend,' which Nietzsche found inexplicable. The German philosopher concludes the same chapter by juxtaposing friendship with enmity: "'Friends, there are no friends!', the dying wise man shouted. 'Enemies, there are no enemies!', shout I, the living fool." And later in the same book, Nietzsche relates friendship to marriage when he writes: "The best friend will probably get the best wife, because a good marriage is based on a talent for friendship."[16]

One of the most interesting characteristics of Indo-European religion is that loving friendship (*philia*) extends to the interaction between the divine and the human levels. We find Plato speaking in the *Symposium* (at 188d) of loving affection between gods and men. In the *Bhagavad Gita* (IV.3), the Lord Krishna calls the man Arjuna his friend. In the Zoroastrian religion, founded by the Prophet Zarathustra, the morally acting man is called a friend of Ahura Mazda, the One Universal God.[17] And in the *Laws*, Plato describes the conduct that recommends itself to God, which he contrasts with the humanist view of Protagoras that 'man is the measure of all things.' He writes: "In our view it is God who is pre-eminently the 'measure of all things,' much more so than any 'man,' as they say. So if you want to recommend yourself to someone of this character [i.e., moderation], you must do you level best to make your own character reflect his, and on this principle the moderate man is God's friend, being like him, whereas the immoderate and unjust man is not like him [God] and is his enemy; and the same reasoning applies to the other vices too" (*Laws*, IV, 716c-d). To the foregoing textual evidence, Hans Günther adds the following observation: "To the belief in the Gods as friends there thus corresponds the Indo-European idea of kinship between the high-minded and morally acting man and the Gods, which is already found in the 9th Nemean Ode of the Theban, Pindar. This kinship rests above all on the view that Gods and men are bound through the same values, through truth and virtue."[18]

---

16. Nietzsche, *Human*, 176, 184, 185.
17. Günther, *Religious attitudes*, 15.
18. Günther, *Religious attitudes*, 15.

Moreover, the notion of loving friendship (*philia*) between God and man is affirmed in the Christian tradition. For instance, Jesus Christ said to his disciples: "You are my friends (*philoi*) if you do whatever I command you. No longer do I call you servants, for a servant does not know what his master is doing; but I have called you friends (*philous*), for all things that I heard from my Father I have made known to you" (John 15:14-15). A close friend of Jesus during his earthly ministry was Lazarus, who is referred to as 'Our friend (*philos*) Lazarus' (John 11:11). We also read in the epistle of St James that Abraham believed God and was called a friend (*philos*) of God (2:23).

Self-giving Love

Finally, there is the love which Jesus Christ taught to the world, namely *agapē*. This word is cognate to the verb *agapaō*, which means to love dearly. Its Latin equivalent is *caritas*, which means 'affection' and from which is derived the word 'charity.'[19] As C.G. Campbell aptly comments, in his teaching on love Jesus not only built upon the precepts of earlier prophets of God such as the Pharaoh Akhenaten in Egypt and Zarathustra in Iran; he also promulgated "the momentous addition that Love, the essential sense of spiritual kinship and unity of men with God and with one another, was the prime necessity in the lives of men for the realization of their Heavenly Father's benign purpose for them. For by Love men were united, and made one, with God and with one another in the great spiritual monad of being."[20]

We could say that *agapē* is the love of God for mankind and the reciprocal love of humans for God.[21] For example, we read in chapter 5 of St Paul's letter to the early Christians in Rome about God's love, *agapē*, for us humans. The great Apostle to the Gentiles also wrote an extended passage on *agapē* in his first letter to the Corinthians. Love is depicted therein as patient and kind; not jealous or boastful; not arrogant or rude; does not insist on its own way; is not irritable or resentful; and does not rejoice in wrong but rejoices in the right; it bears all things, believes all things, hopes all things, and endures all things. Unlike prophecies and knowledge, love never ends. St Paul concludes his treatise on love as follows: "So faith (*pistis*), hope (*elpis*), love (*agapē*) abide, these three; but the greatest of these

19. LSJ, 3; Wheeler, *Latin*, 520.
20. Campbell, *Race and Religion*, 19.
21. Wikipedia: Greek words for love.

is love" (1 Cor 13: 4-8, 13). This is the highest kind of love, aimed at the well-being of another rather than of the self.

Conclusion

We conclude this chapter with some brief remarks about love by Friedrich Nietzsche, whose acute psychological insights compensated for his own setbacks in love, such as the rejection of his marriage proposal by the Russian-German author Lou Salomé, who then proceeded to elope with a former friend of the German philosopher. First, in a passage titled 'Love and duality,' Nietzsche writes: "What else is love but understanding and rejoicing that another lives, works, and feels in a different and opposite way to ourselves? That love may be able to bridge over the contrasts by joys, we must not remove or deny those contrasts."[22] And a final thought-provoking statement in this regard: "What is done out of love always takes place beyond good and evil."[23] It is to a consideration of good and evil that we will now turn.

22. Nietzsche, *Human*, 291.
23. Nietzsche, *Beyond*, 579.

Good and Evil

It has become a commonplace in the modern world to view good and evil as relative terms. After all, if there is no higher reality than humankind, then there could not be any objective standard by which notions such as good and evil may be judged. This approach has been masterfully stated by Fyodor Dostoyevsky in his epic novel, *The Brothers Karamazov*. One of the brothers, the intellectual Ivan, declares that "If God does not exist, everything is permitted." And this rejection of transcendence, combined with an insistence on individual choice as the highest good, has inevitably resulted in nihilism becoming the *de facto* 'religion' of modernism. In the words of the Orthodox theologian David Bentley Hart: "And so, at the end of modernity, each of us who is true to the times stands facing not God, or the gods, or the Good beyond beings, but an abyss, over which presides the empty, inviolable authority of the individual will, whose impulses and decisions are their own moral index."[1] Let us now consider the Hellenic and traditional Christian understandings of good and evil, which represent a clear contrast with moral relativism.

Hellenic Views

In the Platonic understanding, goodness is an essential attribute of the divinity. For instance, in the *Politeia* we find Socrates declaring that God is the sole cause of good (*agathōs*) and not in any way the cause of evil (*kakōs*). In addition, since God is perfect in beauty and goodness, he is eternally without change or variation (379c, 381c). Moreover, in the *Timaeus* the goodness of the Demiurge is stated as the motive for creation: "He was good, and one who is good can never become jealous of anything. And

---

1. Quoted in Myers, "*Music*," 4; see also the treatise *Nihilism: The Root of the Revolution of the Modern Age* (Platina, CA: St Herman of Alaska Brotherhood, Second edition, 2009) by Eugene Rose for an incisive analysis of the nihilist-modernist nexus.

so, being free of jealousy, he wanted everything to become as much like himself as was possible. The god wanted everything to be good and nothing to be bad so far as that was possible, and so he took over all that was visible—not at rest but in discordant and disorderly motion—and brought it from a state of disorder to one of order, because he believed that order was in every way better than disorder" (29e).

Plato concludes his seminal account of the creation of the universe with an eulogy to the created order: "And so now we may say that our account of the universe has reached its conclusion. This world of ours has received and teems with living things, mortal and immortal. A visible living thing containing visible ones, perceptible god, image of the intelligible Living Thing, its grandness, goodness, beauty and perfection are unexcelled. Our one universe, indeed the only one of its kind, has come to be" (*Tim*, 92c). It is clear from this passage that Plato held an appreciative view of the physical world, precisely because it receives its being, goodness, and beauty from the metaphysical world.

Aristotle likewise viewed the universe as good. Although there exists no movement or change in the Godhead, it is yet the final cause of everything. The Prime Mover draws all things to itself through beauty, goodness, and love, and therefore the cosmos is characterized by goodness, beauty, order, and purposefulness. In contrast, evil is the failure of realization—it represents possibility not actualized, matter not formed, and purpose not attained.[2] Against the dualistic cosmology that would later be popularized by the Gnostics, Aristotle denies the existence of an evil principle in the world, since if that which is eternal can have no element of potentiality, it cannot have an element of evil either. Evil is therefore not a necessary feature of the universe but a by-product of the world-process, so that there is no evil apart from specific things.[3]

Matter is viewed by Plotinus as the principle of evil because it is the terminus out of which nothing more can originate. The opposites of good and evil exist due to the contrary principles found in all being. Since the cosmos is the product of the interaction between Intellect and Necessity (as Plato taught in the *Timaeus*), good is that which comes from God, whereas evil is that which comes from the material substrate.[4] However, Plotinus does not view matter as inherently evil. Instead, because matter receives

---

2. Dreyer, *Wysbegeerte*, 133, 137–138.
3. Ross, *Aristotle*, 184.
4. Oosthuizen, *Plotinus*, 127, 130, 132, 134.

the action of soul it is only evil in relation to soul, to the extent that soul is bound by matter (*Enneads* I.8.14).[5] In other words, matter represents relative evil and not absolute evil. For Plotinus, evil is thus viewed as having a parasitic existence (*parahypostasis*), as an inevitable result of the existence of the cosmos. Accordingly, the world is good to the extent in which it participates in being, and it is evil to the extent in which it participates in matter.[6]

The relation between matter and evil was explored by Proclus in his treatise *On the nature and origin of evil*. To begin with, it is argued that just as the Good transcends Being, so evil transcends the Form of Non-being, and is thus even further removed from the Good than is Non-being. Further, in creating this world the Demiurge willed it to be devoid of evil as far as possible, as Plato stated in the *Timaeus* (at 30a). However, Proclus continues, since evil is the destructive element in each thing, and since generation would be impossible without destruction, evil must exist. Paradoxically, since evil thus contributes to the preservation of the universe, it is good by existing. Proclus therefore affirms that evil has a two-fold aspect: that which is strictly evil, as transcending non-being; and the evil that exists mixed with goodness (*On the nature and origin of evil*, 3, 5, 9).

Proclus holds a more nuanced view of matter than Plotinus, who associated it with evil (albeit in a qualified sense) and privation. If matter is indeed evil, then either the Good is the cause of evil or there are two principles of existing things, namely primary Good and primary Evil. Proclus counters these false alternatives with a variety of arguments on which we do not need to dwell, except to note that the role of matter as 'mother' or 'nurse' (i.e., as the receptacle of becoming in Plato's *Timaeus*) in the realm of generation is acknowledged. Accordingly, in the sense that matter came to be because of a good, it is good, but not unqualifiedly so; and in the sense that matter is the lowest of the things that exist, it is evil, but not unqualifiedly so. Ultimately matter is neither good nor evil, Proclus concludes, but it is necessary. And evil does not exist in itself, but as a privation and lack of goodness (*On the nature and origin of evil*, 31, 32, 37, 51).

---

5. Moore, *Plotinus*.
6. Wikipedia: Neoplatonism; Laos, *Metaphysics*, 33.

Christian Views

The early Christian theologians viewed evil as a deficit of being, in contrast to Manichaeism with its view of evil as a principle opposed to God. In the Orthodox perspective, the problem is that of evil-doers, namely humans who revolt against God. As Vladimir Lossky adds, evil is therefore conceived in personalist rather than essentialist terms. Moreover, evil entered the world through the will of man—it is therefore not a nature (*physis*), but a condition (*hexis*). To be more precise, evil is a sickness of the human will, as Gregory of Nyssa held, which makes evil very much a reality. The origin of evil lies in the spiritual world, namely in the will of the fallen angels rebelling against God.[7]

Viewed in ontological terms, evil is the attraction of the will to non-being, the negation of God and creation, and the hatred of grace. Lossky concludes that through the human will, evil becomes a power that infects all of the created order—man's free will therefore carries non-being into God's creation. The Orthodox theologian Hilarion Alfeyev concurs that the problem is one of evil-doers, whose nature was originally good. Therefore, in the Lord's Prayer we do not ask God to deliver us from evil in general, but from *the evil one*, i.e., the evil-doer, a person that embodies evil.[8]

In his exegesis of the scriptural statement that darkness was upon the face of the deep (Gen 1:2) before God's creation of light, Basil of Caesarea takes issue with those, such as the Gnostics and Manicheans, who posited a self-existing evil power in perpetual opposition to the goodness of God. Neither does evil has its origin in God, Basil adds, for something cannot proceed from its contrary: life does not engender death, darkness is not the origin of light, and sickness is not the maker of health. Basil concludes that evil is not a living, animated essence; rather, "it is the condition of the soul opposed to virtue, developed in the careless on account of their falling away from good" (*Hex* II.4). Every rational creature, whether angelic or human, possesses free will to choose between good and evil. Not even goodness is imposed by God, since that would have undermined our freedom. Instead, goodness has to be cultivated at the level of our being.[9]

Dionysius the Areopagite states in the *Divine Names* that the Good is the transcendent Cause of all true being, goodness, light, and beauty. In

---

7. Lossky, *Orthodox Theology*, 80–82.
8. Lossky, *Orthodox Theology*, 132, 136; Alfeyev, *Mystery*, 48.
9. Alfeyev, *Mystery*, 46.

an extended survey of what evil is and is not, Dionysius then writes that evil does not come from the Good, since the Good cannot produce its opposite. Furthermore, evil has neither being nor non-being, but is in fact further removed from the Good than non-being is. Nonetheless, since evil destroys things that have being, and the destruction of one thing is the birth of another, in a paradoxical manner evil contributes to the fulfilment of the world (*DN*, IV.19). Therefore, for Dionysius nothing is evil insofar as it is a being; and conversely, anything is evil insofar as it fails to be.[10]

Since evil does not come from God, Dionysius considers some other sources of evil that have been suggested. He concludes that evil does not inhere in beings, since all beings derive from the Good. Evil is not to be found in the angels either, since even the fallen angels received their being from the Good before they embraced evil. Neither are souls evil by nature, but souls can become evil due to a lack of perfection of the virtues. Regarding the rest of the created order, evil is not to be found among the irrational animals, or in nature as a whole, or in our bodies, or in matter as such. The common assertion that evil is inherent in matter is false, Dionysius counters, since matter also share in the beauty and form of the cosmos (*DN*, IV.21–28).

Dionysius then sums up his conclusions on evil. "Good comes from the one universal Cause, and evil originates in numerous partial deficiencies. The Cause for all good things is one. If, however, evil is contrary to the Good, then evil must have numerous causes. And it is not principles and powers which produce evil but impotence and weakness and an inharmonious commingling of discordances. We have to assume that evil exists as an accident. Thus, evil is contrary to progress, purpose, nature, cause, source, goal, definition, will, and substance. It is a defect, a deficiency, a weakness, a disproportion, a sin. It is purposeless, ugly, lifeless, mindless, unreasonable, imperfect, unfounded, uncaused, indeterminate, unborn, inert, powerless, disordered" (*DN*, IV.30–32).

Following the Neoplatonic and Greek Patristic consensus, Augustine of Hippo agrees that evil is a privation of the good (*De Natura Boni*, IV).[11] This argument also relates to the utility of things for us. For example, poisons are harmful if used wrongly, but they can be wholesome if proper use is made of them. On the other hand, things like food and drink and sunlight delight us, but they can be harmful if used immoderately. And

---

10. Perl, *Theophany*, 58.
11. Camus, *Christian Metaphysics*, 119.

the same fire that burns and consumes can be made useful for cooking and warming. Augustine concludes: "For there is nothing at all which is evil by nature, and 'evil' is a name for nothing other than the absence of good" (*De civ Dei*, XI.22, XII.4).

Augustine also approached the problem of evil from an ontological viewpoint. Since all beings are created out of nothing (Latin, *ex nihilo*), they display an inborn compulsion to return to nothingness.[12] This striving towards non-being is none other than evil, which has no substance. An evil will could not exist in an evil nature, the Latin theologian reasons, but rather in a nature that is good but nonetheless mutable. Evil arises not from the created nature of mankind, but from the fact that humans are created out of nothing (*De civ Dei*, XII.6). It is therefore absurd to blame God for the existence of evil, as many have done over the ages.

However, the Patristic view of evil as devoid of substance or being should not be construed as an underestimation of its malignant presence. The Orthodox theologian Georges Florovsky wrote that although evil is a pure negation, privation, and defect, it is yet a void of nothingness which swallows and devours beings. It never creates, but its destructive energy is enormous. Ultimately, "the meaning of evil is a radical opposition to God, a revolt, a disobedience, a resistance."[13]

Furthermore, Augustine draws a distinction between two types of evil, namely natural evil and moral evil (without using these terms as such). While natural evil pertains to the existential misery of the human condition, moral evil is known as sin. Augustine explains the phenomenon of natural evil by analogy to the necessity of shadows in a painting (*Contre Julianum*, 111, 206).[14] In this way, natural evil is viewed as serving the universal harmony. Referring to such things as fire, cold, and wild beasts, he notes "how splendid such things are in their own places and natures, and with what beautiful order they are disposed, and how much they contribute, in proportion to their own share of beauty, to the universe as a whole, as to a commonwealth" (*De civ Dei*, XI.22). We thus find Augustine in agreement with Dionysius in respect of natural evil.

In contrast to natural evil, moral evil is attributable to the human misuse of its free will, which has been occurring ever since Adam and Eve. As a result, "Because [man] is what he now is, he is not good, nor is it in his

---

12. Moran, *Eriugena*, 213.
13. Quoted in Alfeyev, *Mystery*, 48.
14. Camus, *Christian Metaphysics*, 119.

power to become good, either because he does not see what he ought to be, or, seeing it, has not the power to be what he sees he ought to be" (*De libero arbitrio*, L.3). For Augustine, therefore, "God has given us the free will of Adam, but our will has acquired the desire to serve evil. And we are so profoundly corrupted that it is from God alone that comes all good use of free will."[15] Furthermore, "the good make use of this world in order to enjoy God; but the evil, by contrast, wish to make use of God in order to enjoy this world" (*De civ Dei*, XV.7). And since moral evil has become a pervasive aspect of the human condition, the Latin theologian viewed mankind as a mass of perdition (Latin, *massa damnata*). In other words, all humans are spiritually damned without the divine Grace which alone can bring about a virtuous life and the salvation of the soul.

Only God is being itself and the highest good, Augustine insisted, whereas created beings are less existent than God, and their goodness is variable. Nonetheless, God saw the creation as very good, as we read in Genesis 1:31. This implies that all singular beings were good, and the whole formed a good and beautiful order (*Enchiridion* 3, 9–10). After the fall, suffering occurs due to the corruptible human condition. Animal suffering is said to be the price to be paid for the harmonious whole with its great variety of beings (*De civ Dei*, XI.22, XII.4).[16]

In the final analysis, "the question of the distinction between good and evil and of its origin cannot be solved apart from the prior question as to the relation between God and man, between the Divine and the human freedom, or between grace and freedom." Thus writes the Russian philosopher Nicolas Berdyaev, adding that if there were no distinction between good and evil, there could be no ethics. But if there is such a distinction and if evil exists, then God must be justified, "since the justification of God is the solution of the problem of evil."[17]

Satanic Evil

It is axiomatic in Christian theology that the rampant evil in the human world originated in the primordial rebellion of Lucifer (whose name means 'light-bearing') and his followers against God. This cataclysmic event has been depicted metaphorically as follows: "And a great star fell from heaven,

15. Camus, *Christian Metaphysics*, 119.
16. Knuuttila, *"Time and creation,"* 105.
17. Berdyaev, *Destiny of Man*, 23.

burning like a torch. And a third of the sun was struck, a third of the moon, and a third of the stars, so that a third of them were darkened" (Rev 8:10, 12). This statement has traditionally been understood as indicating that a third of the angelic beings fell away from the light of God into darkness and evil. As a result, Lucifer became known as the devil. This word is derived from the Greek *diabolos*, which means slanderer, cognate to the verb *diaballō*, meaning to accuse falsely. Another name for the devil is Satan, the god of darkness. And ever since this celestial rebellion began, the universe has been an arena for the struggle between the divine and the demonic, between God and Satan.[18]

How far the evil of Satan and his fallen angels differs from the human vices has been emphasized by Alan Watts in his book *Myth and Ritual in Christianity*: "Something must be said here as to the true nature of angelic evil, since most people are not aware of any greater evils than lust, cruelty, murder, drunkenness, greed, and sloth. From the angelic point of view these 'sins of the flesh' are as far from real evil as conventional goodness is removed from true sanctity or holiness. Very few human beings have the courage, the persistence, the very *asceticism* necessary for the perfect service of Satan—which requires that one perform miracles of darkness, as the saints perform miracles of light. From this standpoint, characters such as Jenghiz Khan, the Marquis de Sade, Heinrich Himmler, and Jack the Ripper are mere blunderers. The true Satanist must always have the outward aspect of an angel of light, and will never, under any circumstances, resort to the cruder, violent types of evil. He must be so clever that only an expert in holiness can discern him, for in this way he may far more effectively mislead the sons of men and please his infernal Master, whose supreme craft lies in Deception, and subtle confusion of the truth."[19] Or, as Shakespeare wrote in *King Lear*, "The prince of darkness is a gentleman."[20]

This description of the real servants of Satanic evil holds true for many of the politicians of the 'democratic' world, who habitually perform evil deeds while claiming to be servants of the good. This is done, for example, by waging perpetual war in the name of 'freedom,' 'human rights,' and other liberal-humanist terms of deception. George Orwell had more than an inkling of this brand of true evil when he coined the slogan 'War is peace' in his dystopian novel *Nineteen Eighty-Four*. More recently, the

---

18. Alfeyev, *Mystery*, 46–47; LSJ, 159.
19. Watts, *Myth and Ritual*, 43–44.
20. Quoted in Perry, *Treasury*, 460.

novelist Gore Vidal accurately labelled American foreign policy since 1945 as 'Perpetual war for perpetual peace' in his book of the same title. The American author has aptly commented on this phenomenon: "With the doctrine of pre-emptive war, the Bush administration went far beyond the utopian credos of America's founders—or even of Wilson, Roosevelt, or Reagan. It is, fundamentally, a doctrine of endless war."[21] The former South African president and Nobel laureate Nelson Mandela was therefore correct in his assessment of the United States as a threat to world peace (in a 2002 *Newsweek* interview), to which he added that they have committed unspeakable atrocities in the world (in a speech shortly before the Anglo-American invasion of Iraq in 2003).[22]

That 'freedom' cannot be enforced by means of military intervention, was already recognized by Maximilien Robespierre. In a 1792 speech, the French revolutionary leader made the following remarks: "The most extravagant idea that can be born in the head of a political thinker is to believe that it suffices for people to enter, weapons in hand, among a foreign people and expect to have its laws and constitution embraced. It is in the nature of things that the progress of reason is slow and no one loves armed missionaries; the first lesson of nature and prudence is to repulse them as enemies. *One can encourage freedom, never create it by an invading force.*"[23]

However, being ignorant of history and averse to reason, American president George Bush and British prime minister Tony Blair ordered their military forces to invade Iraq in 2003, on trumped-up charges that this country possessed weapons of mass destruction (unlike the case of their ally Israel, which had long been in possession of such weapons). These men and their cohorts unashamedly lied to the public by providing fake evidence fabricated by their intelligence agencies. In truth, they invaded Iraq to overthrow the government of Saddam Hussein, who had long been a thorn in the flesh of the Western imperialists; and more importantly, for their petrochemical companies to obtain control over the rich Iraqi oilfields. The fact that hundreds of thousands of Iraqis, mainly civilians, have died because of this Anglo-American violation of international law, has been of no consequence to these 'leaders' and their cohorts, who therefore deserve to be treated as war criminals.

21. Quoted in Gray, *Black Mass*, 210.
22. https://en.wikiquote.org/wiki/Nelson_Mandela
23. Quoted in Gray, *Black Mass*, 206 (italics ours).

The endless warmongering by 'democratic' politicians ordering the bombing and/or invasion of smaller countries while pretending to be fighting against evil, regardless of the immense suffering and destruction thus brought about, is a truly Satanic state of affairs. It has been accurately depicted by the rock band Black Sabbath in their anti-war classic, *War Pigs*, released in 1970 at the height of the Vietnam War. They sing about generals gathering in their masses, with their evil minds plotting death and destruction, while the politicians who started the war are hiding away. The final verse mentions the divine judgment awaiting all, with the war pigs crawling on their knees and begging for mercy, while a laughing Satan spreads his wings.

The conclusion of the above song recognizes the tragic fact that Satan is the ultimate winner in wars. Truly, he is the ruler of the world (Greek, *ho archōn tou kosmou*), as Christ taught two millennia ago (John 12:31, 14:30, 16:11). Therefore, as St Paul writes in his letter to an early Christian community in Asia Minor, the spiritual struggle is not against mere human opponents: "For we do not wrestle against flesh and blood, but against principalities, against powers, against the rulers of the darkness of this age, against spiritual hosts of wickedness in the heavenly places" (Eph 6:12). An alternative translation of this Greek text is just as informative: "For our struggle is not against human foes, but against cosmic powers, against the authorities and potentates of this dark age, against the superhuman forces of evil in heavenly realms."[24] References to these cosmic powers occur in several of the Pauline letters, indicating the demonic astral or planetary beings that rule the world.[25]

However, those who are committed to truth and justice have the consolation that these ruling powers of evil will ultimately be defeated, as the Scriptures also teach. An eminent Orthodox theologian has summarized the anticipated victory of good over evil as follows: "After the resurrection of all and the Last Judgement, everything will be centred around God, and nothing will remain outside Him. The whole cosmos will be changed and transformed, transfigured and illumined. God will be 'all in all,' and Christ will reign in the souls of the people whom he has redeemed. This is the final victory of good over evil, Christ over Antichrist, light over darkness, Paradise over hell. This is the final annihilation of death."[26]

24. *OSB*, 1486.
25. *OSB*, 1449.
26. Alfeyev, *Mystery*, 226.

Truth and Knowledge

IN THE TRADITIONAL INDO-EUROPEAN conception, truth is the highest of all values. As noted by Jean Haudry, this is more than just a moral notion, for truth also involves aesthetic and cosmic roles or functions. For example, in both Celtic and Aryan (i.e., classical Indian) societies, the success of a king's reign is dependent above all else on his truthfulness. And in Aryan Iran, the Holy Immortal *Arta*, or Truth, enables humans to distinguish between good and evil: the world of the Good is called *artāvan*, meaning 'which has truth in it,' whereas the world of Evil is called *drugvant*, meaning 'which has lies in it.' Evidently, devotion to the truth is not an option but a duty.[1] It has been remarked that in contrast to the pursuit of truth, modern science derives its authority from the power it gives humans over their environment. Therefore, "to think of science as the search for truth is to renew a mystical faith, the faith of Plato and Augustine, that truth rules the world, that truth is divine."[2]

One of the earliest Indo-European religions which is still practised is Zoroastrianism, founded in Iran by the prophet Zarathustra during the second millennium B.C. Some of its precepts, for example Paradise as posthumous reward for the righteous, and the perennial struggle between Light/Goodness and Darkness/Evil, have exerted a lasting influence in later religions such as Judaism, Christianity, and Islam. Zarathustra taught that the sole God and creator of the world is *Ahura Mazda*, which means Lord of Wisdom. He taught further that Truth is the primary attribute of God and the essential foundation of the Good, whereas the Lie is the primary source of all evil. Accordingly, human beings are called to seek the Right through Truth, and to overcome the evil influences in the human world

---

1. Haudry, *Indo-Europeans*, 57.
2. Gray, *Straw Dogs*, 20.

by devotion to the Truth.³ In the teaching of Jesus of Nazareth, similarly, truth and justice were inextricably linked.

Let us now consider the meaning of truth in the Hellenic understanding. Nicolas Laos explains: "The Greek word *alētheia* is a combination of the prefix a- (signifying lack) and the Greek word *lēthē*, meaning forgetfulness. Therefore, for the ancient Greeks, truth means un-forgetfulness, un-concealment, and disclosure." Laos adds that Martin Heidegger had (correctly) related *alētheia* to the notion of disclosure, or the way in which things appear as entities in the world. Consequently, 'existence' corresponds to 'disclosure.' The Greek philosopher continues: "The term that the ancient Greeks used in order to refer to the event of disclosure was *logos*. Disclosure speaks about and declares the existence of an entity in the world, and, additionally, it refers to a conscious being that is aware of the event of disclosure. Hence, from the perspective of the Greeks' notion of *alētheia*, truth emerges from the relationship between a disclosed entity and the viewer of this disclosure." The term *logos* thus refers to an experiential understanding of truth through participation.⁴ We could say that truth is an ontological event involving an existing thing and a being that perceives it.

How may humans as limited beings know the truth? Knowledge of the truth is only possible by means of the soul, specifically its rational faculty. Heraclitus was the first Western thinker to ascribe cognitive functions to the human soul, which understands and interprets sense impressions. The latter is done correctly when phenomena are understood as manifestations of the *logos*. According to the testimony of Sextus Empiricus, Heraclitus connected intelligence (*nous*) with the *logos*, since what surrounds us is rational (*logikos*) and intelligent (*noētikos*). In this conception, humans become intelligent by drawing in the divine *logos* through breathing.⁵ Nonetheless, reality is complex, as Heraclitus recognized with his statement, "Nature loves to hide" (Fragment 123).

A contemporary of Heraclitus, Parmenides, made a clear distinction between being and becoming, in terms of which being is the object of knowledge while becoming is the object of opinion. In fact, for Parmenides there is a confluence of true being and true knowledge: "For the same thing is [or, is there] for thinking and for being [or, For thinking and being are the same]" (Fragment 3). However, the world of sense perception (i.e., the realm

---

3. Campbell, *Race and Religion*, 19.
4. Laos, *Metaphysics*, 2, 35.
5. McKirahan, *Philosophy*, 146, 147.

of becoming) cannot be the object of knowledge, since it only appears to be real. It thus appears that Parmenides was conscious of the conflict between reason and sense perception, and the illusory nature of the latter.[6] And like Parmenides, Anaxagoras taught that reliance should not be placed on sense perception as a guide to knowledge: "On account of their [the senses'] feebleness we are unable to discern the truth" (Fragment 21).

Plato on Knowledge

Although Plato wrote 35 dialogues and a number of letters which are extant, he did not write any philosophical treatises as such, probably due to his conviction that human language is too defective to fully express truth.[7] It has been remarked that Plato, standing at the end of a venerable tradition of religious thought (contrary to the modern academic view that Western philosophy more or less began with Plato), attempted to express ineffable truths in philosophical terms. This project harboured the implicit danger that Plato's method could become misunderstood as an end in itself, so that the categories of logical thought came to be regarded as embracing the whole of reality.[8]

The dialogue *Theaetetus* represents Plato's only sustained enquiry into the question, 'What is knowledge?' It thus became the founding document of epistemology as a branch of philosophy. In it, Socrates describes his role as that of a 'midwife,' since he 'brings to birth' the ideas of others, develops their presuppositions and consequences, and establishes them as sound or defective. Theaetetus' definition of knowledge as perception is linked by Socrates to Protagoras' doctrine of relativistic truth (i.e., man is the measure of all things), and the theory that all is motion and change, which is finally rejected as unsound.[9] What is important to note is that Plato here opposes two false notions about truth that have achieved dominance in modernist circles, namely relativism and empiricism.

Plato believed that with strenuous intellectual effort it is possible to move away from error and towards truth: "Only when all of these things—names, definitions, and visual and other perceptions—have been rubbed against one another and tested, pupil and teacher asking and answering

---

6. Curd, "*Presocratic Philosophy*"; Blackburn, *Oxford Dictionary*, 268.
7. Cooper, *Plato*, 1635.
8. Sherrard, *Greek East*, 5–6.
9. Cooper, *Plato*, 157.

questions in good will and without envy—only then, when reason (*dianoia*) and knowledge (*epistēmē*) are at the very extremity of human effort, can they illuminate the nature of any object" (*Letter VII*). For Plato, the mind participates in the transcendent Idea, or Form, of an external object, and it thus knows the latter due to its experience of the light of the corresponding Idea. Because of this relation between knowledge and the light of the Idea, Plato's philosophy is the opposite to every form of individualistic subjectivism.[10]

In the dialogue *Timaeus*, Plato reasons that since the world order (*kosmos*) is visible and tangible, it is grasped by sense perception and opinion (28b–c). Moreover, since the universe is perceptible, we cannot have true knowledge (*epistēmē*) of it, but only opinion (*doxa*) or belief (*pistis*) (28b–c, 29d). Plato therefore emphasizes that we cannot have more than a 'likely account' about the physical details of the world's structure. This limitation to our knowledge is due to the great distance, both literal and metaphorical, that separates us from the heavens, on which the rest of the world depends.[11] In addition, the sensible realm participates in both being and non-being. It is therefore the realm of opinion, which lies between knowledge, related to what is, and ignorance (*agnoia*), related to what is not. Those who are lovers of opinion should therefore be distinguished from those who love the truth in each thing, being called lovers of wisdom—in other words, philosophers (*Pol*, 478d–e, 480b).

Plato held that the eternal Forms, or Ideas, can be known through recollection (*anamnesis*), which also enables human communication. This ability is due to the communal knowledge shared by all souls, based on their pre-existence in the realm of Ideas. In the dialogue *Meno*, we thus find Socrates arguing in favour of the immortality of the soul, and that at our birth we already possess all theoretical knowledge. Consequently, through recollection we can draw on prior knowledge, which also applies to our understanding of moral truth.[12]

It was also stated by Plato that human knowledge begins with sight, which led to the invention of number and philosophy: "As it is, however, our ability to see the periods of day-and-night, of months and of years, of equinoxes and solstices, has led to the invention of number, and has given us the idea of time and opened the path to inquiry into the nature of the

---

10. Laos, *Metaphysics*, 34.
11. Cooper, *Plato*, 1225.
12. Dreyer, *Wysbegeerte*, 96; Cooper, *Plato*, 870–871.

universe. These pursuits have given us philosophy, a gift from the gods to the mortal race whose value neither has been nor will ever be surpassed" (*Tim*, 47a–b). In other words, human knowledge began with visual observation, which led to mathematics and thence to philosophy.

For Plato, the reality of the Forms and the physical things that participate in them involves a hierarchy of knowing states, as illustrated by means of the Analogy of the Divided Line in Book VI of the *Politeia* (509d–511e). The subdivisions of the line are, from higher to lower: (i) intelligence (*noēsis*) and (ii) reasoning (*dianoia*), which both perceive the intelligible realm (*to noēton*), and (iii) belief (*pistis*) and (iv) illusion (*eikasia*), which both perceive the visible realm (*to horaton*). In terms of this scheme, intelligence leads to a direct vision of ultimate truth; reasoning is deductive and pertains especially to mathematics; beliefs (also called common sense) are helpful in everyday life but cannot by itself lead to truth; and the illusions filling the unreflecting minds of the many perceive only the shadows and images of things.[13] A significant implication of this schema is that the natural sciences cannot lead to true knowledge, since they deal with mutable objects and not with the immutable Forms.

The philosopher Nicolas Laos has remarked that these different types of knowledge (as Plato further elaborates in his famous Simile of the Cave, in Book VI of the *Politeia*) are also different states of consciousness, namely: (i) intelligence (*noēsis*), which is the comprehension of the true nature of reality; (ii) rule-based reasoning, or logic (*dianoia*), through which one can achieve systematic knowledge of the objects of consciousness; (iii) belief (*pistis*), which is empirical knowledge that enables one to distinguish objects from their shadows, but it lacks the epistemological rigour of *dianoia*; and (iv) illusion, or conjecture (*eikasia*), which provides one with only the most unreliable opinions.[14] It is not difficult to notice that much of what passes as knowledge in the modern world does not go beyond the level of belief, despite the derision of this word by the same modern types with their rejection of metaphysical realities.

Another Orthodox philosopher, Philip Sherrard, has commented that for Plato, man's highest purpose is contemplation of and participation in supra-individual and supernatural realities (i.e., the eternal Forms or Ideas). In this regard, humans differ from their animal relatives. Whereas animals participate in the intelligible order in a passive sense (since the

---

13. Lee, *Republic*, 310–311.
14. Laos, *Metaphysics*, 14.

Ideas are present in sensible objects, including living beings), mankind has the ability to participate therein in an active sense. Sherrard concludes that in Plato's epistemology there are two faculties in humans corresponding to two modes of knowing: (a) the individual faculty of the reason (*dianoia*), which provides relative and contingent knowledge; and (b) the supra-rational intellect (*nous*), which provides absolute knowledge through direct intuition of supernatural realities.[15]

Ultimately, in the Platonic view, it is impossible to have pure knowledge in this earthly life. In order to attain to such knowledge, Socrates reasons, "We must escape from the body and observe things in themselves with the soul by itself. It seems likely that we shall, only then, when we are dead, attain that which we desire and of which we claim to be lovers, namely, wisdom, as our argument shows, not while we live" (*Phaedo*, 66d–e). Socrates here harks back to the precise meaning of the term *philosophia*, namely love of wisdom. The soul is contaminated through its association with the body, he continues, and therefore it must be separated from the body in order to gain true freedom and knowledge. Therefore, "those who practise philosophy in the right way are in training for dying and they fear death least of all men" (*Phaedo*, 67a–e).

In the Platonic understanding, Nicolas Laos writes, "knowledge does not consist in the accumulation of experiences, or of data from the sensible world, but it can be achieved inside the soul; therefore, the *telos* [purpose] of theorizing and education is to turn one's mind away from darkness until he can bear to gaze at the 'sun,' which symbolizes the idea of the Good." Just as the sun, by providing light, makes it possible for sensible things to be seen and for the eye to see them, so the Good provides that which makes the forms able to be known and the intellect able to know them (*Pol*, 508b12–c2). Laos remarks further that the *telos* of Plato's philosophy is psychotherapy, which in the Hellenic understanding consists in psychic order, harmony, and beauty.[16]

Aristotle on Knowledge

Aristotle opens his immensely influential work, the *Metaphysics*, with the statement that all humans by nature desire to know. He explains: "An indication of this is the delight we take in our senses; for even apart from their

15. Sherrard, *Greek East*, 8.
16. Laos, *Metaphysics*, 9; Perl, *Theophany*, 8.

usefulness they are loved for themselves; and above all others the sense of sight. The reason is that this, most of all the senses, makes us know and brings to light many differences between things" (Book I, 980a). However, Aristotle cautions, we do not regard any of the senses as Wisdom (Greek, *Sophia*), even though they give the most authoritative knowledge of particulars. The reason for this limitation is that the senses do not tell us the *why* of anything, for example why fire is hot, but only say *that* it is hot. Instead, Wisdom lies elsewhere, namely in the knowledge about certain principles and causes (*Met* I, 981b, 982a). The influence of Plato and some of the Pre-Socratic thinkers may be discerned in Aristotle's reasoning here.

In the *Nicomachean Ethics*, Aristotle writes that there are five intellectual virtues which enable us to approach truth: (i) science (*epistēmē*), which is knowledge of that which is necessary and eternal; (ii) art (*technē*), which is knowledge of how to make things; (iii) practical wisdom (*phronēsis*), which is knowledge of how to secure the ends of human life; (iv) intuitive reason (*nous*), which is knowledge of the principles from which science proceeds; and (v) philosophical wisdom (*sophia*), which is the union of intuitive reason and science (Book VI, Chapters 3–7).

In the Aristotelian view there are three kinds of knowledge: theoretical knowledge, which is pursued for its own sake; practical knowledge, which is pursued as a means toward conduct; and productive knowledge, which is pursued as a means toward making something that is useful or beautiful.[17] Of these sciences, theoretical knowledge represents the highest level of wisdom. It includes the subdivisions of metaphysics (or theology), natural philosophy (or physics), and mathematics. These are concerned with substances unconnected with matter, natural bodies, and numbers and spatial figures, respectively (*Met* VI.1025b–1026a).

Now, it is most interesting that Aristotle links the pursuit of knowledge and truth with happiness (or, more accurately, well-being, as we have noted). The contemplation of truth consists in metaphysics (or theology, since they are interchangeable to Aristotle), and mathematics. However, the happy life is not one of searching for the truth, but one of contemplation of truth already attained.[18] As Aristotle explains, contemplation is the best activity because reason is the best thing in us, and it is also the most continuous, since we can contemplate truth more continuously than we can *do* anything. He concludes: "For man, therefore, the life according to reason

---

17. Ross, *Aristotle*, 195, 222–223, 242.
18. Ross, *Aristotle*, 239.

is best and pleasantest, since reason more than anything else *is* man. This life therefore is also the happiest" (*Nic Eth* X, 1177a–b).

Following the psychology of Plato, Aristotle viewed reason as one of the elements that constitute the human soul, the others being desire and sensation. Of these, it is reason and desire that control action and truth (*Nic Eth* VI, 1139a). Aristotle adds that moral choice involves both the desire for an end (or purpose) and reason as establishing the means to the end. Although the object of reason is truth, thought as such achieves nothing; only thought directed to an end does. Furthermore, the human being is a union of desire and reason, both of which determine action (albeit in different ways). Ultimately, truth is the aim of reason (*Nic Eth* VI, 1139b).[19]

Knowledge in Neoplatonism

The first of the great Neoplatonist thinkers, Plotinus, similarly acknowledged different levels of knowledge. He did not conceive Intellect (*nous*) as a substance which exercises *noēsis*, the act of intellection; rather, Intellect is that activity itself (*Enneads* V.3.5). In this conception, Intellect is pure consciousness, at the highest level thereof.[20] It may be asked, how does soul mediate between Intellect and the sensible world? As the locus of discursive reason, soul brings the multiplicity of sense impressions which it receives 'from below' under the unity of the forms which it receives 'from above' (*Enneads* V.3.2).[21] It should also be kept in mind that Plotinus ascribed the discursive power of the soul to the presence of Intellect. The soul's thinking is conceived as an image of the intellect's thinking, so that discursive reason (*dianoia*) arises due to intellect (*dia nou*), and not in separation from it (*Enneads* V.3.6).[22] This implies that for reason to provide us with a reliable account (*logos*) of the physical world (*kosmos*), it has to be enlightened 'from above,' by Intellect.

Moreover, for Plotinus the rational knowledge of things and the spiritual destiny of the soul are interlinked: "The demonstrations [of the Good] themselves were a kind of leading up on our way" (*Enneads*, I.3.1). In this view, Albert Camus comments, "To know is to worship in accordance with Reason. Science is a form of contemplation and inner meditation, not a

19. Ross, *Aristotle*, 221–222.
20. Perl, *Theophany*, 85.
21. Perl, *Theophany*, 87.
22. Dillon and Gerson, *Neoplatonic Philosophy*, 93.

construction."²³ It has been remarked elsewhere that Plotinus was not only a metaphysician, but also a natural scientist. Naturally, as a Platonist he viewed the physical world as derived from the intelligible world. Therefore, the contemplation of the natural world reflects the relation between the intelligible *logoi* (reason-principles) and the phenomenal world consisting of form-matter aggregates.²⁴

The priority of the truth that subsists in souls over the opinion (*doxa*) that flows from sense-perception is strikingly described by Iamblichus: "And the former indeed receives its perfection in intelligible and divine forms . . . but the latter looks to that which is formless, and non-being, and which has a various subsistence. The former contemplates that which is, but the latter assumes such a form as appears to the many. Hence the former associates with intellect, and increases the intellectual nature which we contain; but the latter, from looking at that which always seems to be, hunts after folly and deceives."²⁵

Continuing the Platonic epistemology, Proclus agreed that the faculty of sense-perception is unreasoning in several ways. For example, the sun looks small from the Earth. Therefore, the truth can only be apprehended by the higher faculty of understanding. Since the visible world is only a likeness of the intelligible world, any account of it can be no more than a likely one.²⁶ Consequently, in the Platonic perspective there can be no exact science of natural things, for they are always changing.

Nonetheless, the importance of sight should be recognized, even though physical sight is subordinate to spiritual sight. The eminent metaphysical thinker René Guénon has pointed out that both spiritual and physical sight are related to true knowledge (Sanskrit, *vidya*). This is evident from the fact that the classical Indian religious texts, the Vedas, derive their name from the root *vid*, which contains the two-fold meaning of seeing (Latin, *videre*) and knowing (Greek, *oida*). Accordingly, "sight is taken as a symbol of knowledge because it is its chief instrument within the sensible order; and this symbolism is carried even into the purely intellectual realm, where knowledge is likened to 'inward vision,' as is implied by the use of words such as 'intuition' for example."²⁷ This reasoning confirms

---

23. Camus, *Christian Metaphysics*, 89.
24. Martijn, Review of *Physics*, 36–38.
25. Quoted in Taylor, *Introduction*, 110–111.
26. Cornford, *Plato's Cosmology*, 24, 28.
27. Guénon, *Man and his Becoming*, 14.

that the physical cannot be divorced from the metaphysical, which provides its ontological foundation.

Proclus followed Empedocles and Plato in asserting that at every level of reality, like is known by like. Accordingly, the sensible realm is known by sensation, the heavenly realm by opinion or belief, the realm of Soul by discursive reasoning, and the intelligible realm by intellection. When the soul contemplates the universe, Proclus continues, it sees only the images of true beings, but when it turns into itself the soul perceives its own reason-principles (*logoi*); the latter being the projections within the soul of the eternal Forms. In the words of Proclus, "For all things are within us in a manner proper to soul, and by reason of that we have the natural capacity to know everything through awaking the powers within us and the images of all beings" (*Platonic Theology*, I.3).[28] Thus in true Platonic fashion a hierarchy of knowledge is postulated, which from lowest to highest is represented by sensation (*aisthēsis*), opinion or belief (*doxa*), reasoning (*dianoia*) and intelligence (*noēsis*).

In the modern, 'democratic' world everyone is expected to have an opinion, however uninformed it may be, on all kinds of matters. However, in the Hellenic understanding opinion is the lowest power of the rational soul, limited to knowing the universal in particulars. In other words, opinion can only know *that* a thing is (*oti*), but not *why* it is (*dioti*).[29] In an aphorism titled 'Final opinion on opinions,' Friedrich Nietzsche mocked as follows: "Either we should hide our opinions or hide ourselves behind our opinions. Whoever does otherwise, does not know the way of the world, or belongs to the order of pious fire-eaters."[30] In contrast to the low knowledge content of opinion, the Hellenic tradition recognizes two levels of higher knowledge: (a) discursive reasoning (*dianoia*) that strives toward rational, 'scientific' knowledge; and (b) intellection (*noēsis*), which entails a non-discursive dialectic which implies the soul's affinity with the Forms.[31] With its firm ontological basis, this epistemology is indeed superior over the agnostic relativism that characterizes postmodern culture.

28. Dillon and Gerson, *Neoplatonic Philosophy*, 290–291.
29. Taylor, *Introduction*, 105.
30. Nietzsche, *Human*, 371.
31. Uzdavinys, *Orpheus*, 76.

Knowledge in Christian Theology

A markedly different approach to the acquisition of knowledge is encountered in Christian theology, especially its Augustinian strand. The main reason for this divergence from Hellenic thought is the more realistic anthropology of the Christian tradition. In this view, mankind has been spiritually blinded by its ongoing rebellion against God, whether individual humans are conscious thereof or not. This rebellion of the creature against its Creator finds expression in many forms, particularly the deadly sins of pride, greed, lust, envy, gluttony, wrath, and sloth. To this list should be added the ignorance of metaphysical realities among most humans, on which point the Platonists would surely agree.

The early Christian understanding of knowledge (Greek, *gnōsis*; also rendered as a seeking to know, or *cognitio* in Latin),[32] as exemplified in the letters of St Paul and the *Stromata* ('Miscellanies') of Clement of Alexandria, has been summarized as follows. There are three kinds of *gnosis*: (i) a false knowledge which 'puffs up' (1 Cor 8:1); (ii) a true knowledge that admits of degrees and will 'vanish away' (1 Cor 13:8); and (iii) a knowledge that is perfect and eternal. Moreover, true knowledge begins in faith and is borne along by language, so that it may be called doctrinal. However, it cannot be reduced to language, as in the post-modernist sense. "Rather, it pertains to the essence of language in general, and of sacred language especially, *to point beyond itself*, and thereby to serve as the carrier of a gnosis, precisely." Therefore, true gnosis of the 'preliminary' kind and doctrinal gnosis are identical. Finally, the perfect and eternal gnosis of which Clement speaks is the gnosis of Christ himself, which is the knowledge of salvation (Luke 1:77).[33]

The founder of much of Latin Christian theology, Augustine of Hippo, defines reason (Latin, *ratio*) as the logical process according to which the intellect discerns and connects the objects of knowledge. Moreover, in his important work *On the Trinity*, Augustine draws a distinction between *ratio superior*, which discerns ideal reality in and through the human soul and leads to the truth, and *ratio inferior*, which employs the senses to look at the external world of objects and cannot lead to the truth. In this way, the inner truth and certainty of intellectual perception is contrasted with the uncertainty of sense perception.[34]

32. LSJ, 144.
33. Smith, *Christian Gnosis*, 25, 28.
34. Laos, *Metaphysics*, 33.

Since the human soul is created immortal, Augustine reasons, it is independent of the body and superior to it. The soul has a superior mental faculty called the intellect, which knows things in their essences, since the human mind contains copies of the immutable spiritual essences according to which everything is made. Consequently, the choice that we have is between the lower reason and clinging to the natural forms, or the higher reason and contemplating the eternal essences of things.[35]

In Augustinian theology, furthermore, secular knowledge is viewed as an insufficient means leading to the salvation of the soul. Instead, human reason has to be enlightened by faith in God. Thus, in the words of Etienne Gilson, "True philosophy begins by an act of adherence to the supernatural order which will liberate the will from the flesh through grace, and thought from scepticism through revelation."[36] We could say that reason must be illuminated by faith in order to remain rational.

By subordinating reason to faith, yet without rejecting the validity of reason in its own sphere, Augustine laid the foundations of traditional Christian epistemology. In his *Homilies on the Gospel of John* (29.6), the Latin theologian made the celebrated statement, "If thou hast not understood, said I, believe. For understanding is the reward of faith. Therefore, do not seek to understand in order to believe, but believe that thou may understand." Albert Camus aptly comments: "This reason is dulled. It is clarified by the light of Faith. One must believe, not that God exists, but in God."[37] Believe, in order that you may understand—this is Augustine's famous *Credo, ut intelligam*. In other words, rational understanding is the reward of faith in God, if the believer should choose to pursue such understanding.

In the Orthodox Christian understanding, Vladimir Lossky writes, true theology is situated between *gnōsis*, or contemplative and existential knowledge, and *epistēmē*, or scientific and rational knowledge. Theology thus finds itself in the domain of wisdom, which in the Septuagint is designated the divine Wisdom, or Sophia. Lossky adds, "Theology as *sophia* is connected at once to *gnōsis* and *epistēmē*. It reasons, but seeks always to go beyond concepts." This is the only approach to knowledge that does justice to the total transcendence of God by His nature, in the very immanence of

---

35. Sherrard, *Greek East*, 145.
36. Quoted in Camus, *Christian Metaphysics*, 128.
37. Camus, *Christian Metaphysics*, 128.

His manifestation. For this reason, Christian theologians have adopted the apophatic way of 'learned ignorance,' as it has been called.[38]

This concept of learned ignorance (Latin, *docta ignorantia*) should not be confused with a pre-critical ignorance of theological issues. Instead, it harks back to the statement by St Paul that if anyone thinks that he knows anything, he knows nothing yet as he ought to know (1 Cor 8:2). In the same vein, the Jewish-Hellenic thinker Philo of Alexandria wrote that the final aim of knowledge is to hold that we know nothing, since God alone is wise.[39] And for the Renaissance philosopher and theologian Nicholas of Cusa, learned ignorance meant that since humans are unable to grasp the divine infinity through rational knowledge, both reason and a supra-rational understanding are required to approach God.[40]

Apophatic Theology

In the Christian tradition, another approach to knowledge and understanding is that of apophatic mysticism. These terms are derived from the Greek *apophasis*, meaning denial or negation, and *mystikos*, meaning secret or mystical. Its opposite is called affirmative or cataphatic theology, from the Greek verb *kataphainō*, meaning to make or become visible or clear. Since God transcends all names and attributes, all that can we say about God remains incomplete and limited. Thus, in apophatic theology (or the way of negation) the emphasis falls on statements about what God is not, in contrast to cataphatic theology (the way of affirmation) which involves statements about what God is.[41]

Within his grand synthesis of Neoplatonic philosophy and Christian theology, Dionysius the Areopagite opens his concise yet immensely influential treatise titled *Mystical Theology* as follows: "O Trinity! Higher than any being, any divinity, any goodness! Guide of Christians in the wisdom of heaven! Lead us up beyond unknowing and light, up to the farthest, highest peak of mystic scripture, where the mysteries of God's Word lie simple, absolute and unchangeable in the brilliant darkness of a hidden silence. Amid the deepest shadow they pour overwhelming light on what is most manifest. Amid the wholly unsensed and unseen they completely

38. Lossky, *Orthodox Theology*, 14–15, 23.
39. Perry, *Treasury*, 745.
40. Wikipedia: *De Docta Ignorantia*
41. LSJ, 96, 363, 456; Alfeyev, *Mystery*, 24–25.

fill our sightless minds with treasures beyond all beauty" (*MT*, 997a–b). In this passage, the Greek theologian employs some of the ways in which apophatic theology can be expressed, such as the prefix *hyper*, meaning 'beyond' (translated here as 'higher'), and by means of oxymorons, such as 'brilliant darkness.'[42]

Following this picturesque prelude, Dionysius encourages the reader to leave behind everything perceptible and understandable (the Platonic sensible and intelligible worlds), all that is not and all that is (non-being and being), in order to strive towards union with Him who is beyond all being and knowledge (the transcendent One). In this way, "By an undivided and absolute abandonment of yourself and everything, shedding all and freed from all, you will be uplifted to the ray of the divine shadow which is above everything that is" (*MT*, 997b–1000a). A similar terminology is employed by Lorenzo Scupoli (c.1530–1610) in his celebrated work *The Spiritual Combat*: "Know that God is beyond all senses and sensory things, beyond all shape, colour, measure and place; is wholly without form and image and, while present in all things, is above all things; therefore He is beyond all imagining."[43]

In this understanding, Eric Perl comments, "we cannot say what God is not any more than we can say what he is, because God neither is nor is not anything at all." For Dionysius, "God is not merely unknowable but beyond unknowing, not merely ineffable but beyond ineffability." However, this negative theology should not be confused with atheism, for it transcends atheism no less than it does theism. The Catholic philosopher adds that both theism and atheism are modern phenomena which cannot legitimately be read into Neoplatonism (including that of Dionysius).[44]

An interesting argument has been made by Nicolas Berdyaev that atheism may spring from good motives and not only from bad ones. The good as well as the wicked rebel against God, albeit with different motives: the wicked hate God because He prevents them from doing evil, whereas the good are ready to hate Him for allowing the existence of evil. In this way, "the very distinction between good and evil which is the result of the Fall becomes the source of atheism." The traditional doctrines of (affirmative) theology are therefore unable to solve the problem of evil, the Russian philosopher concludes. It is only by means of negative (or apophatic)

42. Alfeyev, *Mystery*, 26.
43. Quoted in Perry, *Treasury*, 721.
44. Perl, *Theophany*, 14–15.

theology, which conceives of God as the infinite mystery that underlies existence, that the pain of life is made endurable.[45]

The Dionysian conception of the interaction between cataphatic theology and apophatic theology has been sketched as follows by the Orthodox theologian Vladimir Lossky. While cataphatic theology provides an imperfect knowledge of God, apophatic theology leads to total ignorance, whereby God is attained through non-knowing (*agnōsia*). The practice thereof, as Dionysius taught, requires leaving behind all that is sensible and intelligible, what is and what is not. This is not a dialectical process, but a purification (*katharsis*), as is illustrated by Moses' purification before ascending the mountain to meet with God. Apophatic theology thus leads to mystical union with God rather than knowledge of Him, for His nature remains incomprehensible. As Dionysius emphasizes, the universal Cause of all is above all affirmation and all negation.[46]

Throughout his *magnum opus*, the Irish philosopher John Scottus Eriugena practises the way of negation when writing about God, without denying the validity of affirmation regarding God. He states, for example: "God is truth; God is not truth; and God is more than truth" (*Per* IV, 757–758). For Eriugena, everything that can be said about God can be contradicted, and even the contradiction can be contradicted. Therefore, God is nothing; God is something; God is not nothing; and God is not something.[47] Nicolas Laos comments that for Eriugena reason prepares the way for faith, so that the latter follows the path of philosophy. Thus, philosophy leads to a cataphatic form of knowledge which underlies apophatic, or mystical, theology.[48] According to the Dionysian tradition within which Eriugena works, the divine darkness of ignorance is a prerequisite for union with the unknowable. This 'unknowing' excludes the sensible world and can therefore not be demonstrated; it also excludes the intelligible world and can therefore not be learnt; and yet it is an ineffable, unitive vision.[49]

The tradition of apophatic mysticism was continued in the fourteenth century by another Greek theologian, Gregory Palamas. In the *Twenty-two Homilies* he writes: "It is truly impossible to be united to God unless, besides purifying ourselves, we come to be outside or, rather, above ourselves,

---

45. Berdyaev, *Destiny of Man*, 23–24.
46. Lossky, *Mystical Theology*, 25, 27–29.
47. Carabine, *Eriugena*, 59.
48. Laos, *Metaphysics*, 35.
49. Sheldon-Williams, "*Greek Christian Platonist*," 470.

having left all that which pertains to the sensible world and risen above all ideas, reasonings, and even all knowledge and above reason itself, being entirely under the influence of the intellectual sense and having reached that ignorance which is above knowledge and (what is the same) above every kind of philosophy."[50]

Vladimir Lossky contends that the apophatic way of Christian theology is more absolute than that of the Hellenic philosophers. For Plotinus, although the One is the Absolute that cannot be named, it is in a certain manner in continuity with the Intellect, and ultimately with the world. In contrast, for Christians there is a radical break between the Trinity and the created world, both in its intelligible and its sensible modalities. The early Christian theologians used the philosophical method of negation in order to posit the absolute transcendence of the living God. As Lossky concludes, "*Apophasis is the inscription in human language, in theological language, of the mystery of faith.*"[51]

The preference for apophatic theology has remained characteristic of Eastern Christianity to this day. As argued by Nicolas Berdyaev, by teaching that God is Being and may be known in concepts, cataphatic theology has denied the fundamental truth that God is mystery, and that mystery underlies all things. In contrast, apophatic theology recognizes that God is higher than Being, and that knowledge of God is beyond Being. Nonetheless, Lossky points out, there is room for both approaches: cataphatic theology revolves around God's descent towards us in His self-manifestation, whereas apophatic theology involves our ascent to God. The interaction between the two is like a ladder on which climbing takes place in opposite directions.[52]

Conclusion

If we briefly step outside of the Hellenic and Christian views of truth and knowledge, we may find an illuminating insight in Nietzsche's aphorism on the relation between age and truth. He writes: "Young people love what is interesting and odd, no matter how true or false it is. More mature minds love what is interesting and odd about truth. Fully mature intellects, finally, love truth, even when it appears plain and simple, boring to the ordinary

---

50. Quoted in Sherrard, *Greek East*, 140.
51. Lossky, *Orthodox Theology*, 24–25.
52. Berdyaev, "*Being and Existence*," 375; Lossky, *Mystical Theology*, 39.

person; for they have noticed that truth tends to reveal its highest wisdom in the guise of simplicity."[53]

Ultimately, the Hellenic notion of the soul's primacy over the body implies that pure knowledge (*gnōsis*) is only attainable after death. As declared by Socrates shortly before his enforced suicide, "It really has been shown to us that, if we are ever to have pure knowledge, we must escape from the body and observe things in themselves with the soul by itself" (*Phaedo*, 66e). Thus, by dying to the body already in this life, the true philosopher (*philosophos*, 'lover of wisdom') acquires knowledge of the noetic realm, and thus becomes akin to the eternal Forms.[54]

In summary, we could say that in the Hellenic tradition the main problem is ignorance, while in the Christian tradition it is sinfulness. For the Hellenists, it is ignorance that prevents us from returning to the One, while for the Christians it is sin that erects a barrier between us and God. Accordingly, the Hellenic spiritual life is aimed primarily at overcoming ignorance, while the Christian spiritual life is aimed primarily at overcoming sin. In the words of Frithjof Schuon, "while the Platonists propound Knowledge because man is an intelligence, the Christians envisage . . . salvation by Grace because man is an existence – as such separated from God – and a fallen and impotent will." Symbolically speaking, if all men are in danger of drowning due to the ancestral fall, the Christian saves himself by grasping the pole held out to him by Christ, while the Platonist saves himself by swimming; but neither way weakens or neutralizes the effectiveness of the other.[55]

We therefore conclude that these Hellenic and Christian approaches are complementary and not contradictory. As further explained by Schuon, for the Hellenists truth is that which is in conformity with the nature of things, while for the Christians truth is that which leads to God. For the Christian gnostics, such as the Alexandrian school, to know God is to love Him, and to love God perfectly is to know Him; thus remaining true to the Pauline theology. And in the related Vedantic teaching, love (Sanskrit, *bhakti*) finds its sublimation in pure knowledge (*jnāna*), these being individual and universal, respectively.[56]

---

53. Nietzsche, *Human*, 242.
54. Uzdavinys, *Orpheus*, 75.
55. Schuon, *Ancient Worlds*, 63, 69.
56. Schuon, *Ancient Worlds*, 60–62.

Time and Eternity

As mentioned earlier, the intelligible world of true being is eternal, whereas the sensible world of becoming is temporal. In other words, eternity applies to the metaphysical world and time to the physical world. The latter, also called the world order (*kosmos*) by Plato, is not eternally existing, but has an origin and therefore came to be (*Tim*, 28b–c). And since time applies only to the realm of becoming, it follows that the realm of being (which includes the eternal Forms) is outside of time.[1] A momentous implication of this reasoning is that only that which is without a beginning in time is also without an end in time. On the other hand, everything which has a beginning in time must also have an end in time. It is therefore impossible for an entity in the physical world to be everlasting or endless.

An interesting distinction is made in the Greek language between two kinds of time, indicated by the words *chronos* and *kairos*. The first word, *chronos*, means chronological or sequential time, from which the term 'chronology' is derived. In other words, *chronos* means a certain time or a period. The second word, *kairos*, signifies the critical moment, a right or opportune time for action, as is indicated by its Latin equivalent, *opportunitas*. The Hellenic writer Aesop depicted Kairos as a swiftly running man with a lock of hair on his forehead (*Fables*, 536). He could therefore be grasped and held while approaching, but once he has passed cannot be pulled back. From these descriptions we can see that the meaning of *chronos* is quantitative, whereas *kairos* has a qualitative nature.[2]

The Traditionalist author Ananda Coomaraswamy explains the metaphysical understanding of time and eternity as follows. Concerning the doctrine of divine creation of the world, he points out that the scriptural phrase 'In the beginning' (Greek, *en archē*; Latin, *in principio*) also means 'in principle,' which is "an ultimate source logically rather than temporally

---

1. Cohen, "*Plato's Cosmology.*"
2. Wikipedia: *Kairos*; LSJ, 341, 790; Laos, *World Order*, 147.

prior to all secondary causes." This phrase is interpreted by Philo of Alexandria as meaning that all things were created simultaneously, but a sequence was written into the Genesis narrative because of their subsequent generation from one another. Referring to Aristotle's notion that eternal beings are not in time, Coomaraswamy adds: "God's existence is, therefore, *now* – the eternal now that separates past from future durations but is not itself a duration, however short. Therefore, in Meister Eckhart's words, 'God is creating the world *now*, this instant.' Again, no sooner has some time elapsed, however little, but everything is changed; *panta rei* [Greek, 'everything flows'], 'You cannot dip your feet twice in the same waters.'"[3] The latter statement is attributed to Heraclitus of Ephesus, who emphasized the ever-changing nature of the sensible world.

Hellenic Views

The relation between time (*chronos*) and eternity (*aion*) is explained by Plato in terms of motion, namely that time is made by the Demiurge as a moving image of eternity. In this way, time came to be together with the cosmos. The correlate hereof is that time and the universe will disintegrate together, should disintegration take place (*Tim*, 37d, 38b). The purpose of the Demiurge in establishing time is that mankind should learn mathematics through calculating the periods of time, namely days, months, and years. The basic unit of reckoning is day-and-night, which is the shortest division of time produced by the celestial revolutions (*Tim*, 39c).[4]

Plato also relates time to the wanderings of the celestial bodies: "Such was the reason, then, such the god's design for the coming into being of time, that he brought into being the Sun, the Moon and five other stars [i.e., planets], for the begetting of time. These are called wanderers (*planeta*), and they came into being to set limits to and stand guard over the numbers of time" (*Tim*, 38b). It has been suggested that Plato wished first to define time to contrast the temporal existence of even the everlasting gods (i.e., the celestial bodies) with the unchanging duration of the eternal model.[5] We could say that the sensible world is the realm of space and time, whereas the intelligible world is the realm of eternity beyond space and time.

3. Coomaraswamy, *Literacy*, 118.
4. Cornford, *Plato's Cosmology*, 115.
5. Cornford, *Plato's Cosmology*, 117.

In his turn, Aristotle linked the reproduction of living beings with eternity. For all living things, "the most natural act is the production of another like itself, an animal producing an animal, a plant a plant, in order that, as far as its nature allows, it may partake in the eternal and divine" (*De An* I.415a–b). Plato similarly asserted that the mortal nature of both humans and animals strives towards immortality by means of reproduction, which is the only means possible for it (*Sym*, 207c–d). Elsewhere Aristotle reasons in a similar vein: "And since soul is better than body and the ensouled is better than the soulless owing to its soul and being is better than not being and living better than not living, for these reasons reproduction (*genesis*) of living things exists. Since it is impossible for it [i.e., a living thing] to be eternal as an individual . . . it is possible for it to be eternal in species. This is the reason why there exists eternally the class of human beings, animals, and plants" (*GA*, I.731b–732a).[6] In this way, reproduction serves to preserve the different kinds of organisms.

For Plotinus the distinction between Being, which is produced by Intellect, and Soul is analogous to that between eternity and time. In the *Enneads* (at III.7), eternity is stated to be the state and nature of real Being, whereas time pertains to the life of the World-soul. Concurring with Plato that time is an image of eternity, Plotinus writes in his treatise *On Time and Eternity* that the state of eternity is timeless, unending, and changeless, whereas time is the activity of the soul in the world. Moreover, Nicolas Laos comments, for Plotinus real Being in its ideal state is unmanifested, while existence is the manifestation of being in the world of becoming. "Hence, time manifests a tendency toward perfection, and eternity manifests the participation of beings in the state of the intelligible world, precisely in a state of ontological completeness."[7] We could therefore say that eternity is the domain of perfection, whereas time is the realm of imperfection.

Not surprising for such a brilliant thinker, Proclus held a nuanced Platonic view on the relation between eternity and time. He writes, "Prior to all eternal entities there is Eternity, and prior to all temporal ones there is Time." Employing the hermeneutical key of participation, Proclus reasons that there are as many eternal things as there are temporal things. "But prior to these are the undivided Eternity and the unique Time; the former is the Eternity of eternities, while the latter is the Time of times, since they

---

6. Gerson, *Aristotle*, 118.
7. Laos, *Metaphysics*, 18–19.

are the generators of their respective participants" (*Elem Theol*, Proposition 53).

It has been remarked that the notion of 'opportune time' (*kairos*) is related to Aristotle's notion of 'right measure' (*metron*), thus giving rise to the temporal categories of 'not yet' or 'too early' and 'never again' or 'too late.' *Kairos* is therefore not only the proper time to act, but is also the temporal point at which the continuity of temporality is replaced by the discontinuity which is caused by the presence of eternity in time. Consequently, in the Neoplatonic understanding, through this process whereby 'horizontal time' is transfigured into 'vertical time,' time undergoes a fundamental qualitative change.[8]

Christian Views

The Eastern Christian theologians concurred with Plato that time came into existence together with the universe, both being created by God 'in the beginning.' Since the celestial bodies move in a circular course, Basil of Caesarea used the example of a circle, which does not appear to have a beginning, but a drawing of it really begins at some point at a certain radius from the center. Therefore, "That which was begun in time is condemned to come to an end in time" (*Hex* I.3). Basil taught further that God first created the intelligible world, which is eternal and infinite, as an abode for the intellectual and invisible natures, such as the angelic beings. Afterwards, God created the sensible world, as a home for beings destined to be born and die. Thus was created the succession of time, "for ever pressing on and passing away and never stopping in its course." This is the nature of time, Basil adds, that the past is no more, the future does not exist, and the present escapes before being recognized. And this is the nature of the creature which lives in time, such as the bodies of animals and plants (*Hex* I.5).

Another Greek theologian, John Philoponus (sixth century), added a scientifically relevant insight to this Platonic view on the simultaneous creation of the cosmos and time. Since both time and motion are measured the one through the other, he reasoned, it is necessary for an observer to record the motion in order to talk about time. Therefore, the existence of time presupposes the creation of the physical world and its recording through the observation of the motion of the celestial bodies.[9]

8. Laos, *World Order*, 148.
9. Kalachanis et al., *Theory of Big Bang*, 35–36.

In the *Divine Names,* Dionysius the Areopagite distinguishes eternity and time. Whereas eternity is uncreated, immortal, and immutable, time is related to the process of change, such as birth, death, and variety. Therefore, in the sacred scriptures, eternity is the home of being, while time is the home of becoming (*DN*, 10:3). Maximus the Confessor also relates time to sensible being (*ta aisthēta*), since its nature is to begin, to endure, and to have an end. However, he postulates a created eternity, the *aeon*, which is outside of time and pertains to intelligible being (*ta noēta*). It is motionless time, the realm of the unchanging structures of the cosmos, the geometry of ideas which govern creation, and the network of mathematical essences. While time is the domain of motion and change, the eternity of the *aeon* is stable and unchanging, so that it makes the world coherent and intelligible. Only the uncreated eternity in which God dwells is incommensurable in relation to both time and the *aeon*.[10]

The first psychological account of time from a Christian perspective was provided by Augustine of Hippo in his *Confessions*. He begins by pondering the nature of time: "What, then, is time? If no one asks me, I know what it is. If I wish to explain it to him who asks me, I do not know. Yet I say with confidence that I know that if nothing passed away, there would be no past time; and if nothing were still coming, there would be no future time; and if there were nothing at all, there would be no present time." The Latin theologian then affirms this relation of time to non-being by remarking that the present time only comes into existence because it passes into the past time—that is to say, the cause of its being is that it will cease to be. Therefore, time only exists as it tends towards non-being (*Conf,* 11:14).

Moreover, for Augustine the measurement of time is possible because the human consciousness anticipates the future, remembers the past, and is aware of the present through perception. In other words, there are three times which co-exist somehow in the soul: memory, experience, and expectation (*Conf,* 11:20). In this sense, time exists as a distension of the soul (Latin, *distentio animi*). This view of time diverges from the Neoplatonic one: for Plotinus, the World-soul spreading out (Greek, *diastasis*) involves time, but for Augustine it is the human soul involving time.[11] With reference to the sound of a voice, the relation between the past and the future is stated as follows by the Latin theologian: "Thus it passes on, until the present intention carries the future over into the past. The past increases by

---

10. Lossky, *Orthodox Theology*, 62; Lossky, *Mystical Theology*, 102.
11. Knuuttila, *"Time and creation,"* 112, 115.

the diminution of the future until by the consumption of all the future, all is past" (*Conf*, 11:27).

One of Augustine's most important contributions to Christian theology is his rejection of millennialism (from the Latin *millennium*, 'a thousand years'), which is also known as chiliasm (from the Greek *chilias*, 'a thousand'). This phenomenon has appeared repeatedly in Christianity and Judaism, usually as messianic movements proclaiming that the earthly kingdom of God was at hand. These movements often caused large-scale social unrest—for example, the Anabaptist revolt which fuelled the German Peasants' War in the early sixteenth century. A secularized version of millennialism is Adolf Hitler's 'Third Reich,' which was envisioned to last for a thousand years.[12] Against this misunderstanding (whether religious or secular) of the relation between time and eternity, Augustine spiritualized the biblical teaching on the end of time, or eschatology. Influenced by Plato's view that spiritual things belong in the realm of eternity, the Latin theologian conceived of the end of time in spiritual terms—in other words, "not as an event that will happen at some point in the future but as an inner transformation that can happen at any time."[13]

Summarizing the traditional Christian understanding, we could say that outside of time there is an eternity which is beyond being. At the end of time, the universe, "called out of non-being into temporal being through the creative word of God," will not disintegrate (*contra* Plato), nor return to non-being, but will become part of the eternity beyond being. And for its part, time will be sublimated into eternity.[14]

Cosmic Cycles

Within this chapter's theme of time and eternity, we should also note the Indo-European notion of cosmic cycles. This is associated with the conviction that instead of the world being the unique creation of a Deity and therefore having a beginning in time, the existence of the cosmos entails a beginning-less and endless succession of world-origins and world-endings. This cyclic cosmogony was taught by early Hellenic thinkers such as Anaximander, Heraclitus, and Empedocles, and by the Roman poet Lucretius in his didactic poem *De rerum natura* ('On the nature of things'). It also found

12. Wikipedia: Millennialism.
13. Gray, *Black Mass*, 11.
14. Alfeyev, *Mystery*, 50.

expression in the Germanic world in the first poem of the *Poetic Edda*, titled *Völuspá*.[15] Let us look at this concept in a little more detail.

In his informative book *The Order of the Ages*, the philosopher Robert Bolton writes about a universal myth which teaches that the world began with a golden age, which was followed by ages of silver, bronze or brass, and iron. He writes, "The qualities of these metals were understood as symbols of the prevailing qualities of the four ages and have no connection with the bronze and iron ages of archaeology, which simply results from the periods when these metals came into general use. The sequence of ages involves the idea of a certain constant deterioration of the world which man cannot prevent, at least on the collective scale. The golden age is said to owe its quality to that of the beginning of the world when nature and the supernatural were still in harmony, and all things had the fullest degree of perfection possible for them."[16]

The cosmic cycle ends with the age of iron, which is vividly depicted by the Hellenic poet Hesiod in his *Works and Days*. In this age, men never rest from labor and sorrow by day, and from perishing by night; strife between family members and throughout society is rampant; might is the only right and reverence will cease to be; the wicked will injure the worthy man, and there will be no help against evil. Finally, this degenerate 'race of iron' will be destroyed by Zeus, the Father of the Gods.[17]

An equivalent to this cyclic schema is found in the scriptures of various other traditions. The biblical book of Daniel (chapter 2) mentions a dream by Nebuchadnezzar, referring to the powerful king who ruled over Babylon from around 605 B.C. until 562 B.C. In this dream, the king saw a figure made of all four of the symbolic elements: it had a head of gold, breast and arms of silver, belly and thighs of brass, legs of iron, and feet of iron and clay. This dream has usually been interpreted as symbolizing the successive empires of Babylonia, Persia, Greece, and Rome, with a final prolongation added to the latter, whereby a fifth element became added to the basic four. The last of these empires is presented in the dream as the most evil of them. As Bolton comments, "This not only illustrates the universality of the four metals as symbols of the world order throughout time, it also shows that the pattern of change governing the world as a whole is continually recapitulated on a smaller scale, since the empires represented

---

15. Günther, *Religious attitudes*, 12.
16. Bolton, *Order*, 63.
17. Bolton, *Order*, 63–64.

by the four main parts of the figure occupy only the period from about 600 B.C. to 400 AD."[18]

In Indian scriptures such as the *Bhagavata Purana*, the four ages are known as the *Krita* (or *Satya*) *Yuga*, the *Tretā Yuga*, the *Dvāpara Yuga*, and the *Kali Yuga*. Bolton remarks that the latter, also called the dark age, is named after Kali, the demon of destruction, and not the goddess Kālī. The whole cycle is called a *Manvantara*, or era of Manu, named after the half-mythical lawgiver at the beginning of the cycle. The temporal durations of the four *Yugas* decline in the ratio 4:3:2:1, while they also follow a declining order of spiritual quality.[19] It is noteworthy that this same ratio also features prominently in the Pythagorean philosophy, where it is called the *tetraktys* (meaning fourness), with the sum of its numbers totaling ten, which is the *decad*.

Some of the salient implications of this downward trend of the gold, silver, bronze, and dark/iron ages have been drawn out by Robert Bolton. He writes: "Social changes such as the rise to dominance of the lower castes [in India] has its parallels in societies with no caste systems. The general mingling of all hereditary social groups is a universal feature of today's world, where it is taken to affirm the value and the freedom of the individual; it passes unnoticed that freedom means nothing without the variety of possibilities which is suppressed by trends toward social uniformity. Even more generally, there is the reductionist outlook which deprives many things of their meaning and confines them to their basically physical functions. Such reductions are brought about by a mentality for which truth and reality are somehow bound to be simple and crude, as though the transcendent simplicity of God [as the One] were being sought in the opposite direction, that of matter."[20] This reductionism may be seen in the rise to dominance of materialism, both conceptual and economic, in the modern world.

At the same time, Bolton adds, the physical wasting away of plant, animal, and human life (in the *Kali Yuga*) develops in parallel with a general loss of the moral and intellectual qualities. For instance, "In the modern world genuine metaphysical knowledge has long since ceased to have any foothold in the prevailing culture, and the void it has left is filled with semi-fictional notions drawn from popularized science." Finally, Bolton writes, "Throughout these texts on the *Kali Yuga*, the unifying factor is the

---

18. Bolton, *Order*, 67.
19. Wikipedia: Kali Yuga; Bolton, *Order*, 91.
20. Bolton, *Order*, 97–98.

relentless contraction in the range of human consciousness, which worsens with the passage of time. This relates to the number of distinct realities which one can be aware of and relate to at a given time. Since the need for physical survival demands attention to material needs and functions, this contraction of consciousness tends to eliminate everything but these functions, before it erodes even them."[21]

This replacement of a spiritual consciousness by a concern for material things inevitably yields disastrous results, as mentioned in the *Vishnu Purana*: "Property alone will confer rank, wealth will be the only source of devotion, passion will be the sole bond of union between the sexes, falsehood will be the only means of success in litigation, and women will be the objects merely of sensual gratification." In addition, Earth will be venerated only for its mineral treasures, while dishonesty will be the universal means of subsistence.[22] No honest observer could deny that this is an accurate portrayal of the state of affairs in much of the human world today.

The present *Kali Yuga* commenced around 3 100 B.C., according to the *Bhagavata Purana* and other Puranic sources. Ultimately, only the god Kalki (the final incarnation of Vishnu) can defeat Kali and bring an end to the dark age. Kalki will appear on a white horse to combat Kali and his forces of darkness, whereupon Brahman will create a new universe and the next Golden Age will begin.[23] This Indian eschatology contains a remarkable parallel with its Christian counterpart, including identical imagery: "Now I saw heaven opened, and behold, a white horse. And He who sat on him was called Faithful and True, and in righteousness He judges and makes war. He was clothed with a white robe dipped in blood, and His name is called the Word of God [*ho logos tou Theou*]. And the armies in heaven, clothed in fine linen, white and clean, followed Him on white horses. And I saw the beast, the kings of the earth, and their armies, gathered to make war against Him who sat on the horse and against His army" (Rev 19:11, 13, 14, 19). Christ and his heavenly beings then defeat the forces of darkness, followed by a thousand years in which Satan is bound. After the latter's final uprising and defeat, the judgment of all who had lived on Earth takes place before God. This is followed by the creation of a new heaven and a new earth (Revelation, chapters 20–22)—a statement again mirroring the classical Indian schema.

21. Bolton, *Order*, 98, 100.
22. Perry, *Treasury*, 466.
23. Wikipedia: Kali Yuga.

Conclusion

The differentiation between time and eternity affects all living beings, for all of them come to be within time. Consequently, the counterpart of being born is having to die. In a very real sense, we are all born in order to die—humans, animals, and plants. For all of us, birth and death are inextricably linked as poles of the same cosmic rhythm, which pulsates between being and becoming, eternity and time, life and death.

Death and Immortality

THERE IS A SAYING that only two things in life are certain: death and taxes. Leaving the latter aside as pertaining to the economic dimension only, we will now consider the relentless certainty of death and, more importantly, the tantalizing possibility of an afterlife. Since all living things are destined to undergo bodily death, the question arises whether it is possible for the individual soul to survive the death of its mortal frame in some way or another. In this chapter we will consider some of the more interesting answers that have been proffered to this question over the ages, in both the Hellenic and Christian traditions.

Bodily Death

In the traditional Christian view, the source of illness, suffering, and death is to be found in the free will of man; or, to be more precise, in its misuse. The Orthodox theologian Vladimir Lossky writes that by choosing an autonomous existence (as symbolized by Adam and Eve), human nature became anti-natural: the spirit now feeds on the soul's autonomous goodness and beauty; the soul feeds on the body and thus the passions are born; and the body feeds on the earth, kills to eat, and dies itself. This is the opposite of the created order, whereby the body is nourished by the soul, the soul by the spirit, and the spirit by God.[1]

In this understanding, physical death is not primarily conceived as a punishment, but as a means of escape provided by a loving God out of the fallen world. Thus, death is not the end of life but its renewal—it prepares the way for the future reunion of body and soul. Lossky explains further: "If human nature disintegrates as a consequence of sin, if sin introduces death into the created universe, the reason for this is not only that human freedom has created a new state, a new mode of existence in evil, but also

---

1. Lossky, *Orthodox Theology*, 82–83.

that God has placed a limit to sin, allowing it to end in death." Human mortality was therefore instituted by God as a pedagogical means—rather mortality than eternalizing evil.[2]

In the early Church there was a strong consciousness of death as a birth into eternal life. In other words, life was viewed as an ascent towards eternity and death as the door of entry into it. We therefore find John Chrysostom in one of his prayers (contained in the Orthodox liturgy) asking God to give us a remembrance of death. This does not at all imply an attitude of morbidity or joylessness, but rather to make us live with all intensity, as if every moment is the last we have. Echoing this mindset, Dostoyevsky wrote in *The Brothers Karamazov* that hell could be summarized as 'too late.' The remembrance of death can help us live in such a way to fulfil relationships without being too late.[3]

But despite this theological reasoning, it cannot be denied that death is horrible—especially when accompanied by much suffering. As Albert Camus eloquently writes (in terms of his 'philosophy of the absurd'), "The absurd man says yes and his effort will henceforth be unceasing. If there is a personal fate, there is no higher destiny or at least there is but one which he concludes is inevitable and despicable." Equally moving is the depiction of death by Nicolas Berdyaev, with his customary ontological approach. Death is the most terrible evil, he writes, for every kind of evil in the last resort means death; it underlies every evil passion, such as pride, greed, and ambition with their deadly results. Death is the evil result of sin, whereas a sinless life would be immortal and eternal. Death is a denial of eternity, resisting God's creation of the world from nothing and striving to return it to non-being.[4]

On the other hand, Anthony Bloom argues, death is the only gate that allows us to escape from the endlessness without God, which is the creaturely infinity that prevents our becoming partakers of the divine nature. St Paul could therefore write in his letter to the Philippians, "For to me, to live is Christ, and to die is gain" (1:21). In the Old Testament it is taught that the dead went to *Sheol*—being the place where God was not, thus implying infinite separation between man and God. With Christ's descent into hell this separation has come to an end—on earth we still experience the pain of separation, but in death there is no longer separation from God. In the

---

2. Lossky, *Orthodox Theology*, 83.
3. Bloom, "*Death*," 85, 87.
4. Camus, *Sisyphys*, 110; Berdyaev, *Destiny of Man*, 252.

Christian view, death is not the end: "Yet, here is also our certainty that death, which is our bereavement, is also a birth into eternity: that it is a beginning and not an end; that it is a great and holy encounter between God and the living soul, which can be fulfilled only in God."[5] And as argued elsewhere, death is the most significant and profound fact of life. The fact of death gives true depth to the question as to the meaning of life. In this paradoxical way, death proves to be the only way out of this sinful world, for immortal and eternal life prove to be only attainable through death.[6]

The inevitability of our bodily death is accepted in the Orthodox Christian tradition by means of a practice called the remembrance of death. For this reason, all Orthodox monks and nuns wear black habits (as distinguished from the Catholic tradition in which the various monastic orders wear differently colored robes), both as a remembrance of death and as a confession of their sinfulness, since black has traditionally been the color associated with evil and death. In a similar vein, whenever a Christian prays the 'Hail, Mary,' he or she concludes with the passage, 'Holy Mary, Mother of God, pray for us sinners now and in the hour of our death.'

Temporally speaking, bodily death occurs within the realm of time, whereas immortality pertains to the realm of eternity, or that which is beyond time. The relation between time and mortality is strikingly presented by Augustine of Hippo in his *magnum opus*: "For from the very beginning of our existence in this dying body, there is never a moment when death is not at work in us. For throughout the whole span of this life—if, indeed, it is to be called life—its mutability leads us towards death. For whatever time we live is subtracted from the whole span of our life, and what remains is becoming smaller and smaller each day. Thus, the whole duration of our life is nothing but a progression towards death." We can therefore say, he adds, that the human being is in death from the very beginning of his/her existence in this body. All our temporal existence is thus nothing else but the progress of death towards its consummation (*De civ Dei*, XIII.10). There is no relativity involved in this relentless progression towards death, the Latin theologian writes in the same passage, since we are all urged onwards with the same motion and rapidity.

Augustine admits that the moment of dying is confusing: before death comes, the soul is in the body and therefore alive; when death has come

---

5. Bloom, "*Death,*" 89–90, 107.
6. Berdyaev, *Destiny of Man*, 249.

and the soul has departed the body, it is dead and not dying.[7] He writes: "We say, then, that there are three separate times—before death, in death and after death—corresponding to three states: living, dying and dead." Ultimately, Augustine continues, the difference between life and death is the presence or absence of the soul in the body, since it is the soul that enables bodily sensation. "Between the two states of being alive and being dead, then, the condition of dying or of being in death disappears." This ambivalence is analogous to the passage of time: "the present is sought but is not found, for the transition from future to past occupies no space." However, this reasoning should not be construed as detracting from the relentless certainty of bodily death, the Latin theologian emphasizes: "Now, however, not only does death indeed exist, but it is so vexatious that it cannot be explained by any kind of speech or evaded by any reasoning" (*De civ Dei*, XIII.11).

Immortality of the Soul

In the traditional understanding, the only context within which personal immortality could possibly be achieved is that of Soul (with the exception of a kind of relative immortality, to be discussed towards the end of this chapter). Since Soul is an immaterial substance, it follows that is not necessarily subject to the contingencies of material existence, of which decay, death, and dissolution are salient features. Consequently, individual souls possess at least the potential to survive bodily death. As could be expected, given that we are all standing on this side of bodily death, the details of any post-mortem existence of souls has been a matter of discussion and debate for thousands of years.

The survival of the individual soul beyond bodily death is affirmed in various spiritual traditions within the Indo-European world-view. The Traditionalist author Ananda Coomaraswamy mentions the following examples thereof. In the *Brhadāranyaka Upanishad* we read that when a man dies, his 'soul' (*nāma*) does not forsake him, since it is without end. In his turn, the Sufi poet Rumi wrote that every shape has its archetype in the placeless (i.e., intelligible) world, so that if the shape perished it matters not, since its original is everlasting. And for the Jewish-Hellenic thinker Philo of Alexandria, the place of immortal life is the intelligible world. We find a similar inter-traditional agreement on the question as to 'where' the soul

7. Knuuttila, "*Time and creation*," 112.

goes when it departs the body. The afore-mentioned *Upanishad* states that he whose mind is attached to mundane things returns to this world, but he whose desire is the Essence (*ātman*) goes to Brahman (i.e., God). And the German mystical theologian Jakob Böhme writes that there is no necessity for the soul to go anywhere, for whichever of heaven or hell is manifested in the soul in this life, in that the soul is judged at the departure of the body.[8]

When this author attended his mother-in-law's funeral service in a leafy Moscow suburb during the summer of 2018, standing in front of her open coffin to pay his last respects to her, he knew with overwhelming certainty that Plato had been right all along: the soul is infinitely more important than the body. He also thought of the scriptural statement, "All flesh is like grass and all its glory like the flower of grass" (1 Pet 1:24), which was movingly set to music by Johannes Brahms in his work *Ein deutsches Requiem* ('A German Requiem'), following the death of his mother in 1865. The phrase 'ashes to ashes, dust to dust' in the English burial service therefore applies to the body only. These words are derived from the text of Genesis 3:19, "For dust you are, and to dust you shall return." This statement is quite literally true, since our bodies consist of the elements oxygen, carbon, hydrogen, nitrogen, calcium, phosphorus, potassium, sulphur, sodium, chlorine, and magnesium. All these elements are necessary for life to exist.[9] And our bodies return to dust after death, either instantly through cremation or gradually through burial and decomposition.

That the body is not only inferior to the soul in terms of lasting value, but also harbours all manner of negative and destructive effects was taught by Plato. In his dialogue *Phaedo*, we find Socrates explaining (while in prison, during the final hours before his death) as follows: "The body keeps us busy in a thousand ways because of its need for nurture. Moreover, if certain diseases befall it, they impede our search for the truth. It fills us with wants, desires, fears, all sorts of illusions and much nonsense, so that, as it is said, in truth and in fact no thought of any kind ever comes to us from the body. Only the body and its desires cause war, civil discord and battles, for all wars are due to the desire to acquire wealth, and it is the body and the care of it, to which we are enslaved, which compel us to acquire wealth, and all this makes us too busy to practice philosophy. Worst of all, if we do get some respite from it and turn to some investigation, everywhere in our investigations the body is present and makes for confusion and fear,

---

8. Coomaraswamy, *Civilization*, 23.
9. Wikipedia: Composition of the human body.

so that it prevents us from seeing the truth." This reasoning leads Socrates to declare that true philosophy is training for death (*Phaedo*, 66b–d, 81a).

This truth on the priority of soul over body was affirmed by Jesus Christ when he taught that one should not fear those who can destroy the body only: "And do not fear those who kill the body but cannot kill the soul" (Matt 10:28); "And I say to you, my friends, do not be afraid of those who kill the body, and after that have no more that they can do" (Luke 12:4). Christ also asked rhetorically, "For what would it profit a man if he gains the whole world, and loses his own soul?" (Mark 8:36). And the great Russian novelist Fyodor Dostoyevsky, a devout follower of Christ (while being a sinner like everyone else), stated the case as follows: "Neither a person nor a nation can exist without some higher idea. And there is only one higher idea on earth, and it is the idea of the immortality of the human soul, for all other 'higher' ideas of life by which humans might live derive from that idea alone."[10]

That at least the higher, rational dimension of the human soul is immortal (Greek, *athanatos*) was widely accepted by the Hellenic thinkers. According to Porphyry's biography, Pythagoras was the first Hellenic thinker to teach that the human soul is immortal, that it can change into other kinds of animals, and that all living beings are related. Furthermore, in the brotherhood (which actually comprised both men and women) founded by Pythagoras, the study of music and mathematics was a necessary activity for purification (*katharsis*) of the soul.[11] Such purification was believed to facilitate the movement of the soul towards union with the Godhead, since pure souls have the best afterlife. Purification was obtained not only physically (e.g., by abstaining from meat), but especially by gaining knowledge through the study of mathematics and the cosmos. The numerical basis of the cosmos facilitates its comprehension by humans—consequently, the human soul becomes orderly (*kosmiōs*) when it understands the order (*kosmos*) in the universe.[12]

One of Plato's most important contributions to Western philosophy and theology is his notion that the soul is ontologically prior to the body, thereby continuing the Pythagorean doctrine on the immortality of the soul. However, during its earthly existence the soul is imprisoned in the

---

10. *A Writer's Diary*, Volume 1: 1873–1876 (1994), p. 734, at https://en.wikiquote.org/wiki/Fyodor_Dostoyevsky

11. McKirahan, *Philosophy*, 84; Dreyer, *Wysbegeerte*, 35.

12. McKirahan, *Philosophy*, 114.

body (*sōma*), so that the latter is described as a tomb (*sēma*) in which the soul is kept until the penalty for its transgressions has been paid. This notion of the soul's imprisonment or entombment is explained by Socrates in the dialogue *Cratylus*, and it is echoed in the dialogues *Phaedrus* and *Gorgias*. Socrates adds that *sēma* also means 'sign,' "because the soul signifies whatever it wants to signify by means of the body" (*Cratylus*, 400c). Therefore, Algis Uzdavinys comments, the body could be viewed as the means whereby the soul indicates (*sēmainei*) its form and purpose. The body as tomb thus functions as an enclosure, keeping the soul within its limits in order that it may be saved.[13]

In view of the foregoing reasoning, we could say that the containment of the soul within a body serves both negative and positive purposes: as deserved punishment for transgressions, and as a vessel for working towards salvation. Plato's conviction that bodily death frees the soul in order to obtain true knowledge is explained in the dialogue *Phaedo, which* was known in the Hellenic world by the title *On the Soul*. Therein Plato continues the Pythagorean teaching on the immortality of the soul, reincarnation, and keeping the soul pure from contamination with the body. As is the case with the dialogues *Gorgias* and *Politeia*, the *Phaedo* concludes with a myth describing the fate of the soul after death.[14]

The basis for the soul's immortality, Plato writes in the dialogue *Phaedrus*, is its capacity for self-movement. As Socrates explains, "Every soul [or 'All soul'] is immortal. That is because whatever is always in motion is immortal, while what moves, and is moved by, something else stops living when it stops moving. In fact, this self-mover is also the source and spring of motion in everything else that moves; and a source has no beginning. And since it cannot have a beginning, then necessarily it cannot be destroyed. But since we have found that a self-mover is immortal, we should have no qualms about declaring that this is the very essence and principle of a soul, for every bodily object that is moved from outside has no soul, while a body whose motion comes from within, from itself, does have a soul, that being the nature of a soul; and if this is so—that whatever moves itself is essentially a soul—then it follows necessarily that soul should have neither birth nor death" (245c–e).

In his great cosmological dialogue, the *Timaeus*, Plato describes the creation of human beings by the gods (i.e., the higher intelligences). It

---

13. Uzdavinys, *Orpheus*, 94.
14. Cooper, *Plato*, 49–50.

commences with an instruction by the Demiurge to the gods: "Weave what is mortal to what is immortal, fashion and beget living things" (41d). Accordingly, as reflection of the intelligible and sensible realms of the cosmos, Plato conceives of the human being as consisting of two main components that differ essentially. On the one hand, there is the rational soul which participates in the realm of the Forms, and which is immortal and the bearer of Intellect. On the other hand, there is the body which is part of the sensible world, and which is mortal and represents the principle of Necessity in the human being.[15] This Platonic view of the human being as comprising an immortal soul and a mortal body would exercise immense influence on Christian thought, in both the Greek and Latin traditions.

We read further in the *Timaeus* that the heavenly gods made human souls of the leftovers from the making of the World-soul, but of a lower grade of purity (41d). Each soul was assigned to a star (41e), so that the number of souls is the same as the number of stars. At death a just soul returns to its companion star, while an unjust soul is reincarnated for a second attempt (42b-c). In other words, those souls that fail to live honourable lives will reincarnate in mortal bodies of a lower order until they also live honourably.[16] It appears that Plato understood the first incarnation of the soul as the same for all, namely as God-fearing living creatures. Thereafter, incarnations are determined by the soul either mastering the passions or being mastered by it, which entails living in righteousness and unrighteousness, respectively (*Tim*, 41e-42d). The soul is therefore responsible for any evil it may suffer—a notion that reflects the Socratic teaching that moral evil is the only real evil.[17]

In the final book of the *Politeia*, Plato considers the immortality of the soul, including the notion of transmigration. To begin with, we find Socrates explaining to Plato's brother Glaucon that unlike the body which can be killed by disease, the soul cannot be killed by its disease, which is wickedness (609a-611a). Glaucon agrees, adding that the soul's wickedness is highly detrimental to others, but it can revitalize and energize its possessor (610d-e). Socrates then points out that if we wish to see the soul as it really it is, we should look at it in the pure state which reason reveals to us, and not in its deformed state through association with the body and other evils. The former state explains the soul's love of wisdom (which is the

---

15. Dreyer, *Wysbegeerte*, 102.
16. Dreyer, *Wysbegeerte*, 102.
17. Cornford, *Plato's Cosmology*, 144.

precise meaning of *philosophia*), not to mention its kinship with 'the divine and immortal and eternal' (611b-e).

As is Plato's custom when dealing with religious or moral truths for which ordinary prose is inadequate, he proceeds to depict the soul's afterlife by means of a myth. It has been suggested that some of the details in this Myth of Er are borrowed from contemporary sources, probably Orphic.[18] Socrates relates the story of a brave man named Er who was killed in battle, and who returned to life as he was lying on the funeral pyre twelve days later. He described the journey of his soul to a strange place, where there were two gaping chasms in the earth, and two chasms opposite and above them in the sky. Between the chasms sat judges who delivered judgment, ordering the souls of the just to take the right-hand road upwards into the sky and the unjust to take the left-hand road downwards into the earth. While they were doing so, Er saw other souls rising out of a chasm in the earth, stained with the dust of travel, and others coming down from a chasm in the sky, pure and clean. These souls share their experiences, on the one hand of a thousand-year journey in the underworld, and on the other hand of the delights and beauty in heaven (*Pol*, 614b-e).

Socrates next summarizes the system of rewards and punishments for which an afterlife is required. For any wrong committed to someone, a penalty must be paid tenfold; in other words, tenfold retribution is done for each crime. And correspondingly, "those who have done good and been just and god-fearing are rewarded in the same proportion." However, those who are incurably wicked, such as mass-murderers and tyrants, are not released after their subterranean journey, but are flung into Tartarus for further punishment (*Pol*, 615a-616a). The latter place-name denotes the subterranean dungeon or abyss that functions as a place of punishment for the wicked, in addition to serving as a prison for the Titans.[19]

After a week of resting for those who have completed their journey, Er accompanied the souls to a place called the Spindle of Necessity. Here, before the three Fates (the daughters of Necessity), the souls are given the opportunity to freely choose their next life on Earth. Thus, Socrates writes, "the fault lies not with God, but with the soul that makes the choice." This is stated to be another reason why the avoidance of extremes is so important, both in this life and the next. Er observed that most of the souls that came down from heaven chose lives without proper examination, which they

18. Lee, *Republic*, 447.
19. Wikipedia: Tartarus.

would belatedly come to regret, whereas the souls that came up from the earth mostly chose better lives, due to their own suffering and the suffering of others they had observed. For example, the soul of Odysseus chose the uneventful life of an ordinary man, having been cured of all ambitions by his former sufferings (as detailed by Homer in the famous epic named after the hero). After all the souls had chosen their next life, they were each allotted a Guardian Spirit to guide it through life. And finally, Er recounted, all the souls except his own were compelled to drink from the river called Lethe (forgetfulness), which caused them to forget everything. They then went to sleep and were taken to their birth (*Pol*, 616b–621b).

Having thus described the afterlife of the soul until its next incarnation, Socrates concludes the dialogue with a splendid admonition: "This at any rate is my advice, that we should believe the soul to be immortal, capable of enduring all evil and all good, and always keep our feet on the upward way and pursue justice with wisdom. So we shall be at peace with the gods and with ourselves, both in our life here and when, like the victors in the games collecting their prizes, we receive our reward; and both in this life and in the thousand-year journey which I have described, all will be well with us" (*Pol*, 614c-d).

Given Plato's affirmation of the reality of an afterlife, it is not surprising that he views philosophy as a preparation for death. As explained by Socrates, "those who practice philosophy in the right way are in training for dying and they fear death least of all men" (*Phaedo* 67e). Algis Uzdavinys comments that since the souls of such 'philosopher-gnostics' are purified of the mortal body and thereby achieve a likeness to the divine, they are encouraged by Plato to examine and mythologize concerning the afterlife (*Phaedo* 61e). It is also relevant to note that Plato's conception of philosophy as a training for death implies a distinction between philosophy as a way of life on the one hand, and its reduction to rationalistic discourse as in the modern, post-Cartesian West on the other hand.[20]

In his turn, Aristotle taught that intellect is a kind (*genos*) that is different from soul (*psychē*), with only the former being separable from the body and thus immortal. While Plato argued that intellect can only exist in soul because it is inseparable from life (*Tim*, 30b and 46d), Aristotle identified life with the activity of intellect, and thus held a narrower view of soul than Plato. In this regard Aristotle was followed by the Neoplatonists,

---

20. Uzdavinys, *Orpheus*, 75–76; Uzdavinys, *Golden Chain*, xi.

who interpreted Plato's teaching on the immortality of soul as referring to intellect.[21]

Some of the Middle Platonists, such as Atticus, concurred with Aristotle that only the rational soul is immortal. They also introduced the concept of a pneumatic vehicle serving as a link between the immaterial soul and the material body. The Greek noun *pneuma* means wind, air, breath or spirit, so that the adjective pneumatic (*pneumatikos*) means spiritual.[22] At bodily death, the Middle Platonists held, both non-rational life and the spiritual vehicle are dissolved, since only intellect is permanent and likened to the gods. Among the Neoplatonists, Porphyry argued that the spiritual vehicle and the non-rational parts of the soul are dissolved into the heavenly spheres from which they were constituted, and which were collected by the soul as it descends. In contrast, Iamblichus viewed both the spiritual vehicle and the non-rational soul as surviving bodily death, since all that is mortal is the bodily element that is fascinated by matter and concerned with mortal things. In other words, the spiritual vehicle survives as a coherent entity after its separation from the rational soul, so that it can be reactivated on the soul's eventual return to the universe.[23]

Interestingly, Augustine of Hippo views death as applying to both the body and the soul, in the latter case those of the wicked. He argues as follows: "For although the human soul is truly said to be immortal, it nonetheless also has a certain kind of death of its own. The soul is called immortal, then, because, at least to some extent, it never ceases to live and feel; whereas the body is called mortal because it can be deprived of all life, and cannot, of itself, live at all. The death of the soul therefore occurs when God forsakes it, and that of the body comes when the soul forsakes it. The death of both, then—that is, of the whole man—comes about when the soul, forsaken by God, forsakes the body" (*De civ Dei*, XIII.2). Since the soul draws its life from God, while the body draws its life from the soul, this death of the soul (which cannot happen to those who live good lives, we are reminded) is called the second death, following the first death which is that of the body (*De civ Dei*, XIII.2).

---

21. Dillon and Gerson, *Neoplatonic Philosophy*, xviii.
22. LSJ, 566–67.
23. Dillon and Gerson, *Neoplatonic Philosophy*, 343.

Purgatory and Transmigration

Observation and reflection lead one to the conclusion that there are three types of humans, in terms of spirituality and morality. First, there is a tiny number who lead lives that can justly be described as saintly. Second, there is a larger number whose lives exhibit regular evil-doing. The third and largest group fall between these extremes of acquired saintliness and habitual wickedness. After all, saintly living may only be acquired by the grace of God, whereas evil-doing flows easily from fallen human nature. Accordingly, any higher justice would have to accommodate three kinds of existence for the soul following bodily death: a state of reward for the saints, or heaven; a state of punishment for the wicked, or hell; and a state of correction or purification, with the potential of progressing to heaven, for most souls. This latter state is indeed recognized in the Catholic tradition, where it is referred to as purgatory (Latin, *purgatorium*).

A similar division of souls following bodily death has indeed been proposed by Plato, recounting what he had learned from Socrates while his mentor was preparing for his enforced suicide. Those who have lived an average life, morally speaking, are taken to a place of purification by means of penalties paid, while also being rewarded for their good deeds. Those who are deemed incurable due to the enormity of their crimes are hurled into Tartarus (the Hellenic version of hell), never to emerge from it. Those who have committed great but curable crimes and felt remorse for the rest of their lives, are taken to places of punishment until they are released by their former victims. Those who are deemed to have lived an extremely pious life, are taken to a pure dwelling place. Finally, those who have purified themselves sufficiently by means of philosophy, are taken to even more beautiful dwelling places. Socrates concludes that since the soul is immortal, "one must make every effort to share in virtue and wisdom in one's life, for the reward is beautiful and the reward is great" (*Phaedo*, 113d–114d).

In the Eastern Orthodox teaching on the afterlife, virtue has sometimes been associated with the rational and vice with the irrational. The influence of Platonism is much in evidence here, as one may deduce from the following extract from the 'Sermon on the Dead' by Gregory of Nyssa (a fourth century theologian and bishop in Asia Minor): "If a man distinguish in himself what is peculiarly human from that which is irrational, and if he be on the watch for a life of greater urbanity for himself, in this present life he will purify himself of any evil contracted, overcoming the irrational by reason. If he has inclined to the irrational pressure of the passions, using for the passions the cooperating hide of things irrational, he may afterward in a quite different manner be very much interested in what is better, when, after his departure out of the body, he gains knowledge of the difference between virtue and vice and finds that he is not able to partake of divinity until he has been purged of the filthy contagion in his soul by the purifying fire."[24] Here the Greek theologian mentions the necessity of a purgatorial state to cleanse the soul from its irrational passions, so that the purified soul may rise to the divine level.

That the post-mortem state of the human soul is not simply a matter of either endless bliss or eternal damnation (or, in popular parlance, heaven or hell) has also been suggested by Augustine of Hippo. After conceding that even in this mortal life some punishments are indeed purgatorial, at least to those who are corrected thereby, he adds that all other punishments are inflicted on us by divine providence, either because of past or ongoing sins, or to reveal our virtues. Augustine continues, "As for temporal punishments, some suffer them in this life only, others after death, and others both now and in the world to come; yet all this precedes that most severe and final judgment. However, not all men who endure temporal punishments after death come into those everlasting punishments which are to follow after that judgment" (*De civ Dei*, XXI:13).

In a similar vein to Gregory of Nyssa, the Latin theologian mentions a purgatorial fire in order to purify the soul towards salvation: "That there should be some fire even after this life is not incredible, and it can be inquired into and either be discovered or left hidden whether some of the faithful may be saved, some more slowly and some more quickly in the greater or lesser degree in which they loved the good things that perish, through a certain purgatorial fire" (*Handbook on Faith, Hope, and Charity*, 18:69). Further on in the same work we read that the souls in this intermediate state are assisted by the prayers of their loved ones still living on Earth: "The time which interposes between the death of a man and the final resurrection holds souls in hidden retreats, accordingly as each is deserving of rest or of hardship, in view of what it merited when it was living in the flesh. Nor can it be denied that the souls of the dead find relief through the piety of their friends and relatives who are still alive, when the Sacrifice of the Mediator [i.e., the Eucharist] is offered for them, or when alms are given

---

24. https://www.churchfathers.org/purgatory

in the Church. There is a certain manner of living, neither so good that there is no need of these helps after death, nor yet so wicked that these helps are of no avail after death" (29:109).[25] This reasoning explains the practice by the Orthodox and Catholic faithful of praying for their departed loved ones, at first for a period of forty days after their repose and then on the annual anniversary thereof.

We suggest that the theological notion of purgatory may be compatible with the Indo-European concept of transmigration of the soul, since both would be meaningless if the soul was not immortal. In the *Bhagavad Gita*, we read of the Lord Krishna explaining to his devotee Arjuna that as the embodied one has infancy, youth, and age in the present body, so will he receive another body. And as a man casts off worn-out garments and takes new ones, so will the embodied one cast off worn-out bodies and pass on to new ones (2. 13, 22). The notion of transmigration is popularly understood as reincarnation, in terms of which an individual soul successively indwells different bodies, until the soul has reached a certain level of perfection. This view has in the modern era been promoted by various movements (Theosophy, Krishna Consciousness, etc.) claiming to be based on Indian philosophy.

However, this conflation of transmigration with reincarnation has been disputed by various Traditionalist authors. For example, Ananda Coomaraswamy has argued that Atman (the World-soul) is in fact the only entity that reincarnates, and not the individual soul. He writes: "Reincarnation—as currently understood to mean the return of individual souls to other bodies here on earth—is not an orthodox Indian doctrine, but only a popular belief." Coomaraswamy quotes Shankara, the philosopher and theologian who formulated the doctrine of *Advaita* Vedanta, to the effect that there is no other transmigrant but He who is both transcendently himself and the immanent Self in all beings, but never himself becomes anyone. The transmigration of each 'individual' *ātman* (or spiritual essence) is therefore a particular case of the transmigration of the universal Spirit, or Brahman. This notion of the divine Self transmigrating through all living beings, as taught in the Vedas and Upanishads, is encountered among thinkers as diverse as Empedocles, Ovid, Rumi, and William Blake.[26]

The notion of a cycle of births (Greek, *kyklos tes geneseos*), was originally probably found among all the Indo-Europeans, including the Celts

---

25. https://www.churchfathers.org/purgatory
26. Coomaraswamy, *Literacy*, 120–121; Coomaraswamy, *Civilization*, 65–66.

and the Teutons.[27] In the Hellenic world the immortality of the human soul was taught pre-eminently by the school of Pythagoras. It was linked to the doctrine of *metempsychosis*, or transmigration of the soul. Through religious devotion, the human soul may rejoin the World-soul whence it originated. Empedocles continued the Pythagorean doctrine on the pre-existence and immortality of the soul. In his view, souls fall from heavenly grace and are condemned to the cycle of birth and rebirth, from which they may be released by means of purification and the acquisition of knowledge. Since human souls reincarnate in the bodies of animals, both Pythagoras and Empedocles taught their followers to abstain from killing animals and eating meat. For the latter, such abstinence also reduces the amount of strife (the opposite of love) in us.[28]

We have already mentioned Plato's notion (in the *Timaeus*), that souls who live honourable lives will return to their companion stars, but the rest will reincarnate in mortal bodies of a lower order until they also live honourably. On the other hand, Augustine of Hippo approvingly mentions that the Neoplatonist philosopher Porphyry rejected the view of Plato and Plotinus that human souls can enter animal bodies, instead holding that human souls can only be inserted into humans (*De civ Dei*, X.30).

Plotinus asserted in the *Enneads* (III, 4.2) that those who have during their lifetime maintained the human level become humans again, while those who have lived wholly according to sense become animals, adding that the spirit of the previous life pays the penalty. This concept of metempsychosis is interpreted by Ananda Coomaraswamy as referring to "the direct or indirect inheritance of the psycho-physical characteristics of the deceased, which he does not take with him at his death and which are not a part of his veritable essence, but only its temporary and most external vehicle. It is only in so far as we mistakenly identify 'ourselves' with these accidental garments of the transcendent personality, the mere properties of terrestrial human existence, that it can be said that 'we' are reincorporated in men or animals: it is not the 'spirit' that pays the penalty, but the animal or sensitive soul with which the disembodied spirit has no further concern." In an explanatory note, Coomaraswamy remarks that soul (Greek, *psychē*; Latin, *anima*) is a two-fold value, the higher powers thereof coinciding with Spirit (*pneuma*) and/or Intellect (*nous*), whereas its lower powers are

---

27. Günther, *Religious attitudes*, 22.

28. Blackburn, *Oxford Dictionary*, 114, 232, 299; McKirahan, *Philosophy*, 88, 258, 286, 290.

associated with sensation (*aesthēsis*) and opinion (*doxa*).[29] Any discussion of rebirth in the traditional conception (whether Hellenic, Indian or otherwise) therefore pertains to these higher dimensions of the soul only.

Relative Immortality through Creativity

When the blind poet Homer composed the *Iliad* and the *Odyssey*, respectively describing the Hellenic war against Troy (which took place around 1200 B.C.) and the perilous homeward journey of King Odysseus of Ithaca, it is unlikely that he could have anticipated to still be widely read almost three millennia later. The same longevity applies to many other masterpieces, whether in literature, music, architecture, or other forms of creative expression. It could therefore be viewed as a kind of relative immortality, particularly so since it is the immortal soul of their human creators that enables the creation of these masterpieces.

As an avowed atheist, Friedrich Nietzsche could not admit to entertaining any thoughts on the immortality of the soul. Instead, he posited obtaining a measure of eternal life through his works, as we read in *Twilight of the Idols*: "To create things on which time may try its teeth in vain; to be concerned both in the form and the substance of my writing, about a certain degree of immortality—never have I been modest enough to demand less of myself. The aphorism, the sentence, in both of which I, as the first among Germans, am a master, are the forms of 'eternity'; it is my ambition to say in ten sentences what everyone else says in a whole book—what everyone else does *not* say in a whole book."[30] And in the Preface to his next book, *The Antichrist*, Nietzsche affirms his belief that he might achieve a share in eternity through his works: "Only the day after tomorrow belongs to me. Some are born posthumously." He proved to be correct in this assessment. From the beginning of the twentieth century, in the years following his death in 1900, Nietzsche began exerting a pervasive influence on Western philosophy, psychology, sociology, and political theory, which is continuing unabated to this day.

Nietzsche's statement on some creators being born posthumously also applies to the case of the late-Romantic composer Gustav Mahler (1860–1911), who during his lifetime was better known as a conductor (especially during his years as music director of the Court Opera in Vienna) than as

---

29. Coomaraswamy, *Civilization*, 61, 67.
30. Nietzsche, *Twilight*, 82.

a composer. This led him to declare, *Meine Zeit wird noch kommen*—'My time will yet come.' His prophetic words became fulfilled during the second half of the twentieth century, when Mahler's music, especially his structurally massive and emotionally intense symphonies, rose to enormous popularity among music lovers worldwide. The same posthumous recognition awaited the novelist Franz Kafka (1883–1924), whose writings received little public recognition during his lifetime. His great novels *Der Process* ('The Trial'), *Das Schloss* ('The Castle'), and *Der Verschollene* ('The Man Who Disappeared') were only published posthumously by Kafka's friend Max Brod, whereupon he became one of the most influential writers of the twentieth century. An interesting coincidence is that both Mahler and Kafka were Bohemian-born, German-speaking Jewish intellectuals. Their time has certainly come, to the benefit of civilized persons worldwide.

Consciousness

IN THE TRADITIONAL INDO-EUROPEAN understanding, all matter is endowed with life. This notion is called hylozoism, from the Greek *hylē* = matter, and *zōē* = life. According to the related concept of pan-psychism (from the Greek *pan* = all, and *psychē* = soul or life), the world (or nature) produces living creatures and therefore should be thought of as itself alive and possessing a world-soul.[1] This implies that wherever there is life, there is consciousness, albeit manifesting at different levels. It would, after all, be irrational to assert that the consciousness of a micro-organism is similar to the consciousness of a saint. Just as there are different levels of soul, so there are different levels of consciousness.

Levels of Consciousness

The difference between plants, animals, and humans with regards to consciousness has been succinctly summarized as follows: "The plant exhibits—at least, not to us—no consciousness, i.e., no *tension* with its environment. The animal exhibits tension, consciousness, individuality. Man has in addition self-consciousness and the ability and necessity of living a higher life in the realm of symbols."[2] Evidently, there is a differentiation in the levels of consciousness among the life-forms on our planet.

According to the Canadian psychiatrist R.M. Bucke, there are three stages in the evolution of consciousness: the simple consciousness of animals; the self-consciousness of the bulk of mankind; and cosmic consciousness. This theory was expounded in the book *Cosmic Consciousness: A Study in the Evolution of the Human Mind* (first published in 1901), which has influenced several well-known psychologists, scientists, and theologians

---

1. Blackburn, *Oxford Dictionary*, 174, 265.
2. Yockey, *Imperium*, 292.

of the twentieth century. Bucke introduces the three 'forms or grades of consciousness' as follows:

1. "Simple Consciousness, which is possessed by say the upper half of the animal kingdom. By means of this faculty a dog or a horse is just as conscious of the things about him as a man is; he is also conscious of his own limbs and body and he knows that these are a part of himself."

2. "Over and above this Simple Consciousness, which is possessed by man as by animals, man has another which is called Self-Consciousness. Through this faculty man is not only conscious of trees, rocks, waters, his own limbs and body, but he becomes conscious of himself as a distinct entity apart from all the rest of the universe. Language is the objective of which self-consciousness is the subjective. Self-consciousness and language (two in one, for they are two halves of the same thing) are the *sine qua non* of human social life, of manners, of institutions, of industries of all kinds, of all arts useful and fine. The possession of self-consciousness and language (its other self) by man creates an enormous gap between him and the highest creature possessing simple consciousness merely."

3. "Cosmic Consciousness is a third form which is as far above Self-Consciousness as is that above Simple Consciousness. With this form, of course, both simple and self-consciousness persist (as simple consciousness persists when self-consciousness is acquired), but added to them is the new faculty so often named and to be named in this volume. The prime characteristic of cosmic consciousness is, as its name implies, a consciousness of the cosmos, that is, of the life and order of the universe. Along with the consciousness of the cosmos there occurs an intellectual enlightenment or illumination which alone would place the individual on a new plane of existence—would make him almost a member of a new species. To this is added a state of moral exaltation, an indescribable feeling of elevation, elation, and joyousness, and a quickening of the moral sense. With these come, what may be called a sense of immortality, a consciousness of eternal life, not a conviction that he shall have this, but the consciousness that he has it already."[3]

---

3. http://www.sacred-texts.com/eso/cc/index.htm

The simple consciousness of animals naturally includes the senses of hearing and sight. For Bucke, language is the primary means whereby self-consciousness is expressed, and since animals do not use language they are said to be devoid of self-consciousness. This aspect of Bucke's theory could be criticized on the grounds that animal sounds such as bird-song and whale-song resemble human music, which evinces at least a degree of self-consciousness. It has to be concluded that self-consciousness is not limited to humankind.

However, Bucke correctly recognizes that within self-consciousness, there exist gradations among individuals in their degrees of intellectual development and talent. Employing the examples of the Buddha Gautama, Jesus of Nazareth, St Paul, Plotinus, Mohammed, Dante, John of the Cross, Francis Bacon, Jakob Böhme, William Blake, and Walt Whitman, among others, Bucke suggests that the next stage of human development, i.e., cosmic consciousness, is gradually spreading throughout all of humanity. As is the case with self-consciousness, there are gradations within the level of cosmic consciousness.[4]

We contend that it is precisely the possession of a rational soul (as Plato, Aristotle, and the Neoplatonists emphasized) that enables humans to rise to higher levels of consciousness than their animal relatives. This includes the potential for spiritual-intellectual (Greek, *noētikos*) awareness, which may be viewed as the traditional equivalent of cosmic consciousness. However, Bucke's expectation that most humans will evolve to the level of cosmic consciousness is unrealistic, since relatively few appear to manifest evidence thereof in their lives. Such an awareness therefore remains a potentiality and not an actuality among most humans. Be that as it may, we suggest that this spiritual-intellectual consciousness manifests particularly in the interaction between religion, mathematics, and music.

Religion

It appears that religion has always been an integral aspect of the human experience. How did it all begin? In his informative book *Race and Religion*, C.G. Campbell explains: "*Homo sapiens* early discovered that there existed invisible forces that were wholly beyond his control and far more difficult to comprehend than his physical problems, and in no way connected with physical nature. For they were evidently non-physical, mystical, and

---

4. Wikipedia: Richard Maurice Bucke.

spiritual powers wholly independent of physical nature, which was none the less inexorably controlled by them. Thus, the religious problem then became his major problem." Consequently, "*Homo sapiens* from the beginning had a religion. His earliest cultural remains in the Upper Palaeolithic, around one hundred and fifty thousand years ago, indicate beyond a doubt that he hoped for spiritual survival in the afterlife."[5] And Frithjof Schuon mentions the interesting argument that just as the wings of birds (and by extension the phenomenon of flight) prove the existence of air, in the same way the religious phenomenon, which is common to all peoples, proves the existence of its content, namely God and the afterlife.[6]

Religion (as encountered in various spiritual traditions, each based on revelation from the divine to the human) is not, as is commonly misunderstood, a man-made system aimed at the control and exploitation of its adherents. That such malpractices have at times occurred, due to the inherent human tendency to evil-doing (or, in theological language, the inherited sinfulness of human nature), does not invalidate the lofty aims of religion in the proper sense of the word. The etymology of the term 're-ligion' is significant, the word being derived from the Latin *religare*, which means to bind fast.[7] That is to say, the ultimate purpose of religion is to reconnect the human to the divine. Thus, through the practice of religion a human being may return to his or her divine source.

In the Traditionalist understanding, God has providentially granted a number of spiritual ways, or religions, to humankind in order to lead the soul of believers back to its Source. As explained by the eminent Middle Platonist philosopher Plutarch, "Nor do we speak of the 'different Gods' of different peoples, or of the Gods as 'Barbarian' and 'Greek,' but as common to all, though differently named by different peoples, so that for the One Reason (Logos) that orders all these things, and the One Providence that oversees them, and for the minor powers [i.e., gods or angels] that are appointed to care for all things, there have arisen among different peoples different epithets and services, according to their different manners and customs" (*Isis and Osiris*, 67).[8]

"Religions may and must be many," writes Ananda Coomaraswamy, "each being an 'arrangement of God,' and stylistically differentiated,

---

5. Campbell, *Race and Religion*, 2.
6. Schuon, *Divine*, 6.
7. http://latin-dictionary.net/definition/33235/religo-religare-religavi-religatus
8. Quoted in Coomaraswamy, *Literacy*, 57–58.

inasmuch as the thing known can only be in the knower according to the mode of the knower." The authentic religions possess a common metaphysical basis, while the cultures based thereon are the dialects of a common spiritual and intellectual language.[9] This approach should not be confused with New Age 'spirituality,' since the Traditionalist authors emphasise the necessity of adherence to a specific, authentic religion in order to attain salvation. Among authentic religions count Hinduism, Zoroastrianism, Judaism, Buddhism, Taoism, Christianity, and Islam.

Another popular misconception is that religious faith requires an irrational acceptance of unproven assumptions. As a matter of fact, the Greek word *pistis* means 'faith' as well as 'trust.' This linguistic correlation suggests that faith comprises both belief and trust in something, which in the case of theistic religion is God. The traditional Christian confession of faith, as promulgated at the ecumenical councils of Nicaea (325) and Constantinople (381), is instructive in this regard. It opens with the statement: "We believe in one God, the Father Almighty" (*Pisteuomen eis ena Patera pantokratora*, in the Greek original). It could equally well be rendered as 'We trust in one God.' This Creed, as it came to be known (from the Latin *Credo*, meaning 'I believe'), has been recited during every Christian liturgy since the fourth century. Faith in God is therefore not only an intellectual assent to the truth of something, but it is equally an existential trust in the goodness and providence of God.

Even that great iconoclast among modern philosophers, Friedrich Nietzsche, derided the self-assured 'realists' who reject belief in anything of a transcendent nature. In *Thus spoke Zarathustra*, he writes: "For thus you speak: 'We are complete realists, and without belief or superstition': thus you thump your chests—alas, even without having chests! But how should you be *able* to believe, you motley-spotted men!—you who are paintings of all that has ever been believed! You are walking refutations of belief itself and the fracture of all thought. *Unworthy of belief*: that is what *I* call you, you realists! You are unfruitful: *therefore* you lack belief. But he who had to create always had his prophetic dreams and star-auguries—and he believed in belief!"[10]

Yet another misconception is that religion is opposed to true spirituality; in other words, one is either religious or spiritual. This false dichotomy is especially popular among adherents of the so-called New Age movement,

---

9. Coomaraswamy, *Civilization*, 18.
10. Nietzsche, *Zarathustra*, 143.

which allows 'spiritual searchers' to concoct their own 'spirituality' from elements of various traditions. These eclectic compilations have been wittily described by the French author Augustin Chaboseau (in a book on Theosophy, but equally valid in our context) as bits of Vedanta, morsels of Taoism, pieces of Egyptianism, samplings of Mazdaism, fragments of Christianity, scraps of Brahmanism, shreds of Gnosticism, dregs of Hebrew Kabbala, all of it endowed with remnants and sprinkled with crumbs from thinkers as diverse as Plato, Spinoza, Paracelsus, Swedenborg, Hegel, Schopenhauer, and Darwin.[11]

To the New Age adherents, religion is authoritarian, dogmatic, and bad, whereas spirituality is free, open-minded, and good. For example, in her 'manual of happiness' (as the book is subtitled), the Lebanese philosopher Abir Taha affirms the necessity of faith, but at the same time contrasts religion with spirituality. Whereas religions offer certainties and crude, simple, and even childish answers to the great questions of philosophy and the unfathomable mysteries of life, spirituality is said to open our minds and free our souls by connecting us with the higher Consciousness that governs the cosmos. Unlike religion, Taha writes, spirituality affirms that man is intimately linked to nature and God. In addition, spirituality is posited as a 'third way' between crude religiosity and atheist materialism.[12]

However, authentic religion is by its very nature spiritual, since it deals primarily with higher, non-material realities such as Spirit, soul, and ultimate destiny. In addition to being spiritual, religion has to be authoritarian and dogmatic (within the requirements of reason and proportion) due to the prevalence of human ignorance and sinfulness. In the Orthodox and Catholic traditions, spiritual authority is exercised by means of ordained bishops and priests, according to the Apostolic Succession. In terms of this practice, all the bishops of the Church over the past two thousand years stand in unbroken continuity with the earliest Church, having received their consecration from two or more existing bishops extending back to the Apostles, who were empowered by Christ to establish the Church. This unparalleled continuity enables the bishops, and the priests ordained by them, to preserve the faith and practice of historic Christianity.

As far as religious dogma is concerned, this is necessary to guard against the perennial possibility of error. The Greek word *dogma* means that which one thinks true, or a resolution. For the Church, it means an

---

11. Perry, *Treasury*, 470.
12. Taha, *Resolutions*, 38–39.

unchangeable truth, accepted by faith and binding for Christians. The opposite of dogmas are heresies, from the Greek word *hairesis*, which means taking for oneself, or choosing. Heresies are thus theological opinions taken out of the context of the Church's teaching and opposed to it.[13] The importance of right belief is evident from the word 'orthodoxy,' which is derived from the Greek *orthodoxia*, meaning right doctrine. The teachings of the Church have not been invented on an *ad hoc* basis, but were arrived at through a lengthy struggle against heresies. Each of the ecumenical councils held during the first Christian millennium were convened to debate a specific heresy, thereby formulating the official doctrine of the Church on various issues. For example, at the first and second ecumenical councils held at Nicaea and Constantinople in 325 and 381, respectively, the heresy of Arianism was condemned and the Christian teaching on the divine Trinity affirmed.[14]

Writing in the early years of the Weimar republic, the German philosopher Oswald Spengler emphasized that authentic religion cannot be separated from metaphysics. He states that "religion is metaphysic and nothing else." However, "this metaphysic is not the metaphysic of knowledge, argument, proof (which is mere philosophy of learnedness), but lived and experienced metaphysic—that is, the unthinkable as a certainty, the supernatural as a fact, life as existence in a world that is non-actual, but true. Jesus never lived one moment in any other world but this. He was no moralizer, and to see in moralizing the final aim of religion is to be ignorant of what religion is." Here we find Spengler taking issue with the reduction of religion to morality, as has become fashionable in modern, liberal Protestantism. He continues, "Religion is, first and last, metaphysic, other-worldliness (German, *Jenseitigkeit*), awareness of a world of which the evidence of the senses merely lights the foreground. It is life in and with the super-sensible. And where the capacity for this awareness, or even the capacity for believing in its existence, is wanting, real religion is at an end."[15] In other words, an authentic religion has to remain grounded in its metaphysical foundations to be of salvific value to its practitioners.

---

13. LSJ, 21, 177; Alfeyev, *Mystery*, xiii.

14. Arianism refers to the teaching of an Alexandrian priest called Arius, who held that Christ was begotten by the Father at a point in time and is thus subordinate to the Father. It has resurfaced repeatedly over the centuries and is taught by various modern cults claiming to be Christian.

15. Spengler, *Decline*, 288–289.

An American follower of Spengler, the political thinker Francis Parker Yockey, contends that from the viewpoint of spiritual content, religion is the highest of all human forms of thought. He also concurs with Spengler that religion is divine metaphysics. Furthermore, "Religion is not a method of social improvement, it is not a codification of knowledge, it is not ethics—it is the presentation of a sacred ultimate reality, and all of its phases flow from this." Religion is thus to be distinguished from philosophy, which is a different direction of thought. Even in the case of a theistic philosophy, Yockey writes, the philosophy is situated on this side of religion and gives a purely natural explanation to its subject-matter. In contrast to both religion and philosophy, natural science is directed to finding interrelations between phenomena and generalizing the results, but it does not attempt to give ultimate explanations.[16] Unfortunately some scientists have attempted to use the provisional findings of the natural sciences to make philosophical and theological statements concerning ultimate reality.

The ultimate identity of religion and metaphysics is similarly affirmed by Ananda Coomaraswamy, who mentions eminent thinkers from various traditions in support thereof. He writes: "Both, considered as Ways, or praxis, are means of accomplishing the rectification, regeneration and reintegration of the aberrant and fragmented individual consciousness, both conceive of man's last end as consisting in a realisation by the individual of all the possibilities inherent in his own being, or may go farther, and see in a realisation of all the possibilities of being in any mode and also in possibilities of non-being, a final goal. For the Neoplatonists and Augustine, and again for Erigena [a variant spelling of Eriugena], Eckhart and Dante, and for such as Rūmī, Ibn ʿArabi, Śaṅkarācarya, and many others in Asia, religious and intellectual experience are too closely interwoven ever to be wholly divided."[17]

It has been accurately stated that the great division in the modern era is not between adherents of different religions as in earlier times, but between religion and atheistic materialism. The latter, "which abolishes belief in God altogether, thereby eliminates spiritual values from the minds of men and leaves humanity a prey to cruelty, injustice and oppression."[18] A similar stance has been assumed by Hilarion Alfeyev, a prominent Russian Orthodox theologian and a gifted composer. He believes that the

16. Yockey, *Imperium*, 237–238.
17. Coomaraswamy, *Civilization*, 20.
18. Mendl, *Divine Quest*, 3.

fundamental conflict of our time is not between the Western world and Islam, as has long been held by sectors of the Western media and their allied politicians, but between faith in God and atheism. Allied to atheism, for all practical purposes, is the Western secular civilization with its moral relativism and suicidal ideology.[19]

Interestingly, although being an atheist himself, the British philosopher John Gray contends that modern atheism is in fact a Christian heresy, differing from other heresies mainly in its intellectual crudity. For example, although Karl Marx viewed religion as the opiate of the masses, he also admitted that it expressed the deepest human aspirations. And the French Positivists, who strove to replace Christianity with a Religion of Humanity, understood that religion provides an answer to universal human needs.[20]

As far as the interaction between religion and mathematics is concerned, the significance of the numbers three, four, seven, and twelve has always been recognized in the Jewish and Christian religions. It is immediately apparent that a numerical regularity is involved here: the sum of three and four is seven, while the product of three and four is twelve. Examples of these numbers are not hard to find:

i. The Christian Godhead comprises a Trinity of Father, Son, and Holy Spirit. The Hebrew Scriptures are divided into three parts: the Law, the Prophets, and the Writings. The Christian Church is served by three levels of ordained ministers, namely bishops, priests, and deacons.

ii. There are four evangelists in the New Testament: St Matthew, St Mark, St Luke, and St John. In the apocalyptic visions recorded in the books of Ezekiel, Daniel, and Revelation, four living beings are described by the authors: a lion, an ox, a man, and an eagle. These beings have since the early Christian era been viewed as representing the evangelists: St Matthew/man, St Mark/lion, St Luke/ox, and St John/eagle.

iii. According to the Genesis account, the universe came to be over a period of seven days, of which six entailed God's creative activity followed by a day of rest. This temporal structure became the model for the week of seven days, including a day of rest on Saturday (for Jews) or Sunday (for Christians). In the Church there are seven sacraments, or mysteries as they are called in the Orthodox tradition. In the Book

---

19. Alfeyev, *"Western secular civilization."*
20. Gray, *Black Mass*, 267.

of Revelation, important messages from Christ are conveyed to each of seven Christian congregations in Asia Minor.

iv. In the Old Testament, the Israelite nation consisted of twelve tribes descended from twelve patriarchs, being the sons of Jacob/Israel. In the New Testament, twelve disciples were initially called by Christ; they were later to become apostles and the first bishops of the Church.

Reflection on religious issues naturally leads to theology (Greek, *theologia*), which means discourse on God or the gods. Religious believers who are opposed to theology, even condemning it as the enemy of faith, are therefore mistaken, for an authentic religion requires a balance between its mystical and rational dimensions. Moreover, theology is linked to mathematics according to Aristotle's useful classification of the theoretical sciences, which is defined as aiming at knowledge for its own sake. In the *Metaphysics* (Book VI, chapter 1), Aristotle explains that the theoretical sciences are divided into physics, mathematics, and theology (or metaphysics). Physics deals with things that exist separately but are not immovable (natural bodies), mathematics with things that are immovable but do not exist separately (numbers and spatial figures), and theology with things that both exist separately and are immovable (substances which exist free from any contact with matter, of which the highest is God).[21]

Mathematics

Mathematics is one of the closest approximations to the universal Mind that the human mind can attain to. It has long been recognized that the structure of the cosmos is based upon mathematical laws. The numerical basis of cosmic manifestation is echoed, for example, in the biblical statement that God ordered all things by measure, number, and weight (*Wisdom of Solomon*, 11:20). This verse is read by Thomas Aquinas as meaning that "by measure the amount or mode or degree of perfection in each thing, by number the diversity and plurality of species that results from these degrees of perfection, and by weight the diverse attractions to specific goals and activities, agents and patients, and properties resulting from the diversity of species." Aquinas also refers to the statement by Boethius (in the *Arithmetic*) that "everything laid down in the primeval nature of things seems to have been formed by reason of number" (*Summa contra Gentiles*, 3.97–98).

21. Ross, *Aristotle*, 65.

In Western philosophy, the mathematical regularity underlying the cosmos was first expounded by Pythagoras and his followers. There can be little doubt that Pythagoras acquired at least some of his mathematical knowledge in Egypt, where he studied during a sojourn of around twenty years (according to the Neoplatonists Porphyry and Iamblichus). This Egyptian knowledge included a decimal system with numbers the equivalent of one, ten, one hundred, one thousand, and ten thousand, but no symbol for zero.[22] The pre-eminence of ancient Egypt in mathematics received an interesting explanation from Aristotle. In the *Metaphysics*, he wrote that the sciences which do not aim at giving pleasure or at the necessities of life (i.e., the theoretical sciences) were discovered first in the places where humans began to have leisure. He concludes, "This is why the mathematical arts were founded in Egypt; for there the priestly caste was allowed to be at leisure" (Book I, 981b).

The point of departure for Pythagorean philosophy was the discovery that concordant musical intervals can be expressed mathematically. As Kitty Ferguson comments, "the first natural law ever formulated mathematically was the relationship between musical pitch and the length of a vibrating harp string."[23] How did this come about? Pythagoras and his students noticed that certain ratios of string lengths always produce the harmonic intervals of the octave (2:1), the fifth (3:2), and the fourth (4:3). The sum of these four numbers (one, two, three, and four) is the sacred number ten, the *tetraktys* (Greek, 'fourness'). This scheme is geometrically represented by four rows of pebbles arranged from four at the base to one at the summit, thus forming an equilateral triangle consisting of ten pebbles. It was also discovered by the Pythagoreans that a tetrehedron, or four-sided solid, could be constructed out of four equilateral triangles. And a tetrahedron is precisely the shape of a pyramid, which thus also contains four faces and four points.[24] An important implication of these discoveries by Pythagoras and his followers is that the mentioned harmonic intervals affirm an indissoluble link between music and mathematics.

Moreover, such observations of mathematical regularity led to the conviction that the number ten underlies the cosmos. The followers of Pythagoras recognized that the number ten contains the formulas for lines, surfaces, and solids: one is a point, two points form a line, three points

---

22. Ferguson, *Pythagoras*, 21–22.
23. Ferguson, *Pythagoras*, 62.
24. Ferguson, *Pythagoras*, 65, 69–70.

produce a triangle, and four points compose a pyramid. In this way, geometrical figures are generated out of numbers, while the physical world is generated from geometrical figures. The sequence of generation of the cosmos is as follows: numbers produce points, which produce lines, which produce plane figures, which produce solid figures, which produce sensible bodies—the latter consisting of the four elements fire, water, earth, and air. Pythagoras taught further that earth is made from cube, fire from pyramid, air from octahedron, water from icosahedron, and from dodecahedron is made the sphere of the whole. Accordingly, the physical world is accounted for in terms of basic kinds of matter, while these are analyzed in terms of a finite number of simple geometrical bodies.[25]

It has been remarked that the Pythagorean cosmology is based on a different approach than the striving by some of their Hellenic predecessors to ground physics in terms of an undifferentiated principle (*archē*) that is shared by all things (such as water for Thales and air for Anaximenes). By instead focusing on form, physical natures are provided with an intelligible grounding in different geometrical structures.[26] This notion anticipates Plato's and Aristotle's insistence on the priority of form over matter in the constitution of physical reality, which in the case of living beings is found in the priority of soul over body.

In the Pythagorean understanding, reality is divided into three levels: intelligible, physical, and intermediate. The intermediate level is the realm of the mathematical, and therefore Plato defines the properties of Soul based on geometrical figures (Proclus, *Commentary on Timaeus*, 1). It has been commented that for Plato, mathematical number expresses quantities, while the Idea (or Form) of number expresses essences and thus determine quality. In this way mathematical number differs from the Idea of number, but it also differs from the sensible phenomena that we describe quantitatively. Mathematical number thus represents an intermediate level between the Forms and the sensible world.[27] This understanding is of Pythagorean provenance, and its appropriation by Plato is most likely due to the Athenian thinker having studied as a young man with the followers of Pythagoras in southern Italy.

The Pythagorean doctrine that things resemble numbers also anticipates Plato's doctrine that sensible things resemble or imitate the intelligible

25. McKirahan, *Philosophy*, 100–102.
26. Blackburn, *Oxford Dictionary*, 300.
27. Dreyer, *Wysbegeerte*, 98.

Forms. This understanding of cosmogony as involving the imposition of order onto disorder by means of numbers has been summarized as follows: "More generally, numbers, geometrical figures, the physical *kosmos*, and musical scales are generated similarly: all come to be when limit is imposed on the unlimited. All are instances of order, perhaps even of sequential order, which exists in different realms. And they all have numerical aspects that are basic: the number of sides of a triangle, the number and distances of the heavenly bodies, the ratios of the lengths of strings."[28]

According to Plato's cosmology in the *Timaeus*, the Demiurge (i.e., the universal Intellect) imposes rationality onto chaos by means of geometric figures. First, the Demiurge took a portion from the whole of the mixture which are the components of Soul (Existence, the Same, and the Different), then he took another portion twice as large, then a third three times as large as the first, followed by a fourth portion twice as large as the second, a fifth three times as large as the third, a sixth eight times that of the first, and finally a seventh portion twenty-seven times that of the first (35b). The sequence of these portions of the World-soul are one, two, three, four, nine, eight, and twenty-seven. The first four of these numbers represent the *tetraktys*, while nine is the square of three, and eight and twenty-seven are the cubes of two and three, respectively. Plato probably ended the sequence with cubes because only three dimensions are required in the creation of physical reality. Through these connected geometrical proportions, the Demiurge establishes in the Soul the source of the harmonious order it has to impart to the three-dimensional body of the cosmos.[29]

The significance of geometry is further evident from the fact that Plato denies the physical kinds (water, air, fire, and earth) the status of elements. Instead, the kinds are generated from triangles, and even these are reducible to numbers.[30] As we read in the *Timaeus*, each kind of matter (earth, air, fire, and water) is constructed by the Demiurge out of particles, and each particle is a regular geometrical solid. There are four kinds of particles corresponding with the four kinds of matter, and each particle is composed of specific triangles. A recent commentator remarked that in this scheme the (elemental) particles represent the molecules of the theory, while the (constituent) triangles are its atoms.[31] Given this pervasive sense

28. McKirahan, *Philosophy*, 112.
29. Ferguson, *Pythagoras*, 130–131; Zeyl, *Timaeus*, 1239.
30. Cornford, *Plato's Cosmology*, 162.
31. Cohen, "*Plato's Cosmology.*"

of the cosmos being constructed according to geometrical forms, it is little wonder that the celebrated remark, 'God is always geometrizing' (*aei ho theos geometrei*), has been attributed to Plato. This also explains the sign displayed above the entrance to Plato's Academy: "Let none ignorant of geometry enter here."[32]

It is clear that in the *Timaeus*, Plato emphasizes mathematical relationships as the basis for cosmic order. Through this seminal work the Athenian philosopher laid down the foundations for the sciences of astronomy, physics, chemistry, and physiology.[33] That the Pythagorean-Platonic numerical cosmology found its ultimate expression in the *Timaeus* should be viewed as a happy outcome, since this was the only Platonic dialogue known to the Latin West during the Middle Ages. In this way, Andrew Wilson-Dickson remarks, Christians were able to accept the 'pagan' notion of a universe that is organized in every detail by numbers and their proportions (including geometry). He writes further, "By marrying a study of astronomy with biblical references to heaven, the picture emerged of a universe created and sustained by God, whose planets created a cosmic music through their harmonious movement. Like the Greeks before them, Christians understood astronomy and music to be inextricably bound together by their common basis in number."[34]

Of unknown authorship but attributed to Iamblichus is a Neoplatonic work titled *The Theology of Arithmetic*, in which the mystical, mathematical, and cosmological symbolism of the first ten numbers is elaborated. It opens with the statement that the monad (i.e., one) is the non-spatial source of number, being called monad due to its stability. In fact, the Greek noun *monas* is derived from *menein*, which means 'to be stable.'[35] The author adds, "Everything has been organized by the monad, because it contains everything potentially: for even if they are not yet actual, nevertheless the monad holds seminally the principles which are within all numbers, including those which are within the dyad [i.e., two]." The monad is thereby associated with God, who is seminally everything that exists, is self-generated, and is the cause of permanence in natures (Chapter One: On the Monad).

32. Lundy, *Sacred Geometry*, 63.
33. Cooper, *Plato*, 1224.
34. Wilson-Dickson, *Brief History*, 57.
35. Waterfield, *Theology of Arithmetic*, 35.

The relation between being and non-being, which we touched upon earlier, may also be depicted in numerical terms. Although the number zero (or rather, the absence of number indicated by it) was unknown in Hellenic numerology, a symbol for zero was (independently) invented at least three times, namely by the Babylonians, the Mayans, and the Indians. Among the latter, the zero was associated with the void (Sanskrit, *Sunya*), thereby denoting the (ultimately unknowable) abyss of non-being, which is simultaneously the pregnant ground of all being. Accordingly, both zero and one are situated on the borderline between the absence and presence of being. It is also noteworthy that the symbols for zero and one combine to form the so-called Golden Section, symbolised by the Greek letter Φ (*phi*). It represents the division of a line, so that the ratio of the lesser part to the greater part is the same as the ratio of the greater part to the whole. In numerical terms this division always produces either 0.618 or 1.618, ratios that often appear in organic life.[36]

Hellenic mathematics has been related to the transformation of chaos into cosmos by Oswald Spengler. In terms thereof, formless matter (such as the stone used by a sculptor) is chaos, or something which is not yet actualized. The opposite state thereof is that of cosmos, which is a harmonic order. "The sum of such things constitutes neither more nor less than the whole world," Spengler writes. Therefore, Hellenic mathematics is fundamentally solid geometry.[37] This transition from chaos to cosmos is brought about through the geometrical extension of number by the Demiurge, as Plato depicted in the *Timaeus*.

Spengler reasoned further that since number is the symbol of causal necessity, it contains the ultimate meaning of the physical world. Number is moreover the primary element on which all mathematics is based. That the German philosopher views mathematics as both a science and an art is evident from the following tribute: "It [mathematics] is a science of the most rigorous kind, like logic but more comprehensive and very much fuller; it is a true art, along with sculpture and music; it is, lastly, a metaphysic of the highest rank, as Plato and above all Leibniz show us."[38] Not only mathematics is viewed as a metaphysical reality by Spengler, but religion is similarly conceived as inseparable from the metaphysical (as we have had occasion to note earlier).

36. Lundy, *Sacred Number*, 56; Lundy, *Sacred Geometry*, 86.
37. Spengler, *Decline*, 46–47.
38. Spengler, *Decline*, 42–43.

It was also remarked by Spengler that some of the greatest Western mathematicians have been brought to their discoveries through a profound religious intuition, as was the case with Pythagoras and Plato. For instance, Nicholas of Cusa was guided from the notion of the divine infinity in nature to the elements of the Infinitesimal Calculus, and Leibniz from the infinite extent of the Godhead to his notion of *analysis situs* (the mathematical field now known as topology) for the interpretation of pure space. Spengler comments, "And Kepler and Newton, strictly religious natures both, were and remained convinced, like Plato, that it was precisely through the medium of number that they had been able to apprehend intuitively the essence of the divine world order".[39] This coherence of mathematics with religion confirm both as indisputable manifestations of spiritual-intellectual consciousness.

In an epochal 1931 essay, the Austrian mathematician and logician Kurt Gödel (then only twenty-five years old) published his celebrated Incompleteness theorems. He demonstrated that, for any computable axiomatic system which is powerful enough to describe the arithmetic of the natural numbers: (a) if such a system is consistent, it cannot be complete; and (b) the consistency of axioms cannot be proved from within their own system. Interestingly, Gödel described himself as a theist and believed in an afterlife.[40] Evidently, this mathematical genius had no difficulty in reconciling his intellectual quest with faith in a personal God. It has been commented that for Gödel, who was philosophically a Platonist, "important epistemological questions require philosophical methods that transcend formal mathematical methods and necessarily lead scholars to the fields of metamathematics and metaphysics."[41]

Clearly, mathematics and the natural sciences employing it are by their nature unable to provide us with a complete description of reality. Nonetheless, it should be recognized that mathematics, being intermediate between the intelligible and sensible realms, is able to elevate the human mind from the physical to the metaphysical. But this is even more so the case with music, being more accessible than mathematics through involving all the elements of the human soul.

---

39. Spengler, *Decline*, 52.
40. Wikipedia: Kurt Gödel.
41. Laos, *Metaphysics*, 16.

Music

In his thought-provoking book *Twilight of the Idols*, the German philosopher Friedrich Nietzsche paid homage to the vital role of music by writing that without music, life would be a mistake. And the Alsatian theologian, organist, and Nobel laureate Albert Schweitzer stated that there are two means of refuge from the miseries of life, namely music and cats.[42] Anyone who is sensible enough to be both a music lover and a cat lover would surely agree with this lucid assessment of their existential value. Leaving our feline companions aside for the moment, let us now consider the importance of music.

Music is here understood in the Platonic sense, namely as a meaningful combination of harmony, melody, and rhythm. This threefold scheme reflects the elements of the human soul, which are the reason, the emotions (both positive and negative), and the bodily needs or appetites. Accordingly, the harmony of music is accessible to the reason, its melody to the emotions, and its rhythm to the body. There is no question of 'equality' among these elements of the soul, since Plato taught that the rational soul should be in control of the other elements. For example, in the dialogue *Phaedrus* the soul is depicted as consisting of three parts, represented by a charioteer (i.e., reason), a good horse with self-control (i.e., positive emotions), and a bad horse (i.e., negative emotions) that needs to be disciplined by the charioteer (253d–254d). Employing the same imagery as Plato, the Jewish-Hellenic thinker Philo of Alexandria wrote that "when Mind as charioteer rules the whole living being, as a governor does a city, then life holds a straight course."[43]

The Hellenic and early Christian understanding of music was much influenced by the teaching of the Pythagorean school. These initiates produced a variety of appropriate songs to conduct the dispositions of the soul in a useful manner. For instance, before going to sleep certain songs were used to purify the reason from the tumult of the day, thus procuring tranquil sleep. Certain instrumental sounds were also used to heal the passions of the souls and even bodily diseases. Pythagoras is therefore credited by

---

42. Nietzsche, *Twilight*, 9; https://www.goodreads.com/author/quotes/47146.Albert_Schweitzer

43. Quoted in Coomaraswamy, *Civilization*, 10.

his Neoplatonist biographer Iamblichus with producing through music the most beneficial correction of human manners and lives.[44]

Pythagoras taught further that our individual reason should be illuminated 'from above' by the universal Mind, so that we can control our emotions: "Leaving thyself always to be guided and directed by the understanding that comes from above, and that ought to hold the reins" (*Golden Verses*, 69). The implication hereof for music is that harmony should be the dominant element, without denying a proper place to melody and rhythm. As a matter of fact, Robert Mendl writes, the two earliest elements of music were rhythm and melody, both linked with dancing.[45] And Plato remarked that even rhythm is a gift from heaven to help us, for most humans have lost all sense of measure and are lacking in grace (*Tim*, 47d–e).

The immense power of music on the soul, and hence on society, has been fully recognized by Plato. In discussing the role of music in education, Socrates explains that beauty and ugliness result from good rhythm and bad rhythm, respectively. Moreover, as is the case with good literature, good music depends on goodness of character, which includes a well-formed mind. This is why musical education is so important, "for rhythm and harmony penetrate deeply into the mind and take a most powerful hold on it, and if education is good, bring and impart grace and beauty, if it is bad, the reverse." Socrates therefore cautions against musical innovations, for the music and literature of a state cannot be altered without major political and social changes (*Pol*, 400c–e, 401d, 424c).[46]

The combination of harmonic, melodic, and rhythmic elements in a piece of music is called its texture. During the historical course of Western music, several different textures have developed, including the following types:

i. Monophonic: a single melodic line without any accompaniment. A well-known example hereof is the Gregorian chant of the Western Church during the so-called Middle Ages;[47]

---

44. Perry, *Treasury*, 683–684.
45. Mendl, *Divine Quest*, 8.
46. Lee, *Republic*, 161–163, 191.

47. We say so-called Middle Ages, since the conventional division of Western history into 'ancient', 'medieval', and 'modern' periods is an ideological scheme which serves the modernist, anti-traditional agenda. It has been effectively subverted by Oswald Spengler with a cyclic model of history in his *magnum opus*, translated as *The Decline of the West*.

ii. Biphonic: two distinct melodic lines, with the lower sustaining a drone (or constant pitch) while the other line creates a more elaborate melody above it. In the Western world this texture appeared with the organum (see below) of the late medieval period;

iii. Polyphonic: multiple melodic voices (usually four, namely for soprano, alto, tenor, and bass) which are largely independent from or in imitation with one another. This is the characteristic texture of Renaissance music and it is also prevalent during the Baroque period;

iv. Homophonic: multiple voices of which one, the melody, stands out prominently while the others form a background of harmonic accompaniment. This is the characteristic texture of the Classical period and continues to predominate in Romantic music. Moreover, by the twentieth century, nearly all Western popular music is homophonic.[48]

It is noteworthy that the development from monophonic to polyphonic singing followed certain physical realities. Starting with the monophonic music of Gregorian chant, the natural division of men's voices into bass and tenor (i.e., the lower and higher registers) enabled choristers to sing the same chant at a pitch that suited them. Accordingly, the earliest organum in the Church was in two parts, with the Gregorian melody reproduced at an interval below. Later a fourth above and an octave below came to be added, which led to descant (or counterpoint) singing. In this way polyphonic music came into being, which corresponded with the elaborate, soaring architecture of the Gothic cathedrals in northern Europe.[49] Thus, in music one again encounters a coherence of the metaphysical and the physical.

The interaction between religion and music is particularly evident in the forms of sacred and liturgical music. In his informative book *The Divine Quest in Music*, Robert Mendl contends that the manifestation of God in music differs from that in other arts, due to a fundamental divergence. The method of music is different from those of religious literature, painting, sculpture, and architecture, since music does not necessarily rely on association or imitation, but on representation. Music can thus be religious or spiritual by virtue of the intrinsic character of the composition itself.[50] We would add that among all the arts, music (as traditionally understood) provides the most powerful link between the human and the divine levels,

---

48. Wikipedia: Texture.
49. Mendl, *Divine Quest*, 29.
50. Mendl, *Divine Quest*, 4.

on account of its innate capacity for our participation, through hearing and understanding, in the higher levels of reality."

The musicologist Andrew Wilson-Dickson outlines the spiritual context of music as follows: "The links between worship and music are deep-seated, for both spring from a God-implanted desire to search for truth and order. Music is a manifestation of that search in the mental and physical realms, while worship is its expression in the cosmic. What is more, God has ordered his creation in such a way that the unfolding of its truths is profoundly satisfying, both mentally and emotionally."[51] This understanding reflects Plato's view that music involves our mental, emotional, and physical dimensions through harmony, melody, and rhythm, respectively. Wilson-Dickson continues: "Music, like the other arts, is itself a response to the pattern and order of God's creation. The composer Vaughan Williams was therefore able to observe that 'music is the reaching out towards the utmost realities by means of ordered sound.'"[52]

In a talk given in 2011 at the Catholic University of America in Washington, D.C., the Russian Orthodox theologian and composer Hilarion Alfeyev explored the relation between spirituality and artistic creativity. He said, "If creativity is dedicated to God, if the creative person puts his efforts into serving people, if he preaches lofty spiritual ideals, then his activity may aid his own salvation and that of thousands around him. If, however, the aim of creativity is to assert one's own ego, if the creative process is governed by egotistical or mercenary intentions, if the artist, through his art, propagates anti-spiritual, anti-God or anti-human values, then his work may be destructive for both himself and for those about him." Alfeyev added that genuine art is that which serves God either directly or indirectly. The music of Bach is clearly dedicated to God, even when it is not intended for worship (one thinks, for example, of Bach's concertos and keyboard works). On the other hand, the works of Beethoven and Brahms may not directly praise God, yet they are capable of elevating the human person morally and educating him or her spiritually. And this means that they also serve God, albeit indirectly.[53]

An interesting correspondence between the spiritual element in music and the human soul has been pointed out by Robert Mendl, namely that neither can be reduced to concrete, scientific terms. He adds that there is

---

51. Wilson-Dickson, *Brief History*, 14.
52. Wilson-Dickson, *Brief History*, 14–15.
53. Alfeyev, "*Music and Faith.*"

no watertight division of music into sacred and secular, or music which manifests divine inspiration and that which does not. However, there is a great deal of music which clearly lacks divine inspiration (e.g., by being mechanical or superficial), whereas the sacred quality of most of Beethoven's instrumental art, for example, is undeniable.[54] We would add that much of the instrumental music of Buxtehude, Bach, Mozart, Schubert, Brahms, Bruckner, Mahler, and Sibelius, to name some prominent examples, is spiritual in character.

In the Jewish and Christian traditions, the worship of God has always included music, particularly singing. Following the example of the Hebrew scriptures known as the Old Testament, the New Testament treats music as sacred. Examples include the following:

i. The *Magnificat* (its Latin title) of the Virgin Mary, in which she praises God for His mercy (Luke 1:46–55). It opens with the exclamation, "My soul magnifies the Lord, and my spirit has rejoiced in God my Saviour";

ii. The singing of hymns, psalms, and spiritual songs by Christians, as recommended in the Epistles (Eph 5:19, Col 3:16, Jas 5:13);

iii. The singing by the saints in heaven (Rev 5:9, 14:3, 15:3).[55]

As usual, etymology is instructive. In his letters, St Paul uses the Greek terms *psalmos* (psalm), which is derived from the verb *psallō*, 'to move by a touch'; *hymnos* (hymn), which is derived from the verb *hymneō*, 'to sing praise'; and *ōdē* (song), which has variously been translated as inspired, spiritual, or sacred song. A hymn was defined by Augustine of Hippo as a song containing praise of God. Thus, a hymn contains the three elements of *song* and *praise* of *God*; if any of these are missing, it does not count as a hymn.[56]

We read in St Paul's first letter to the Corinthians, "I will sing with the spirit, and I will also sing with the understanding" (14:15). The latter term translates the Greek *nous*, which also means mind. In a thoughtful essay on the meaning of music, Ken Myers comments as follows: "St Paul's assertion of the possibility of mindful singing . . . is a recognition that music can be an intelligible and intelligent act, and act that appealed to the

---

54. Mendl, *Divine Quest*, 5–7.
55. Mendl, *Divine Quest*, 27.
56. Wilson-Dickson, *Brief History*, 35, 36.

understanding and not just the feelings or to an inward disposition." Myers remarks that it's not only the lyrics that can involve the mind, but the musical form itself is intelligible. He adds, "Music has a unique capacity to involve the spirit, the emotions, the body, and the mind, and whenever we eliminate or neglect the involvement of any one of these, we diminish the gift that music is."[57]

Interestingly, Augustine of Hippo admitted experiencing a conflict between the singing that gives pleasure to the ears and what is being sung. He advised that singing should be done with a clear and skilfully modulated voice, "so that by the delights of the ear the weaker minds may be stimulated by a devotional mood" (*Conf*, Book X.33). The Latin theologian's musical interest and knowledge is evident from an essay titled *De musica* written some years earlier. And concerning Gregorian plainchant some 700 years later, Bernard of Clairvaux wrote that it should be pleasing to the ear and move the heart, while enhancing the sense of the words.[58]

As we mentioned earlier, Plato taught (in the dialogue *Timaeus*) that the Demiurge orders the universe through the transformation of chaos into cosmos. Moreover, our senses of sight and hearing enable us to perceive its harmonious arrangement. This notion of a divinely established cosmic harmony was widely accepted among the early Christian theologians. For example, Clement of Alexandria (c.150–215) related vocal music to God's creative activity, writing that God's creative song "ordered the universe concordantly and tuned the discord of the elements into a harmonious arrangement, so that the entire cosmos might become through its agency a consonance."[59] As Ken Myers remarks, "Clement believed in a fundamental relationship between the aural harmony of music and the harmonious arrangement of all of Creation as ordered by the Logos." And because music has the capacity to echo the cosmic order and thus harbours a formative power, Clement (like other Church Fathers) was concerned about the power of music to form or deform the soul.[60]

Characteristically, Plotinus provided music (and the arts in general) with a metaphysical grounding. He writes that the harmonies we hear are created by unheard harmonies which awaken the soul to the consciousness of beauty, thereby showing it the one essence in another kind. This

57. Myers, "*Music*," 9–10.
58. Mendl, *Divine Quest*, 28.
59. Wilson-Dickson, *Brief History*, 16.
60. Myers, "*Music*," 11–12.

is possible, "for the measures of our music are not arbitrary, but are determined by the Principle whose labour is to dominate matter and bring pattern into being" (*Enneads* I.6.3).[61] Arguing along similar lines, the fourth-century theologian Gregory of Nyssa held that "the order of the universe is a kind of musical harmony, richly and multifariously toned, guided by an inward rhythm and accord, pervaded by an essential 'symphony'; the melody and cadence of the cosmic elements in their intermingling sing of God's glory, as does the interrelation of motion and rest within created things." As a result, Ken Myers writes, the harmony of the created order may be experienced by those with attentive senses.[62]

The Platonic and Christian conception of a cosmic order created by God led the Christian Roman philosopher Boethius (early sixth century) to write about three types of music: that of the universe (*musica mundane*), that of the human being (*musica humana*), and that which is created by certain instruments (*musica instrumentis constituta*). Thus, Andrew Wilson-Dickson comments, "even the humble *musica instrumentis constituta* was linked through the music of the human soul ultimately to the music of the spheres, for all three were part of the same divinely controlled system. Humanity had therefore to strive to make music which synchronized with this harmoniously vibrating universe and which would thereby form a worthy part of God's great symphony of proportions."[63]

The patron saint of music in the Catholic and Orthodox traditions is St Cecilia, whose feast day falls on 22 November. Of noble Roman birth, she was martyred for her Christian faith in Sicily during the reign of the 'enlightened' Emperor Marcus Aurelius (author of the celebrated *Meditations*), sometime between 176 and 180. Cecilia was said to have praised God by vocal as well as instrumental music, thus linking both forms of musical art to religion in the person of a saint and martyr, as Robert Mendl notes. Odes for annual celebrations of St Cecilia's Day have been produced by several composers, including Purcell and Handel. The significance of St Cecilia for the relationship between music and religion is that she united in herself a double personality: an enormously brave and devout woman who died rather than renounce her faith, and the patron saint of both vocal and instrumental art. Mendl concludes his fine tribute to St Cecilia as follows: "Thus the godlike nature of great music, both that which is avowedly

---

61. Quoted in Perry, *Treasury*, 679.
62. Myers, "*Music*," 13.
63. Wilson-Dickson, *Brief History*, 57.

'sacred' and that which is not, reflects the character of music's own votaress who lived about 1 800 years ago."[64]

During the fourth century, the Christian religion experienced a spectacular reversal of fortunes due to the Emperor Constantine granting Christians freedom of worship through the edict of Milan in 313 A.D. From having to endure sporadic yet fierce persecution by the Roman authorities during the previous three centuries, Christianity rose to imperial religion within a few decades after the Milanese edict. As the Church became established throughout the empire and beyond, a variety of liturgical traditions arose that reflected the languages in different geographical areas. While Greek had been the common language throughout the early Church, the Western churches (e.g., those in Spain, Gaul, and Britain) in due course adopted Latin for worship, with the Eastern churches mostly retaining the vernacular (e.g., Greek, Arabic, and Coptic).[65]

As a result of these developments, in the Eastern Christian territories such as the Near East, Asia Minor, and Greece, so-called Byzantine chant was practised; in Northern Italy, it was Ambrosian chant, named after the famous Bishop Ambrose of Milan; in the Frankish lands, it was Gallic chant; and in the Iberian Peninsula, it was West Gothic or Mozarabic chant. Gradually, due to political reasons the music of the Roman liturgy, known as Gregorian chant, became the dominant liturgical music across Western Europe and remained so until the Protestant Reformation of the sixteenth century.[66] Gregory the Great, who was Pope of Rome from 590 to 604, played a key role in the ascendancy of Gregorian chant, which is named after him. Gregory did so by encouraging conformity in styles of worship, so that the various Latin liturgies mentioned above mostly became absorbed into the Roman liturgy. Remarkably, two of the ancient liturgies managed to survive this drive towards conformity and can still be heard today: the Mozarabic liturgy in the cathedral of Toledo and the Ambrosian liturgy in the cathedral of Milan.[67]

Regarding the liturgical music of Eastern Christianity, Byzantine chant is still used in the Greek Orthodox Church today. It is biphonic in texture, consisting of a melodic line supported by a drone line called the *ison*, providing a constant pitch upon which the melody rests. In contrast,

---

64. Mendl, *Divine Quest*, 34–39.
65. Wilson-Dickson, *Brief History*, 40.
66. Hughes, *European Music*, 3–4.
67. Wilson-Dickson, *Brief History*, 43.

the Russian Orthodox Church uses mainly polyphonic chant, consisting of different yet consonant parts for sopranos, altos, tenors, and basses, thereby establishing splendid harmonies (when properly sung, of course). Both of these Orthodox traditions share the custom of unaccompanied singing, since the early Christian theologians (known as Church Fathers) forbade the use of musical instruments during worship.[68] The wisdom of this Orthodox practice became apparent during the twentieth century, when at first the Protestant denominations and later also parts of the Catholic Church introduced secular instruments such as guitars and drums into their 'worship' services.

An interesting argument has been made by Friedrich Nietzsche, to the effect that music (i.e., apart from mere rhythm) is a latecomer in every culture. He writes: "Among all the arts that are accustomed to grow on a definite culture-soil and under definite social and political conditions, music is the last plant to come up, arising in the autumn and fading-season of the culture to which it belongs. At the same time, the first signs and harbingers of a new spring are usually already noticeable, and sometimes music, like the language of a forgotten age, rings out into a new, astonished world, and comes too late." The German philosopher then provides the following examples: the art of the Dutch and Flemish musicians evokes the soul of the Christian middle ages; the music of Handel reflects the soul of Luther and his fellow Reformers; the music of Mozart, who in 'golden melody' expressed the age of Louis XIV; the music of Beethoven and Rossini, singing out the world of the eighteenth century; and finally the music of Wagner, which expresses both rapid cultural decay and the reaction that delights in indigenous, national, 'primitive' manners. Nietzsche adds: "This spirit [i.e., of Wagner's music] wages the last campaign of reaction against the spirit of illumination which passed into this century [i.e., the nineteenth] from the last, and also against the super-natural ideas of French revolutionary romanticism and of English and American colourlessness in the reconstruction of state and society."[69]

As was the case in literature, visual art, and other expressions of higher culture in the twentieth century, music in the Western world also

---

68. It has been pointed out that the early Christians shunned instrumental music and dancing due to the context of debauchery within which such activities often occurred in Roman society; Wilson-Dickson, *Brief History*, 39.

69. Nietzsche, *Human*, 321–322; his mention of Dutch and Flemish musicians presumably refers to the great Flemish composers of the Renaissance, such as Desprez, Dufay, Ockeghem, and Willaert.

underwent a radical rupture from the forms and conventions of the preceding millennium. This breach with tradition inevitably harboured spiritual repercussions of a negative nature. As observed by Hilarion Alfeyev, "In the twentieth century, the art of music was wrenched from any religious association. During the epochs of Impressionism and the Avant-garde, interest in anything to do with religion seems to have faded altogether. Avant-garde composers renounced the final elements that linked music to faith—the elements of harmony and of beauty as fundamental for musical creativity. Cacophony and disharmony became the constructive fabric with which musical works were built."[70] Fortunately for lovers of truth and beauty, a relatively small number of composers (including Alfeyev) have continued the Western art music tradition throughout the twentieth century and into the twenty-first.

One of the salient features of post-Romantic music is its domination by Soviet composers, hailing from Russia and other Soviet republics. This is also a paradoxical phenomenon, for religious activity was proscribed by the communist-ruled Soviet Union from 1918 onwards. The fierce persecution by the authorities of the Russian Orthodox Church, by far the largest religious organization in the country, is well known among those who are historically aware. And yet this oppressive situation did not prevent musical giants such as the composers Prokofiev, Khachaturian, and Shostakovich from rising to global prominence, not to mention a host of brilliant conductors, singers, pianists, violinists, cellists, and other musicians who lived and worked in the USSR.

It is noteworthy in this regard that culture can be a powerful bearer of Christian piety, as Hilarion Alfeyev has argued. Thus, in Russia during the Soviet era when religious literature was inaccessible, people learnt about God from the works of the Russian classics. For example, it was impossible to obtain the works of the mystical theologian Isaac the Syrian, yet people had access to the writings of the Elder Zossima in *The Brothers Karamazov*, which were inspired by the works of Isaac the Syrian. This is due to the fact that Russian literature, art, and music of the nineteenth century, albeit secular in form, preserved a deep inner link with its original religious underpinnings, i.e., Orthodoxy. In this way, Alfeyev concludes, "nineteenth-century Russian culture throughout the Soviet period fulfilled the mission which, in normal circumstances, would have been the work of the Church."[71]

---

70. Alfeyev, *"Music and Faith."*
71. Alfeyev, *"Music and Faith."*

In addition, although the Soviet Union was officially a godless state, the Western ruling elites were certainly not holding the moral high ground during the Cold War era, their pietistic rhetoric notwithstanding. As Nicolas Laos has pointed out, these Western elites have not hesitated to pursue amoral strategies such as the global drug offensive, cultural subversion, international organized crime, and the doctrine of 'friendly tyrants.' Therefore, if one bears in mind that the only sinners whom Christ utterly condemned were the hypocrites (Matt 23:13), then it could be concluded that the godlessness of the Western political establishment was even worse than that of the Soviet political establishment.[72]

It has been remarked by Hilarion Alfeyev that the real return of composers to the sphere of religious faith came only at the end of the twentieth century, after decades of mostly discord and cacophony. This change of direction was prompted, at least partially, by the longing of audiences for a music that united simplicity and profundity; in other words, "a music that could transport one beyond the boundaries of earthly existence into communication with the world above." It is therefore not fortuitous that by the end of the twentieth century the Western world experienced an upsurge of interest in Church music, particularly Gregorian chant.[73]

We may gauge the accuracy of our correlation between musical and psychic elements as mentioned at the beginning, by considering the stages through which Western music has passed over the past thousand years:

i. At the threshold of this period we encounter the transcendent sound-world of Gregorian chant in liturgical music, which continues to uplift the soul towards the higher realms.

ii. The next stage is the music of the Renaissance, characterised by rich harmonies that elevate the souls of those listening to the work of Palestrina, Byrd, Victoria, and their contemporaries.

iii. This is followed by the music of the Baroque from Monteverdi onwards, in which contrapuntal harmony reaches its zenith. By the late Baroque, composers such as Bach, Handel, and Vivaldi are already weaving beautiful melodies into their vocal and instrumental harmonies.

iv. They are succeeded by the masters of the Classical era, notably Haydn, Mozart, and early Beethoven. In their marvellous compositions there

72. Laos, *Metaphysics*, 199.
73. Alfeyev, "*Music and Faith.*"

is an abundance of pleasing melody, while rhythmic elements are becoming more noticeable than before.

v. This combination increases during the Romantic era, which lasts from mature Beethoven through Schubert, Rossini, Chopin, Mendelssohn, Schumann, Liszt, Verdi, Wagner, Brahms, Bruckner, Dvorák, and Tchaikovsky, and well into the twentieth century with the so-called Late Romantics. Among the latter count Puccini, Sibelius, Mahler, Elgar, Rachmaninov, and Richard Strauss, all of whom refused to be carried along by the abandonment of melody which became fashionable during the early decades of the twentieth century. However, to their lasting credit, some modern composers have continued creating works that contain pleasing melodies, and of course harmony and rhythm. Prominent examples thereof are the great Soviet composers we have already mentioned.

vi. Since the beginning of the twentieth century, much of the music in the Western world has been dominated by the element of rhythm. This includes such popular genres as jazz and rock (although, to be fair, some rock music from the 1960s to the 1980s are quite melodic).

Thus, in Western music there has occurred a shift of emphasis from harmony (in Renaissance and Baroque music) to melody (in Classical and Romantic music) and finally to rhythm (in modern music), without denying the presence of any of these elements in the other eras. In the Platonic understanding, it thus appears that much of humankind (since most of the inhabited world has been dominated by Western powers for the past five hundred years) has over the past millennium degenerated from being guided by reason (harmony) to being controlled by emotions (melody) and finally being dominated by bodily needs (rhythm). This phenomenon also serves to undermine the myth of 'progress' on which the modernist world-view rests, and according to which the present is in all respects better than the past.[74]

This section began with Plato and it is proper to conclude it with the Hellenic intellectual titan, thus closing the musical circle. The exalted view Plato had of music is evident from his statement that hearing, like sight, is a gift from heaven. He adds that hearing has been granted to humans

---

74. The 'progress' myth has been thoroughly demolished by some of the Traditionalist thinkers. See, e.g., the essay by S.H. Nasr titled "Progress and Evolution. A Reappraisal from the Traditional Perspective," in *Parabola* (Volume VI, Number 2, 1981).

both to enable speech and, guided by intelligence, to perceive the harmony in music, which in turn was not given for the sake of irrational pleasure. Instead, harmony is meant to correct any discord which may have arisen in the soul and to make it concordant with itself (*Tim*, 47c–d). The Jewish-Hellenic philosopher Philo of Alexandria (who played a crucial role in the transmission of Platonism into the early Church) similarly rejected the notion of music as primarily giving pleasure to the senses. The view of the Neoplatonic philosophers Plotinus and Porphyry that music is an approach to the divine by means of ecstasy, was approved by the Greek theologian John Chrysostom. This fourth-century Archbishop of Constantinople and compiler of the liturgy used ever since in all the Orthodox churches, added that church music should help to lift the souls of men towards God, and not serve for entertainment.[75] It is not difficult to surmise what these prominent thinkers and teachers would have made of the cacophony that has characterized much of what has been presented as music in the Western world since the early twentieth century, and even more so the sonic filth of the twenty-first century.

---

75. Mendl, *Divine Quest*, 27; the term 'ecstasy' is derived from the Greek noun *ekstasis*, which literally means 'a standing out of'; i.e., through ecstasy one can stand outside oneself. It is noteworthy that Friedrich Nietzsche viewed the physiological state of ecstasy as a prerequisite for artistic creativity (*Twilight*, 52).

Man and Woman

ONE OF THE MOST conspicuous features of humankind is that it consists of men and women, and not of genderless persons. In the traditional Christian understanding, God created humankind from the outset as male and female. As part of the creative activity on the sixth day, "God created man in His own image; in the image of God He created him; male and female He created them" (Gen 1:27). The Greek word for 'man' is *anthrōpos* (the equivalent of the Latin *homo*), which means a man, a woman, or mankind in general.[1]

It may justly be asked, why did God create man and woman? The Orthodox theologian Hilarion Alfeyev has provided an illuminating answer: "Because a solitary monad cannot love, being alone, God created not a single unit but a couple, with the intention that love should reign among people." However, the love between a couple is not yet perfect, for the couple consists of two opposing principles, thesis and antithesis. This needs to be fulfilled in a synthesis, which is the birth of a child. Hence the divine command to the first human couple to be fruitful and multiply (Gen 1:28). Moreover, the fully realized family of husband, wife, and child is a reflection of the divine love in Father, Son, and Holy Spirit.[2]

The Polarity of Male and Female

In his epochal work *The Decline of the West*, Oswald Spengler outlines sexual differentiation in the organic continuum of plant-animal-human as follows: "A fathomless secret of the cosmic flowings that we call Life is their separation into two sexes. Already in the earth-bound existence-streams of the plant world they are trying to part from one another, as the symbol of the flower tells us—into a something that *is* this existence and a something

---

1. LSJ, 63; Wheeler, *Latin*, 525.
2. Alfeyev, *Mystery*, 59.

that keeps it going. Animals are free, little worlds in a big world—the cosmic—closed off as microcosms and set up against the macrocosm. And, more and more decisively as the animal kingdom unfolds its history, the dual direction of dual being, of the masculine and the feminine, manifests itself." In this way, there is a dual significance of all living things.[3]

What is the fundamental difference between male and female, viewed 'from above', so to speak? Oswald Spengler writes: "The feminine stands closer to the Cosmic. It is rooted deeper in the earth and it is immediately involved in the grand cyclic rhythms of Nature. The masculine is freer, more animal, more mobile—as to sensation and understanding as well as otherwise—more awake and more tense." As applied to the human world, "The man *makes* History, the woman *is* History." Accordingly, sociopolitical history is mainly masculine, reaching back deep into the animal world and receiving its highest symbolic expression in the life-courses of the great Cultures. In contrast, the feminine is the primary, the eternal, the plant-like, the culture-less history of the generation-sequence which passes unaltered through the being of all animal and human species; the feminine is therefore synonymous with Life itself.[4]

Due to this fundamental difference between male and female, Spengler continues, the two kinds of History, i.e., cosmic flow as such and the successive individuals in it, are fighting for power in man and woman. "This secret and fundamental war of the sexes has gone on ever since there were sexes, and will continue—silent, bitter, unforgiving, pitiless—while they continue. In it, too, there are policies, battles, alliances, treaties, treasons." Another German philosopher, Friedrich Nietzsche, explained this underlying 'war of the sexes' in psychological terms: "The same emotions are in man and woman, but in different *tempo*; on that account, man and woman never cease to misunderstand each other."[5]

From a Traditionalist perspective, it has been argued that woman is opposable to man in a similar way as the chivalrous type is opposable to the sacerdotal type, or as the practical type is opposable to the intellectual type. Although recognizing that the two human sexes differ fundamentally (and not only on the physiological level, as the egalitarian dogma would have

---

3. Spengler, *Decline*, 354.
4. Spengler, *Decline*, 354–355.
5. Spengler, *Decline*, 355; Nietzsche, *Beyond*, 571.

it), Frithjof Schuon adds that woman is the equal of man from the point of view of the human condition and so also of immortality.[6]

The Russian philosopher Alexander Dugin has differentiated the socio-political dimension of gender from its biological dimension, writing as follows: "It is acceptable to consider 'a gender' in sociological terms, in other words, gender as a socially-constructed phenomenon. This is in contrast to the anatomical 'sex' inherent in biological terms. Gender is a social convention which can change from society to society. At the same time, the political formulation of gender is the social norm, which is approved as an imperative on the basis of political power. Therefore, gender is both a social phenomenon and a political one. Political, because we are dealing with the management of social norms regulated by a society: community, police, and so on, the retreat from which leads to a variety of sanctions."[7]

Patriarchy and Matriarchy

The relation between gender and rule is expressed in the systems called patriarchy (rule by one or more males) and matriarchy (rule by one or more females). Although patriarchy is common among the 'higher' (in the sense of more neurologically complex) animals such as the class of *Mammalia*, the phenomenon of matriarchy is by no means unknown. As a matter of fact, matriarchal societies are found among both mammals and insects. Examples include killer whales, elephants, bonobos (a type of great ape formerly known as the pygmy chimpanzee), spotted hyenas, mole rats, meerkats, honeybees, and ants. And since human beings are descended from animal ancestors, at least on the physiological level (and in many cases also on the behavioural level), it is not surprising that both patriarchal and matriarchal systems have developed in human societies.

In at least parts of the so-called ancient world, societies were matriarchal. This view has been postulated by the Swiss anthropologist Johann Bachofen in his seminal book *Das Mutterrecht* (1861), or 'Mother Right' in English. In it he demonstrated that motherhood is the source of human society, religion, and morality. Stated in socio-political terms, matriarchy was the primordial condition of human society, while patriarchy emerged later in opposition to it. According to Bachofen, the Sun is a masculine principle, symbolizing spirit; the Earth is a feminine principle, symbolizing matter;

6. Schuon, *Castes*, 33–34.
7. Dugin, *Theory*, 184–185.

and the Moon is an intermediate principle between the masculine and the feminine. Moreover, the maternal principle is the source, while the masculine principle is the goal. Matter and maternity are interconnected, Nicholas Berdyaev comments, while matriarchy is associated with communism (in the 'primitive' understanding of this word). Interestingly, the latter link was recognized by the early Marxists, including Friedrich Engels in his 1884 treatise *The Origin of the Family, Private Property, and the State*.[8]

A distinction between materialism and idealism flows from the worldviews of matriarchy and patriarchy. In matriarchal orders, Danie Goosen writes, everything is reduced back to matter. (Significantly, the word 'matter' is derived from the Latin *materia*, which is cognate to *mater*, 'mother'). In the modern world, the matriarchal-materialist link finds expression in capitalism and Marxism, both of which view ideas and religions as merely a function of material forces, whether these serve individual or class interests. In contrast, patriarchal orders strive to ground things in ideas instead of matter. Accordingly, the spiritual becomes more important than the physical, the eternal more important than the temporal, the transcendent more important than the immanent, and the active more important than the passive. Moreover, the materialistic monism of matriarchy is replaced by hierarchical dualism in patriarchy. The latter ontology differs from gnostic dualism in that the lower forces (e.g., the physical and the immanent) are recognized as integral to the whole.[9] The Platonic teaching on the physical receiving its reality from the metaphysical is evident in this reasoning.

It has been argued that matriarchal societies tended socially towards a democratic equality, whereas patriarchal societies inclined towards an aristocratic inequality. Both orders probably originated in hunter-gatherer societies, with the emphasis falling on gathering in matriarchal and hunting in patriarchal societies. Another difference between these social orders lay in their world-views, according to the political philosopher Eric Voegelin. In matriarchal societies, a monistic unity prevailed between the earthly and the heavenly. Since society was conceived as an integral part of the primeval unity, reality was passively experienced. In contrast, patriarchal societies distinguished between the earthly and the heavenly, the human and the divine, the immanent and the transcendent. An active engagement with reality replaces a passive reception thereof. And while matriarchy emphasized the eternal 'now,' patriarchy insists on a distinction between past

---

8. Wikipedia: Johann Jakob Bachofen; Berdyaev, *Destiny of Man*, 62–63.
9. Wheeler, *Latin*, 527; Goosen, *Gemeenskap*, 124–126.

and present. This in turn facilitated a historical consciousness, which in the patriarchal order of classical Greece produced Herodotus and Thucydides, who thereby became the fathers of Western historiography.[10]

The primary religious symbol of matriarchal societies was the Moon, so that we can speak of lunar matriarchy. In contrast, patriarchy was associated with the Sun, so that we can speak of solar patriarchy.[11] Matriarchy thus pertained not only to political rule, but also to religious authority—hence the prevalence of mother-goddesses and priestesses in matriarchal societies. A prominent example of such a deity was the Mesopotamian goddess Ishtar, whose widespread worship only waned with the expansion of early Christianity. Despite the similarity in their names, she should not be confused with the Germanic goddess Eostre (or Ostara), from whom the word Easter would eventually derive, denoting the central festival of the Christian tradition.

With the settlement of the Indo-Europeans in Europe and the Indian subcontinent during the Bronze Age, patriarchal societies became the norm. Again, this applies to both political rule and religious authority. The mother-goddesses and priestesses were gradually replaced by father-gods and male priests, although not without protracted resistance from the female versions and their followers. This occurred, for instance, in the case of the Celts, whose lands extended in a broad swathe across Europe by the third century B.C., from Ireland in the north-west to Asia Minor in the south-east. Although as an Indo-European people the Celts were patriarchal, their socio-political organization was somewhat more complicated, as Hans Günther points out: "Throughout the broad areas under their rule—and the Galatians penetrated as far as Asia Minor—the Celts formed only a thin upper layer holding sway over pre-Indo-European peoples governed by matriarchal family systems, whose linguistic forms deeply influenced the Celtic dialects, and whose spiritual beliefs transformed the original religious attitudes of the Celts."[12]

Of paramount importance in the substitution of matriarchy with patriarchy is the Indo-European concept of a heavenly Father as Supreme Being. The earliest Indo-European name for God was *Dyaus Pitar* (or *Dyeus Pitar*) in Sanskrit, which was in use among the Indo-Aryans by not later than 1500 B.C. In Greek, this Divinity became known as *Zeus Pater*, or

---

10. Goosen, *Gemeenskap*, 121–124.
11. Dugin, *Theory*, 184.
12. Günther, *Religious attitudes*, 4.

Father Zeus, and in Latin as Jupiter, from *Ious Pater*. All these names for the supreme deity were of common origin and bear the same meaning, namely Sky-Father or Heavenly Father. Related to this terminology is the Greek *theos*, the Latin *deus* and the Germanic *tiwas*—all of which means god, or God in the theistic traditions.[13]

Similarly, in the biblical traditions of Judaism and Christianity, Father is one of the names for God. For example, the prophet Isaiah writes: "Look down from heaven, and see from your habitation, holy and glorious. Doubtless you are our Father. You, O Lord, are our Father" (63:15–16). On the other hand, the Hebrew word for the divine Spirit, which took part in the creation of the world (Gen 1:2), is *ruah*, which is a feminine word. To this observation, a leading Orthodox theologian adds that one should not literally apply gender categories to God, for there is no gender in the Godhead. All the biblical names for God are attempts to grasp the transcendent mystery which is beyond all names. Nonetheless, it is incumbent on the Church to preserve biblical God-language, in order to prevent its entire spiritual, theological, and mystical tradition from undergoing irrevocable alteration.[14]

Throughout his earthly ministry, Jesus Christ spoke about a benign heavenly Father who creates all things and cares for them. This is epitomized in the prayer which He taught his followers, beginning with the phrase *Pater hēmōn ho en tois ouranois*, which means 'Our Father who art in the heavens.' Known as the Lord's Prayer, it has from the outset been prayed by the faithful in every Orthodox and Catholic liturgy. Interestingly, the original Greek text gives 'heavens' in the plural and not the singular 'heaven' as in the usual translation of the Lord's Prayer. This is based on the belief that there are various heavenly levels, or heavens, as is suggested by the statement of St Paul that he had at a certain juncture in his life been transported to the third heaven (2 Cor 12:2).

Together with the worship of God as a heavenly Father, a male priesthood developed as a natural corollary. This is especially evident in monotheistic traditions such as Zoroastrianism, Judaism, Christianity, and Islam. In the historic Christian tradition, which has been preserved in Orthodoxy and (in this regard) in Catholicism, all the bishops and priests have from the outset been male. The reason for this is that Christ chose only male disciples to become the first Apostles, who in turn became the first bishops of

---

13. Campbell, *Race and Religion*, 9–10; Wikipedia: *Dyeus*.
14. Alfeyev, *Mystery*, 20.

the Church. And that this preference has nothing to do with 'cultural prejudice' among the early Christians, is evident from the fact that many of Christ's most devoted followers were women. In fact, mainly women attended His crucifixion, and it was to a woman (Mary Magdalene) that the risen Christ first appeared.

In this context, the Traditionalist author Frithjof Schuon writes that woman is the equal of man in respect of sanctity, but not in respect of spiritual functions, adding: "No man can be more holy than the Blessed Virgin, and yet any priest can celebrate Mass [called Liturgy in Orthodoxy] and preach in public, which she could not do." Nonetheless, woman assumes an aspect of Divinity towards man: "her nobility, compounded of beauty and virtue, is for man like a revelation of his own infinite essence" which he would like to attain. Also noteworthy is the statement by the Roman historian Tacitus, that the Germans discerned something sacred and visionary in women. This is even suggested in the German language, in which the Sun (*die Sonne*) is feminine, whereas the Moon (*der Mond*) is masculine.[15]

It is a fact that traditional European society, including pre-modern Christianity, has been mostly patriarchal. Alexander Dugin adds that European society was patriarchal even before the appearance of Christianity (due to the Indo-Europeans settling in much of Europe, as we mentioned earlier). This socio-political reality implies that behind modernity and its conception of gender, stands Western patriarchy which eventually became global patriarchy. It is therefore not surprising that this patriarchy has heavily influenced the structure and political understanding of gender in modernity.[16] However, after several millennia of patriarchy, the Western world has during the twentieth century embarked upon a return to matriarchy, as we will now discuss.

Feminism

Broadly speaking, feminism began as a peaceful movement aimed at securing the right for women to vote in elections on an equal footing with men. Eventually (and perhaps inevitably, since psychic balance is an impossibly difficult state for most humans to attain), feminism became a militant drive to place women in positions of power, while vilifying men who refuse to bow the knee before feminists as being chauvinists.

15. Schuon, *Castes*, 34, 95.
16. Dugin, *Theory*, 184.

The feminist ideology is one of the most auspicious manifestations of liberalism in the modern era. The intimate relation between liberalism and feminism has been stated by Francis Parker Yockey: "Liberalism is, in one word, weakness. It wants every day to be a birthday, Life to be a long party. Liberalism is an escape from hardness into softness, from masculinity into femininity, from History to herd-grazing, from reality into herbivorous dreams, from Destiny into Happiness." Feminism itself is only a means of feminizing man, Yockey adds: "If it makes women man-like, it does so only by transforming man first into a creature whose only concern is with his personal economics and his relation to 'society,' i.e., a woman."[17]

It is noteworthy that the feminist movement arose in male-dominated, liberal Western societies. According to Alexander Dugin, the 'classical' liberalism of eighteenth- and nineteenth-century Europe posited the rational, rich, adult white male as the norm, and even as a natural phenomenon. In time, however, the area of gender increased to include the peasants, the poor, women, and non-white persons. How did this process of social change apply to the case of women? The Russian philosopher explains: "For women, 'manly' characteristics start to be attributed to them: a businesswoman is one who manifests male qualities; white females become 'citizens.' Thus, 'the woman' starts to be thought of as 'the man.' So, liberal feminism, or the aspiration to give women freedom, means to identify a woman as a man and thus equalise them socio-politically, that is, represent a woman as a man socially."[18]

By proclaiming the equal authority of husband and wife in the household, the feminist movement has installed a second steering wheel in the car (symbolically speaking), as an astute business acquaintance in Cape Town remarked towards this author many years ago. Not surprisingly, the domestic car is now dysfunctional due to the presence of two guidance systems. But not to be deterred, the militant feminists have simply assumed sole control of the car, leaving the hapless husband to be the navigator (if he should be so honoured by his master) or often just another passenger in the car.

In the modern West, feminism has also succeeded in militarizing womanhood by having women trained as soldiers on an equal footing with men. As Yockey observes, "And yet what does Liberalism do ultimately to a

---

17. Yockey, *Imperium*, 222–223.
18. Dugin, *Theory*, 185–186.

woman: it puts a uniform on her and calls her a 'soldier.'"[19] Of course, some women have throughout history been willing to fight in order to protect their families and homes, and they deserve due credit for their courage. A prominent example thereof in the modern era is the large number of female partisans in the Soviet Union, who took part in fighting the fascist invaders during the Great Patriotic War (1941-45). Large numbers of Russian and Ukrainian women paid with their lives as a result, and many were honoured by the Soviet state for their sacrifices.

However, the current liberal-feminist militarization of Western women is a different matter altogether, since they are being trained together with their male colleagues primarily for the invasion of other countries, even though it is presented, predictably so, as 'national defense.' This undermining of the fundamental male-female polarity of humankind can only harbour disastrous effects. In Yockey's words, "Liberalistic tampering with sexual polarity only wreaks havoc on the souls of individuals, confusing and distorting them, but the man-woman and the woman-man it creates are both subject to the higher Destiny of History."[20] These terms, man-woman and woman-man, are indeed an accurate depiction of the current state of affairs in much of the Western world, pertaining to both appearance and behaviour—all of which are media-promoted and judicially enforced.

With his keen perception of modern society, Friedrich Nietzsche already in the late nineteenth century foresaw the coming masculinization of Western women. He concedes that in the more civilized European countries women could in a few centuries be educated to become men; not in the sexual sense, but in every other sense. When that occurs, women will have assumed all the male virtues and strengths, and of course also all the male weaknesses and vices. But during the intermediate stage, the real male emotion will be anger over the fact that all the arts and sciences will be overrun by dilettantism, bewildering chatter will talk philosophy to death, politics will be more fantastic and partisan than ever, and society will be in complete dissolution because women, who used to be the guardians of the old customs, will be intent on standing outside custom in every way.[21] This last prediction has indeed been fulfilled in the modern feminist movement, with militant women often taking the lead in the ultra-liberal assault on civilized values. The liberal-feminist project to turn women into men was

19. Yockey, *Imperium*, 223.
20. Yockey, *Imperium*, 223.
21. Nietzsche, *Human*, 194–195.

also ridiculed by Nietzsche: "When woman possesses masculine virtues, she is enough to make you run away. When she possesses no masculine virtues, she herself runs away."[22]

By the twenty-first century, most Western countries have become dominated by feminism, at least in the public sphere. This pertains to party-politics, journalism, education, and social services, to name some prominent examples. These are all areas of life that exert considerable influence on a population, which explains the desire to control them among those who are ideologically driven, such as liberals and feminists. For example, all British schools are required by law to participate in the promotion of so-called 'British values.' These 'values' include 'alternative lifestyles' such as homo-, bi-, and trans-sexuality. Interestingly, the only reported public opposition to this enforced degeneracy has come from Muslim parents.

Another conspicuous manifestation of feminism in the late twentieth century has been the appearance of female bishops and priestesses in the Anglican denomination, which has thereby sealed its long-developing rejection of the Christian tradition. This innovation has been accompanied by the Anglican acceptance of homosexual 'marriages,' against the clear teaching of the Bible and in violation of the laws of nature. That this media-promoted and legally-sanctioned practice is incompatible with the Christian faith is clear from its unequivocal condemnation by St Paul: "For this reason God gave them up to vile passions. For even their women exchanged the natural use for what is against nature. Likewise also the men, leaving the natural use of the woman, burned in their lust for one another, men with men committing what is shameful, and receiving in themselves the penalty of their error which was due" (Rom 1:26–27).[23]

Even outside of religious considerations, the male-female polarity is one of the most fundamental aspects of cosmic reality, so that any rejection thereof (as in same-sex unions) represents a revolt against the natural order. However, the departure from Christianity by the Anglicans is not really surprising, given the fact that this denomination was conceived and born in the adultery and bloodlust of a tyrannical Tudor monarch of the sixteenth century.

---

22. Nietzsche, *Twilight*, 8.

23. See also the powerful 'Homily against homosexuality' by the Greek theologian John Chrysostom, building on the mentioned Pauline text, at Wikipedia: John Chrysostom.

So far, the Orthodox and Catholic churches have faithfully preserved the all-male clergy as inherited from the earliest Church, as well as the practice of heterosexual marriage which is treated as a sacrament. The historical practice of only men holding the office of priest or bishop is based on the concept of spiritual fatherhood, as Hilarion Alfeyev has pointed out. A woman can be a mother, wife or daughter, but she cannot be a father. And while motherhood is in no way inferior to fatherhood, its mission and vocation are different. Therefore, if the Church were to lose this fatherhood it would become a family without a father. In addition, the Christian family is viewed as a smaller version of the Church, so that the husband is the head of the family. Again, that this has nothing to with inequality is evident from St Paul's teaching that the wife should submit to her husband in all things, while the husband should love his wife as himself and be willing to give himself up for her (Eph 5:22–28). This text is read in every Orthodox wedding service, thus confirming the Christian view of marriage as the love of man and woman paralleling the love of Christ and the Church.[24]

Women of God

Lest the foregoing disputation against feminism be misconstrued as an expression of misogyny, we hasten to emphasize the vital role that has been played by numerous God-fearing women over the ages. The most eminent of them all is the Virgin Mary, who is venerated as the Mother of God in the Orthodox and Catholic traditions, on account of her giving birth to Jesus Christ. In a beautiful Orthodox hymn, she is praised as more exalted than the Cherubim and the Seraphim (the highest levels of the celestial beings). Curiously, as Hilarion Alfeyev observes, the Protestant denominations that have entrusted the priestly functions to women neither venerate the Mother of God nor pray to her. Nonetheless, if fatherhood is realized in the Church in the episcopate and the priesthood, motherhood is personified *per excellence* in the Mother of God.[25]

Although she was only a teenage girl, Mary did not hesitate to submit to the will of God when the Archangel Gabriel announced to her that she would be overshadowed by the Spirit of God and bear the Son of God. "Let it be with me according to Thy word," she replied (Luke 1:38), undoubtedly aware of the stigma that would attach to her for showing the signs of

24. Alfeyev, *Mystery*, 107–108; Wikipedia: Marriage in the Eastern Orthodox Church
25. Alfeyev, *Mystery*, 109.

pregnancy while still unmarried. Much honour is also due to her fiancée, Joseph, for his unwavering love towards Mary and his courage in accepting her as his wife under these demanding circumstances, which endangered both of them according to the legal provisions of the Torah (the Jewish Law). By the grace of God, Christ was thus born of a Virgin and grew up as the God-man in order to fulfil his cosmic destiny, namely to reconcile the created order with its Creator.[26]

Further examples of God-fearing women venerated as Christian saints are not hard to find. Mary Magdalene travelled with Jesus of Nazareth and his disciples, and became the first person to whom the risen Christ appeared; Thekla of Iconium was a traveling companion and fellow preacher of St Paul on his missionary journeys; Anastasia of Rome was brutally tortured and beheaded during the persecution of Christians under the emperor Decius; Catherine of Alexandria was fiercely tortured and beheaded at the age of eighteen, after converting hundreds of people to Christianity; Nina of Georgia played a key role in the establishment of Christianity in that Caucasian land; Macrina of Caesarea profoundly influenced her brothers, the famous theologians Basil of Caesarea and Gregory of Nyssa, with her sanctity; Helena of York, mother of the emperor Constantine the Great, discovered the cross of Christ during a pilgrimage to Palestine; Mary of Egypt became a Christian while visiting Jerusalem after an extremely immoral life in Alexandria, followed by half a century of solitary living in the Jordanian desert as penance; Genevieve of Paris led a mass prayer which caused the Huns of Attila to withdraw from the city; Brigid of Kildare founded several convents and became a patron saint of Ireland; Olga of Kiev became a Christian during a visit to Constantinople, thus setting an example to her grandson Vladimir I, who adopted Orthodox Christianity as religion for the Russian lands; and Ludmila of Bohemia, a princess who played an active role in the establishment of the Christian religion in that land and was eventually strangled to death on the orders of her daughter-in-law. Several of these saints are honoured in Orthodoxy with the title of Equal to the Apostles. And that this phenomenon of God-fearing women has not remained behind in the distant past is amply demonstrated in the lives of modern saints such as Xenia of St Petersburg and Matrona of Moscow.[27]

---

26. The process of cosmic reconciliation brought about by Christ has been brilliantly described by Maximus the Confessor; see Lossky, *Mystical Theology*, 137.

27. See the website OrthodoxWiki for details of their lives.

Conclusion

In the final analysis, feminism should be rejected as being an assault on femininity, just as male chauvinism should be rejected as being a distortion of masculinity. We contend that feminism and male chauvinism are two sides of the same coin, namely an unbalanced view of gender. Just as chauvinism views men as innately superior to women, so feminism views women as innately superior to men. Both views should be condemned as being unbalanced, if not infantile. Between the poles of feminism and chauvinism lies realism, which accepts that men and women are fundamentally different although sharing the same human nature. In other words, men and women are different in function yet equal in value. We leave a final thought to that great psychologist among philosophers, Friedrich Nietzsche, who wrote: "The perfect woman is a higher type of human than the perfect man, and also something much more rare."[28]

---

28. Nietzsche, *Human*, 185.

Aristocracy and Democracy

THE TERM 'POLITICS' is derived from the Greek noun *polis*, meaning city-state. In the Hellenic understanding, politics is a collective striving to establish a community whose existential purpose (*telos*) is not limited to the management of needs (as is the case in most of the modern world), but is rather an attempt to live in harmony with the principle of truth. In other words, Nicolas Laos writes, "the *telos* of politics is to help humanity to exist authentically through and within a social system."[1] Moreover, since true being (i.e., the way of eternity and immortality) depends on participation in the *logos*, if a human being seeks to be immortal he or she should imitate the *logos* by organizing society "as an event of participation in the order, harmony, and decency of the relations that constitute the eternal cosmic beauty. This is the essence of politics and the way of the ancient Greek *polis*."[2] According to this reasoning, the practice of politics may not be divorced from the notions of truth, order, harmony, and beauty.

In much of the modern world it is commonly accepted that a democratic government is always and everywhere preferable to an aristocratic one. Before assessing the validity of this assumption, let us consider the etymology of these terms. 'Aristocracy' is derived from the Greek *aristos*, which means best, and *kratein*, which means to rule. 'Democracy' is derived from *dēmos*, which means the common people, and *kratein*.[3] Therefore, in the literal sense of the words, aristocracy means rule by the best, while democracy means rule by the common people—or, less flatteringly, rule by the mob (in Greek, *hoi polloi*, 'the many'). In the memorable words of Oscar Wilde: "Democracy means simply the bludgeoning of the people by the people for the people."[4] It has also been remarked that the mob is the

---

1. Laos, *Metaphysics*, 1–2.
2. Laos, *Metaphysics*, 3–4.
3. LSJ, 102, 158, 391.
4. https://www.brainyquote.com/quotes/oscar_wilde_124808

stratum of a population which is totally incapable of cultural attainment; it is therefore referred to as *profanum vulgus* in Latin, meaning the common masses or herd.[5]

Plato's Political Philosophy

The first Hellenic thinker to undertake a systematic investigation into various forms of government was Plato, who thereby became the founder of political philosophy in the Western world. This has been achieved mainly through his dialogue *Politeia* (usually translated as *Republic*), which is subtitled 'On Justice.' In this work, Plato analyzes a variety of governmental forms in terms of their contribution to justice or their deviation therefrom. Employing his mentor Socrates as primary speaker, Plato first outlines the ideal state, which is an aristocracy ruled by philosophers who had received lengthy and rigorous training, enabling them to rule with wisdom and justice. He then proceeds to describe four types of imperfect society, namely timarchy, oligarchy, democracy, and tyranny.

Before considering Plato's teaching on the ideal state, we should note his view of justice (*dikaiosynē*) in the state and the individual. The four main qualities of the state are wisdom, courage, self-discipline, and justice (*Pol*, 427e). As Desmond Lee comments in his translation of this seminal dialogue, this is the first appearance in Hellenic literature of the four cardinal virtues.[6] The correlation between state and individual is then affirmed by Socrates: "We are bound to admit that the elements and traits that belong to a state must also exist in the individuals that compose it" (*Pol*, 435e). Therefore, justice in the individual corresponds with justice in the state: he is wise and brave due to his reason and spiritedness, respectively; he is disciplined to the extent that spiritedness and appetite are subordinated to reason; he is just on account of the harmony which exists when all the elements perform their proper function; and he is unjust in the absence of such harmony (*Pol*, 441c–d).[7] Thus, for Plato, "the cosmic, civic, and individual orders are naturally governed by one and the same law of justice; and among the accepted senses of 'just' is that of 'civilized.'"[8]

---

5. Yockey, *Imperium*, 259.
6. Lee, *Republic*, 197.
7. Lee, *Republic*, 218.
8. Coomaraswamy, *Literacy*, 145.

However, that justice in the Platonic conception has nothing to do with equality has been affirmed by the Christian Neoplatonist thinker Dionysius the Areopagite. In the *Divine Names* he writes that "the divine righteousness in this is really true righteousness, because it assigns to all things what is proper according to the rank of each of the beings, and preserves the nature of each in its proper order and power" (*DN*, VIII.7). As Eric Perl comments: "Justice, properly understood, means not equality but due proportion, a place for everything and everything in its place."[9] Clearly, this balanced view of justice is worlds removed from the modern Western obsession with 'equality,' so much so that in a country such as Britain there is actually an Equality Act, of which the provisions are enforced by the judicial system. In practice, this means submission to the irrational dictates of so-called political correctness.

Plato's view of the just relation between the state and the individual has been summarized as follows. For the individual, justice as highest virtue exists primarily in the harmony among the different components of the soul, so that all are brought under the rule of reason. Likewise, for the state, justice as supreme virtue exists in the harmonic whole among the different classes comprising the state. The guarantor of justice in the state is the philosopher-ruler, whose knowledge of the Ideas is realized in his or her own life and in the guidance of the state. Eminent among the Ideas is the Idea of the Good, which manifests in the loyalty, the good morals, and the binding traditions according to which the guardians and the workers live. And as far as the later concept of rights and freedom of the individual are concerned, we could say that it lies in the latter's rightful place in the state as determined by his or her abilities. In this harmonic schema, the goodness of the state and the goodness of the individual goes hand in hand.[10]

The Three Classes

In the *Politeia*, Plato distinguishes between three classes of citizens in the state, (broadly speaking) corresponding to the three levels of the soul: the reason, the higher emotions, and the appetites. The highest class in the state are the rulers (*archontes*), whose power is absolute. Their primary virtue is wisdom (*sophia*), by means of which the state must be guided and formed. The second class are the auxiliaries (*phylakes*), whose duty is to defend the

---

9. Perl, *Theophany*, 73.
10. Dreyer, *Wysbegeerte*, 116–117.

state. Their virtues are courage, bravery, and manliness (*andreia*). The lowest class are the workers (*dēmiourgoi*), which include all who are neither rulers nor auxiliaries, for example, farmers, artisans, traders, teachers, and artists. Self-control and moderation (*sōphrosyne*) are virtues of the workers. However, it should be kept in mind that Plato does not limit any of the mentioned virtues to one class.[11]

Plato's division of society closely follows the traditional Indo-European concept of three social functions, namely priests, warriors, and cultivators. In addition to the guardians (i.e., rulers and auxiliaries), Plato actually mentions a variety of socio-economic functions: producers, merchants, sailors, retail traders, and manual laborers.[12] The latter are described as those who have no great mental powers to contribute, but whose physical strength makes them suitable for manual labor for which they are paid wages (*Pol*, 371e). These manual laborers are the 'wage-slaves' of an industrial society and the equivalent of the Indian class of *Shudras*, the fourth level in the hierarchy of castes.[13]

The mentioned social functions are derived from the principle of doing what it is ours to do, Plato reasons, which is precisely the principle of justice. Since a city and a human being are called just or unjust by the same standards, justice is realized when each of the several parts of the community performs its own task. And since people have different natures, everyone is bound to perform that social service for which his or her nature is best adapted. In this way, the real needs of society will be satisfied in the best way possible. Conversely, if a producer or merchant tries to enter the warrior class, or if a warrior tries to enter the legislative class, or if a single person tries to do all of these at the same time, it will bring about the ruin of the state, thus being injustice (*Pol*, 433a–434c).[14]

The Traditionalist author Frithof Schuon has pointed out that there exists a hierarchy of mental types: the contemplative or sacerdotal, the combative or princely, the practical or industrious, and the obedient or loyal. Of course, these predispositions can always combine; and it also does not mean that the three superior types are devoid of loyalty, but that the fourth type often has this one quality only. This psychological schema is eminently compatible with both the Indian caste system and Plato's social functions.

11. Dreyer, *Wysbegeerte*, 111–112.
12. Haudry, *Indo-Europeans*, 38–39; Lee, *Republic*, 119.
13. Coomaraswamy, *Civilization*, 147.
14. Coomaraswamy, *Literacy*, 146; Perry, *Treasury*, 337.

Moreover, Plato's view of the human being as consisting of an immortal soul (i.e., its rational level), two parts of a mortal soul (i.e., its spirited and appetitive levels), as well as a body, correlates with the normal number of four castes that must cooperate for the benefit of the whole community.[15]

According to Plato, the ideal state is ruled by a class of guardians, which is divided into rulers and auxiliaries. While the rulers exercise supreme authority in the ideal state, for which they receive rigorous training, the auxiliaries perform executive, military, and police duties as ordered by the rulers. It is important that the guardians are not entitled to possess private property or have a family life, since their happiness lies in service to the whole community.[16] In addition, the guardians have the duty to ensure that extremes of wealth and poverty are avoided in the third class (i.e., the workers and producers), which can possess property. The primary task of the guardians is to maintain the education system unchanged, Plato insists, *"for on education everything else depends, and it is an illusion to imagine that mere legislation without it can effect anything of consequence."*[17] However, given the pervasive reality of human stupidity combined with arrogance, Plato's wise advice on the primacy of education over legislation will probably remain neglected.

Education

In the main, Hellenic education had three subdivisions: reading and writing, physical education (or gymnastics), and literary education which was called *mousikē*. The latter included poetry for recitation and music to be played. Socrates held that elementary mathematics, such as arithmetic and geometry, should be included in elementary education. The purpose of primary and secondary education is training of the character, as well as enabling moral and aesthetic judgement.[18] This elementary education lasted until age eighteen and was followed by two years' military training. Anyone who is familiar with what goes through as 'education' in some countries today, will realize how inferior it is to classical Hellenic education. This is perhaps an opportune point at which to note Nietzsche's aphorism on the size of an education system: "The education system in large states will

---

15. Schuon, *Divine*, 85; Coomaraswamy, *Civilization*, 9.
16. Lee, *Republic*, 177, 183.
17. Lee, *Republic*, 187 (italics ours).
18. Lee, *Republic*, 129, 161, 349.

always be mediocre at best, for the same reason that the cooking in large kitchens is at best mediocre."[19] In other words, when quantity prevails over quality, then education (and much else) will be mediocre.

Plato deserves lasting credit for advocating compulsory education for all boys and girls, which was a revolutionary concept in his era. This should take place under control of the state, with all three classes receiving the same elementary education. The workers then receive further training in their vocations, while the guardians continue with a more theoretical education as preparation for the study of dialectic, or philosophy. Through dialectic a knowledge of the eternal Forms, or Ideas, may be obtained. Although the education of the workers leads to a lower level of knowledge, namely opinion (*doxa*), this should not be held in disdain, for it equips the workers with the skills needed for their work as service and it cultivates a sense of loyalty to the state. Finally, only the rulers proceed to the highest level of study and true knowledge (*epistēmē*), which is knowledge of the Ideas.[20] And since dialectic is the coping-stone of the educational system, Socrates cautions, it is not to be introduced at any earlier stage (*Pol*, 534e).

As one would expect, the education of the philosopher-ruler is described in detail by Plato. In addition to the elementary education as mentioned, the candidate has to study no less than five mathematical disciplines, namely arithmetic, plane and solid geometry, astronomy, and harmonics. These studies are aimed at the training of mind, with the vision of the Good as ultimate objective.[21] In the *Politeia*, it is sketched as follows:

i. Arithmetic draws the mind upwards and forces it to argue about numbers in themselves, instead of being confined by discussions relating to visible or tangible objects (525d);

ii. Plane geometry also draws the mind upwards to the truth, and also has the incidental advantage of being useful in war, for example in military manoeuvres (526d, 527b);

iii. Solid geometry entails a progression from plane geometry to solid bodies, i.e., from two to three dimensions, for example cubes (528b);

iv. Astronomy is solid geometry in motion; it leads the mind from the earth to the heavens (528d, 529a). Although the stars that decorate the sky are the most perfect of visible things, Socrates adds, they are still

---

19. Nietzsche, *Human*, 201.
20. Dreyer, *Wysbegeerte*, 114–115.
21. Lee, *Republic*, 326.

inferior to the true realities, i.e., "the relative velocities, in pure numbers and perfect figures, of the orbits and what they carry in them, which are perceptible to reason and thought but not visible to the eye" (529c–d);

v. Harmonics: Socrates agrees with the Pythagoreans that just as our eyes are made for astronomy, so our ears are made for harmony. Astronomy and harmonics are therefore sister sciences (530d).

The immensely demanding training of those who will become rulers is evident not only from the content of the curriculum, but also from its duration. Between the ages of twenty and thirty, selected candidates undertake the mathematical disciplines; after further selection, it is followed by five years of dialectic; and this is followed by fifteen years of practical experience as guardians, while continuing the study of dialectics. Finally, after fifty years of education and training, those who have survived all these tests are fully qualified philosopher-rulers.[22] They will spend the bulk of their time in philosophy, and by rotation will do their duty as rulers. They will rule, not for the sake of honour, but as a matter of necessity (*Pol*, 540b). Contrary to the modernist view that Plato was a misogynist, we find Socrates stating that some of the philosopher-rulers will be women, if they (like the male rulers) possess the requisite natural capacities (*Pol*, 540c).

Imperfect Societies

Following his delineation of the education of the philosopher-rulers, Plato undertakes a survey of various imperfect societies. These are summarized by Desmond Lee as follows:

a. Timarchy (or timocracy), which is effectively a military aristocracy, of which Crete and Sparta are mentioned as examples in the *Politeia*;

b. Oligarchy (literally, rule of the few; from the Greek *oligos*, 'few'), of which wealth is the criterion of merit; it thus means rule by the wealthy, with an underclass of criminals and malcontents;

c. Democracy, of which the salient characteristics are equality of political opportunity and unbridled freedom for the individual, as exemplified particularly in the case of Athens;

---

22. Dreyer, *Wysbegeerte*, 115; Lee, *Republic*, 347.

d. Tyranny, spawned by the conflict between rich and poor in a democracy, which leads to a tyrant's rise as popular champion; it is further characterized by the tyrant's private army and the growth of oppression.[23]

In terms of Plato's political philosophy, the modern Western world ought to be viewed as a combination of oligarchy and democracy. On the one hand, its economies are dominated by large corporations, which have the financial power to decisively influence the politicians serving their interests. On the other hand, its societies are encouraged by the mass media (which mostly also serve the interests of the financial elites) to indulge in extremes of libertinism, naturally in the name of 'freedom' and 'rights.' Interestingly, as far as oligarchy is concerned, Socrates remarked that "Love of money and adequate self-discipline in its citizens are two things that can't co-exist in any society; one or the other must be neglected" (*Pol*, 555c).

Plato had a personal reason for holding a dim view of democracy, in addition to his customary reasons of principle. It was the authorities of democratic Athens, after all, who had condemned his beloved mentor Socrates to death, on charges of having corrupted the city's youth and of impiety towards the gods. It is admitted, nonetheless, that its diversity of characters, like the different colors in a patterned dress, makes democracy appear as the most attractive of all societies (*Pol*, 557c). However, when one delves beneath the glittering surface a rather different picture emerges. As Socrates remarks, "In democracy, there is no compulsion either to exercise authority if you are capable of it, or to subject to authority if you don't want to; you needn't fight is there is a war, or you can wage a private war in peacetime if you don't like peace; and if there is any law that debars you from political or judicial office, you will none the less take either if they come your way. It's a wonderfully pleasant way of carrying on in the short run" (*Pol*, 557e–558a).

Further indictments of democracy follow in the *Politeia*. For instance, democrats look down on the high principles laid down for the ideal state; thereby ignoring the reality that except for those with exceptional gifts, no one could grow into a good man without upbringing in a good environment and trained in good habits (558b). Ignorant of principles, "Democracy with a grandiose gesture sweeps all this away and doesn't mind what the habits and background of its politicians are; provided they profess themselves the

---

23. Lee, *Republic*, 359, 366, 368, 373, 382.

people's friends, they are duly honoured" (558b–c). Accordingly, democracy is "an agreeable anarchic form of society, with plenty of variety, which treats all men as equal, whether they are equal or not" (558b).

Always striving to be fair and balanced in judgment, Plato describes the democratic character as versatile, but nonetheless lacking in principle. Moreover, the democrat makes no distinction between necessary and unnecessary desires.[24] As explained by Socrates, necessary desires are those we can't avoid, or whose satisfaction benefits us. In contrast, unnecessary desires are those we can get rid of with practice, and whose presence either does us no good or positive harm (*Pol*, 558e, 559a). It is not difficult to see that the media-driven consumerist culture of the present era entails mostly such unnecessary desires.

Stages of Socio-political Degeneration

In Plato's understanding, the imperfect forms of government succeed each other according to their inner dynamic. Consequently, just as the excessive desire for wealth leads to the downfall of oligarchy, so the excessive desire for liberty leads to the downfall of democracy (*Pol*, 562b–c). Extremes of liberty occur, of which various examples are mentioned by Socrates (562d–563b):

i. Rulers behave like subjects and subjects like rulers, in both private and public life;

ii. Children and parents change places, so that parents stand in awe before their children, while the children do not respect their parents;

iii. Teachers fear and pander to their pupils, who in turn despise their teachers;

iv. The young imitate their elders and set themselves up against them, while the elders ape the young and mix with them on terms of easy fellowship;[25]

v. Slaves have the same liberty as their owners;

vi. There is complete equality in relations between the sexes.

24. Lee, *Republic*, 377.
25. As remarked by Nietzsche: "Young people are arrogant because they go about with their own kind, each of whom is nothing, but wishes to be important" (*Human*, 316).

In the final stage of democratic excess, Socrates adds, the slightest vestige of restraint is resented as intolerable. This degeneration manifests as a disregard for all laws, whether written or unwritten. The resultant anarchy then becomes the root from which tyranny springs (*Pol*, 563d–e). 'The slightest vestige of restraint is resented as intolerable'—is this not an apt description of the ideological disease of ultra-liberalism, which has infected most of the modern Western world? Those affected by this cultural aberration apparently believe that they have the right to behave exactly as they please, without any consideration of its effects on others. The predictable result of this unwholesome attitude towards life, which is relentlessly promoted by the Western mass media, is anti-social behaviour that inevitably and negatively affects those who respect traditional values such as responsibility, discipline, moderation, and fairness. Regarding the importance of moderation, it was observed by Friedrich Nietzsche that free-thinking, when it has become a quality of character, produces moderation in behaviour. It does so by reducing covetousness, focussing energy on the advancement of spiritual ends, and showing the danger of sudden changes.[26]

It remains for Plato to explain how tyranny arises from democracy. First, a popular leader emerges from the escalating social chaos and leads the mob against the property owners. Next, he demands a personal bodyguard which the mob grants him, because they fear for his safety. Finally, he overthrows all opposition and grasps the reins of state as complete tyrant (*Pol*, 566a–d). A striking example of this transition from democracy to tyranny in the modern era is the rise to power of Adolf Hitler, whose propaganda machine presented him as the champion of the German working class during the socio-economic chaos of the Great Depression (1929–33). Initially the storm-troopers of the SA (*Sturmabteilung*, 'Storm Detachment'), served as his personal bodyguard, but after its leadership was eliminated on Hitler's orders in 1934 the more fanatical SS (*Schutzstaffel*, 'Protection Squadron') assumed that role. In the meantime, within months of his National Socialist party coming to power early in 1933, all other parties were banned and Hitler became the undisputed ruler of Germany, with all of the destructive consequences that would follow for Europe from 1939 onwards.

According to the traditional Indo-European understanding, there is a certain inevitability to this historical sequence of socio-political degeneration. In this regard, the French linguist Jean Haudry mentions the

---

26. Nietzsche, *Human*, 210.

classical Indian and Hellenic views of the course of human history. Having gone through golden, silver, and bronze ages, humankind is now in the iron age with its emphasis on labor, production, and reproduction. Haudry quotes from a work by the historian Jean-Pierre Vernant in illustration: "The picture of the peasant infatuated by *Hybris* [a Greek term meaning wanton violence, riotousness, insolence, etc.],[27] characteristic of the present age of iron in its decline, represents essentially a revolt against order, a topsy-turvy world in which every hierarchy, every rule of life, every value is turned upside down." Haudry adds that the Germanic and Celtic peoples also conceived the end of the world in this way, reflecting the picture drawn by Hesiod in his *Works and Days*. Furthermore, "Decadence and subversion go hand in hand, and have as common principle the degradation of character. The process is exactly parallel to that described by Plato, *Republic* 547 ff., with reference to the Hesiodic myth: it is by a progressive deterioration of character that man descends from aristocratic 'timocracy' (government of honour) to plutocratic oligarchy and thence, by the operation of envy, to democracy, a regime of egalitarianism and anarchy which makes tyranny inevitable, as only this latter is capable of ensuring the survival of the community in the state of degradation into which it has fallen."[28] In summary, we could say that freedom without discipline leads to anarchy, while discipline without freedom leads to tyranny.

Later Thoughts

In a later dialogue, *Politikos* (translated as 'Statesman'), Plato presents the statesman as a possessor of specialist knowledge of how to rule justly, in the best interests of the citizens of the city-state (*polis*). As John Cooper comments, this dialogue reflects Plato's 'second thoughts' on politics, which appear to be somewhat different from the theory of philosopher-rulers (as advocated in the *Politeia*). Moreover, it anticipates the system of laws and government in the *Laws* (Greek title: *Nomoi*), which is Plato's longest work and the product of his last years.[29] Therein the philosopher argues that the laws of the state should be supreme, with both rulers and ordinary citizens subject thereto. These laws include not only those promulgated by the authorities, but also the moral and religious norms. Such a body of laws

27. LSJ, 723.
28. Haudry, *Indo-Europeans*, 35–36.
29. Cooper, *Plato*, 294–295.

functions as a sacred guidance, as Plato describes it, leading all citizens into goodness, and thereby establishing order and justice in the state.[30]

In the *Laws*, Plato also suggests that the laws of a free, self-governing state should have 'preambles' to explain the purposes for which they are instituted, since commands backed by threats are not appropriate to a free person (Book IV). An elaborate argument is presented to prove the existence of the gods and to establish a law forbidding the denial of their due reverence, as well as appropriate punishments for transgressions (Book X). Here Plato again finds himself in agreement with Pythagoras, who taught that we should "first worship the Immortal Gods, as they are established and ordained by the Law" (*Golden Verses*, 1). It is noteworthy that Plato's Academy was engaged not only in higher education and research, but also in giving concrete advice on laws and constitutions. The *Laws* should therefore be read for its theoretical ideas as well its practical applications.[31]

Moreover, in the same dialogue Plato proposes a mixed form of government in order to prevent the evils of tyranny, the powerful rich (in a plutocracy), and the masses (in extreme forms of democracy). In such a mixed state, the opposing powers are combined and brought into balance with each other. These include a ruler, but one subject to the law in order to prevent tyranny. It also includes a free people, but similarly subject to the law in order to prevent the arising of unbridled masses, such as those that dragged Athens into the abyss. Plato's later political philosophy furthermore allows for the private possession of property, subject to strict rules; permits monogamous marriage for all, again strictly regulated by law; suggests a more differentiated division of labor, including slavery; and emphasizes the supreme importance of religion for morality and hence the good order of the state.[32]

It has been convincingly argued that the difference between Plato's views of the state in the *Politeia* on the one hand, and the *Statesman* and the *Laws* on the other, does not involve a change of mind, as some commentators have asserted, but is in fact attributable to Plato's metaphysics. The state of the *Politeia* is the Idea-state, or the state as it is supposed to be. In contrast, the state of the *Statesman* and the *Laws* is the deficient resemblance of the Idea-state; in other words, the state existing in the empirical reality. And just as the sensible world always remains deficient in comparison to

30. Dreyer, *Wysbegeerte*, 118.
31. Cooper, *Plato*, 1318–1319.
32. Dreyer, *Wysbegeerte*, 118–119.

the intelligible world, so the empirical state always falls short when compared to the ideal state.[33]

Aristotle's Political Philosophy

Plato's most famous student, Aristotle, opens his work titled *Politics* by declaring that the state is the highest form of community and that it aims at the highest good (1252a).[34] It is also significant that Aristotle applies his well-known insistence on final causality (i.e., that all things come to be for a certain end or purpose; in Greek, *telos*) to the state. He argues that the state came into existence out of earlier communities (such as families and towns) for the sake of a good life. The state is therefore just as natural as the earlier forms of society, for it is the end (or purpose) of them, and the nature of a thing is its end. Aristotle concludes: "Besides, the final cause and end of a thing is the best, and to be self-sufficing is the end and the best. Hence it is evident that the state is a creation of nature, and that man is by nature a political animal (*zōon politikon*)" (*Pol* I, 1252b–1253a).

That man is the ultimate political animal (more so than other gregarious animals) is related by Aristotle to his power of speech. Although voice is found in other animals, for example in communicating experiences of pleasure or pain, only man has been gifted by nature with the power of speech. This capacity is intended, Aristotle continues, to set forth the expedient and the inexpedient, and likewise the just and the unjust. Consequently, humans alone have a sense of good and evil, and it is the association of living beings who possess this sense that constitutes a family and a state (*Pol* I, 1253a). In addition, Aristotle views man as a rational being striving towards knowledge and virtue. Such a specifically human existence is only possible in the state, which is therefore the highest realization of human rationality.[35]

The foregoing reasoning leads Aristotle to famously declare that in order to live alone, one has to be an animal or a god: "But he who is unable to live in society, or who has no need because he is sufficient for himself, must be either a beast or a god: he is no part of a state" (*Pol* I, 1253a). Much later, Nietzsche added that there is yet a third alternative for living outside

---

33. Dreyer, *Wysbegeerte*, 117–118.

34. In this brief survey of Aristotle's political philosophy, we have relied much on the useful summaries provided by Benjamin Jowett in his translation of the *Politics*.

35. Dreyer, *Wysbegeerte*, 145.

society. In *Twilight of the Idols*, he writes: "Aristotle says that in order to live alone, a man must be either an animal or a god. The third alternative is lacking: a man must be both – a philosopher."[36] Moreover, for Aristotle communal living depends on justice. He writes, "A social instinct is implanted in all men by nature, and yet he who first founded the state was the greatest of benefactors. *For man, when perfected, is the best of animals, but, when separated from law and justice, is the worst of all.* But justice is the bond of men in states, for the administration of justice, which is the determination of what is just, is the principle of order in political society" (*Pol*, I.1253a; italics ours).

Forms of Government

In Book III of the *Politics*, Aristotle classifies forms of government according to their commitment to the common well-being, or their failure therein. A distinction is first made between true governments which aim at the common interest, and deviant governments which regard only the interests of the rulers. This basic division is then subdivided according to the numbers involved in ruling, so that the following schema appears:

a. True forms: monarchy (one ruler), aristocracy (a few rulers), and timocracy (many rulers);

b. Deviant forms: tyranny (one ruler), oligarchy (a few rulers), and democracy (many rulers).[37]

For Aristotle the difference between oligarchy and democracy lies not only in the numerical proportion of the rulers to the ruled. There is also an economic difference: oligarchy is the rule of the rich, whereas democracy is the rule of the poor (*Pol* III, Chapter 8). This view is reiterated in Book IV of the same work, in which Aristotle notes that in a democracy the many are also the poor, whereas in an oligarchy the few are also the wealthy. Nonetheless, both oligarchy and democracy are viewed by him as important forms of government, with their internal variations arising from differences in the character of the rich and the poor by whom they are ruled (Chapter 3). The worst kind of democracy, Aristotle continues, is that in which all offices are open to all, and the 'will of the people' overrides all law.

---

36. Nietzsche, *Twilight*, 5.
37. Ross, *Aristotle*, 258–259.

On the other hand, the worst kind of oligarchy is that in which offices are hereditary and their holders are uncontrolled by law. In contrast to both oligarchy and democracy stands aristocracy, in which (strictly speaking) only the best men are citizens. Aristotle suggests that many so-called aristocracies are really examples of timocracy, which represents a compromise between democracy and oligarchy (*Pol* IV, Chapters 4, 5, 7 and 8).

What is the best state for Aristotle? He argues that the average city-state (*polis*) is best served when the middle class holds power, thereby achieving a mean between the rule of rich and poor (i.e., oligarchy and democracy). As a matter of fact, Aristotle writes, stable government is only possible where the middle class exceeds one, or both, of the others (*Pol* IV, 296b). This applies also to cases where democracy and/or oligarchy must be accommodated, since no government can succeed without the support of the rich and/or the many (*Pol* IV, Chapters 11 and 12).

Aristotle further remarks that every city-state is composed of quality and quantity: "By quality I mean freedom, wealth, education, good birth, and by quantity, superiority of numbers. Quality may exist in one of the classes which make up the state, and quantity in the other. For example, the meanly-born may be more in number than the well-born, or the poor than the rich, yet they may not so much exceed in quantity as they fall short in quality; and therefore, there must be a comparison of quantity and quality" (*Pol* IV, 1296b). This passage by Aristotle has been related to the traditional Indo-European tripartite division of society into priests/rulers, warriors, and producers. Jean Haudry contends that the former two functions pertain to the world of quality, since they depended on a small elite; whereas the third function belongs to the domain of quantity, since it concerns the masses of 'commoners' and the plenteous supply of material goods.[38]

We should also note that the rule of law is of paramount importance to Aristotle. The maintenance of good laws is vital, for on it depends stability of government and the good order of the state.[39] He writes: "And the rule of the law ... is preferable to that of any individual. On the same principle, even if it be better for certain individuals to govern, they should be made only guardians and ministers of the law. Therefore he who bids the law rule may be deemed to bid God and Reason alone rule, but he who bids man rule adds an element of the beast; for desire is a wild beast, and passion

38. Haudry, *Indo-Europeans*, 93.
39. Dreyer, *Wysbegeerte*, 148.

perverts the mind of rulers, even when they are the best of men. The law is reason unaffected by desire" (*Pol* III, 1287a).

Education

In the final part of the *Politics* (Books VII and VIII), Aristotle discusses the educational system of the ideal state, thus following Plato's example but differing in the details thereof. Since happiness lies in the perfect exercise of virtue, Aristotle writes, and the latter is acquired through nature, habit, and reason, it follows that the latter two are the fruits of education. In general, citizens should be educated to obey when young and to rule when old (Book VII, Chapter 14). What a contrast this approach to pedagogy represents with the modern Western system of 'education,' whose *laissez faire* approach (by parents and schools) inevitably produces vast numbers of 'educated' youth without a sense of responsibility, self-discipline, respect, or any other virtue for that matter.

It is reasonable to state that both the raising of children by their parents and formal education by their teachers should involve a combination of love and discipline. Love without discipline often leads to misbehaviour, even violently so, given the reality of fallen human nature; while discipline without love may lead to the suppression of personality and the stifling of creativity. However, during the twentieth century the Western world came to reject discipline, which it erroneously views as authoritarian. It also confused love with a 'letting go' approach, whereby children may behave as they please. This unbalanced approach to education is therefore part of the social dimension of liberalism, just as *laissez faire* capitalism is its economic dimension and party-political democracy is its political dimension.

Let us return to some aspects of Aristotle's pedagogy. Education should follow the natural order of human development, which involves training of the body first, then dealing with the appetites, and finally training the intellect. In a marked contrast to the irrational modern practice that children should be pampered from birth, Aristotle prescribes physical training for infants and young children. This should be followed by moral education by means of suitable tales, pictures, plays, and so forth. Then, from five to seven years of age, children should be prepared for intellectual training; in other words, formal education in the classroom (*Pol* VII, Chapters 15 and 17).

Given the vital role of the state in ordering civilized life, it is not surprising that Aristotle requires all education to be placed under the control of the state. In a similar vein as Plato, he writes: "No one will doubt that the legislator should direct his attention above all to the education of youth; for the neglect of education does harm to the constitution" (*Pol* VIII, 1337 a). Furthermore, since education should be the same for all citizens, it should be public and not private. Regarding the subjects taught to children, it has to include reading, writing, drawing, gymnastics, and music. Interestingly, Aristotle held that music should not be taught as mere amusement (as is generally the case in the modern era), but that children should rather listen to music as performed by professional musicians. The importance of music lies in the fact that it is both a moral discipline and a rational enjoyment (*Pol* VIII, Chapters 1, 3 and 5).

Ultimately, for Aristotle the supreme practical science is politics, of which ethics is a major dimension. As David Ross comments, Aristotle's ethics are social and his politics are ethical. Thus, in the *Politics*, the good life of the state exists only in the good life of its citizens, while in the *Nicomachean Ethics* the individual man is essentially a member of society. We find the latter work opening with the statement that every art, enquiry, action, and pursuit is aimed at some good; and the good is that at which all things aim (*Nic Eth*, 1094a). Evidently, Aristotle's ethics is teleological, since all action aims at something other than itself.[40]

Augustine's Political Philosophy

Unlike Plato and Aristotle, the most influential Latin Christian theologian did not devote a book or treatise to what is now called political philosophy. However, it is possible to obtain a glimpse into Augustine of Hippo's political views through his immense body of writings on theology, psychology, ethics, and philosophy of history.[41] These views have remained highly relevant, as is the case with most other aspects of his thought.

In his celebrated work, *The City of God against the Pagans*, Augustine makes a categorical distinction between the Earthly City and the Heavenly City.[42] He writes that these two cities have been created by two loves: the

---

40. Ross, *Aristotle*, 195–196.
41. Weithman, "*Augustine*," 234.
42. These are also referred to by commentators as the City of Man and the City of God, respectively.

earthly by love of self, extending even to contempt of God; and the heavenly by love of God, extending to contempt of self (XIV.28). Moreover, the citizens of the Earthly City are produced by a nature vitiated by sin, while the citizens of the Heavenly City are produced by grace, which redeems nature from sin (XV.2). It should be noted that Augustine does not identify the Heavenly City with the visible Church. In the *City of God*, he writes that the good and the reprobate are mingled in the Church, like fish caught in the same net and swimming together until they are brought ashore (XVIII.49). Therefore, every political society includes citizens of both cities. And since no visible society or institution can be identified with either city, the distinction between them is an eschatological rather than a political one.[43]

As conceived by Augustine, human life is marked by original sin, and therefore the City of Man and the City of God can never be united. John Gray explains this view further: "Evil has been at work in every human heart since the Fall of Man; it cannot be defeated in this world. This doctrine gave Christianity an anti-utopian bent it never completely lost, and Christians were spared the disillusionment that comes to all who expect any basic change in human affairs. In Augustinian terms, the belief that evil can be destroyed, which inspired medieval millenarians and resurfaced in the Bush administration, is highly unorthodox. By de-literalizing the hope of the End, Augustine preserved eschatology while reducing its risks."[44] It is clear in the light hereof that all utopian projects are doomed to failure, since they strive to establish 'heaven on earth' in purely human terms.

In the Augustinian view, history is not the unfolding of an ongoing contest between the Earthly City and the Heavenly City. Such a dualism is discounted by his conviction that even those who are destined to spend eternity with God are drawn into the conflicts of this temporal existence. Consequently, everyone needs the restraint which governments are supposed to provide. This also explains the Latin theologian's lack of interest in forms of government, in contrast to Plato and Aristotle for whom it was of central concern. As Paul Weithman further remarks, Augustine is more interested in how God's providence works through political history than in the social forces and institutional forms involved therein.[45]

However, Augustine did touch upon the concepts of people and commonwealth. In the *City of God*, he defines a people as "an assembled

---

43. Weithman, "Augustine," 236–237.
44. Gray, *Black Mass*, 11.
45. Weithman, "Augustine," 237.

multitude of rational creatures bound together by a common agreement as to the objects of their love" (XIX.24). He adds that the better the objects of this agreement, the better the people; and the worse these objects, the worse the people. An interesting qualification is made in this regard by Augustine. Referring to the Romans, as well as the Athenians, Egyptians, and Assyrians of earlier times, he writes that none of them obeyed the divine command that sacrifices should be offered to Him alone. "Thus, because the soul cannot in that case rightly and faithfully govern the body, nor the reason the vices, there can be no true justice in that city" (XIX.24). Here the Latin theologian again shows his Platonic provenance: the existence of justice depends on the subordination of the body to the soul, and of the vices to the reason.

Although Augustine believed that ideal justice cannot be realized in political society, he would certainly recognize the possibility of incremental improvements. To this remark, Paul Weithmann adds that the Latin theologian wrote that human law should conform to divine law (*On true religion*, 31.58).[46] And regarding the size of states, Augustine argued elsewhere that if men were peaceful and just, all kingdoms would be small. Therefore, waging war in the service of empire-building may appear happy to wicked men, but to good men it is only a necessary evil. In the final analysis, it is always preferable to live in concord with one's neighbors than to subdue a wicked neighbor by means of warfare (*De civ Dei*, IV.15). If this sound advice could be taken to heart by neighboring nations involved in long-standing conflicts, such as the Israelis and the Palestinians, a peaceful solution may be at hand.

An interesting divergence between Augustine's political thought and the contemporary disciplines engaged in the study of politics has been pointed out by Paul Weithman. In the case of these disciplines (e.g., political science), political activity is assumed to be a rational undertaking.[47] This applies to rational behaviour, rational decision-making, rational exchange of opinions, rational grounds for institutions, and rational principles of justice. In contrast, Augustine's political interest is focussed on "the divine and psychological forces which govern human life, but which human reason cannot fully penetrate or control." Moreover, Augustine viewed political activity as merely symptomatic; it is only one way by which humans express

---

46. Weithman, "*Augustine*," 244.

47. Although such an assumption certainly does not apply to the mob, as will be discussed in the next section.

orientations that lie deep within themselves.[48] There can be little doubt that the Latin theologian, with his acute psychological insight, held a more accurate view of political behaviour than modern scholars with their emphasis on human rationality.

The Rise of Modern Democracy

In his epochal book *The Decline of the West*, the German philosopher Oswald Spengler outlined the transformation of Western culture due to the urbanization that accelerated during the early modern era. To begin with, the unity of the bourgeoisie, the class representing urban 'freedom', was based on a negative freedom, since they longed to be free from something. Likewise, the power of Money wanted a free path to business success. However, the power of the mob (French *canaille*, German *Pöbel*) then came to the fore in the great cities. They are described by Spengler as a mass of rootless fragments of population, containing elements drawn from all classes and conditions, from derailed nobles to uprooted peasants. The mob harbours power far greater than their numbers, since they are always ready to do anything, and are devoid of all respect for orderliness, (ironically) even that of a revolutionary party. As a result, it is from them that events acquire the destructive force which distinguishes the French Revolution of 1789 from the English Revolution of 1688 (since the latter was an overthrow of the monarch arranged by the British parliament).[49]

The negative role of the mob in modern democracy had earlier been lambasted by Friedrich Nietzsche. In *Thus Spoke Zarathustra*, he writes: "Life is a fountain of delight; but where the rabble also drinks all wells are poisoned. But I once asked, and my question almost stifled me: What, does life have *need* of the rabble, too? And I turned my back upon the rulers when I saw what they now call ruling: bartering and haggling for power—with the rabble!"[50] The classic study of crowd psychology, which manifests as mob behaviour, remains Gustave Le Bon's *Psychologie des Foules* (literally, 'Psychology of Crowds'), which has been translated as *The Crowd: A Study of the Popular Mind*. In it, the French polymath argues persuasively that in a crowd the capacity for reason and critical judgment are replaced by impulsiveness, irritability, and excessive sentimentality, while individuals

48. Weithman, "*Augustine*," 248–249.
49. Spengler, *Decline*, 364.
50. Nietzsche, *Zarathustra*, 120–121.

ARISTOCRACY AND DEMOCRACY

immersed in a crowd soon find themselves in a state of fascination that resembles hypnotism.[51] One only has to think of the behaviour of crowds at political rallies, and even more so at sport events, to appreciate the accuracy of this assessment.

Another interesting observation made by Oswald Spengler is that France obtained all its revolutionary ideas from England, just as it had received the style of its absolute monarchy from Spain. Starting in the 1790s, the English nobility then unleashed its twenty-year long war against France and mobilized all the monarchs of Europe to bring about the fall not so much of Napoleon as of the Revolution, since the French revolutionary leaders had dared to introduce the private opinions of English thinkers into practical politics. What was called 'opposition' in England was nothing more than the attitude of one aristocratic party while another was running the government.[52]

The negative, anti-Western role that Britain has for centuries been playing in international politics is depicted as follows by an American follower of Spengler: "While Germany in the East, and Spain in the South, were protecting the body of the Western Culture from the Barbarian [which means the nations outside this Culture, regardless of their own cultural level], England was forming a national feeling based purely on contrast with other Western nations, and without feeling for the deep, total contrast between the Culture-peoples and the Barbarian. This exaggerated national feeling was to have fateful consequences for the entire West, including England, in the era of World Wars."[53]

As a matter of fact, since the Tudor era the British ruling elites have engaged their country in wars successively against the Spanish, the Dutch, the French, the Russians, and the Germans. During this time, they were also waging wars around the world to expand and preserve their empire. This includes unprovoked wars against the Zulu and Boer nations in South Africa, both of which initially inflicted unexpected defeats on the British armies before being overwhelmed by the enemy's numerical superiority. However, the British empire fell apart around the middle of the twentieth century, and since then their ruling elites have enlisted the British military in the service of the American empire, in a desperate attempt to remain relevant in international affairs. This project includes incessant

---

51. Wikipedia: The Crowd: A Study of the Popular Mind.
52. Spengler, *Decline*, 368, 371.
53. Yockey, *Imperium*, 360.

war-mongering aimed at Russia, which together with China has taken the lead in the establishment of a multipolar world order; the latter being perceived as a threat to the unipolar world order which the Anglo-American elites have long been striving to enforce.

What is the role of parliaments in this perspective? Oswald Spengler writes that Parliamentarianism was a brief transition between the late Cultural period with its mature forms and the age of great individuals in a formless world. It is not difficult to find examples of such great individuals in the twentieth century, regardless of what they stood for. The interactions and conflicts between them, and the international political heritage thereof, still reverberates in our time. By the beginning of the twentieth century, Spengler continues, Parliamentarianism had assumed the role that was previously assigned to the monarchy. Thus it became an impressive spectacle for the masses, while the center of gravity of major policy, which had already shifted from the Crown to elected representatives, was passing from the latter to unofficial groups and the will of unofficial personages (especially the Money power and its propaganda media, we would mention here); this development was all but completed by the outbreak of the First World War.[54] It therefore appears that the parliamentary pretension to represent the will of a country's population is just that—a pretension.

The Two Political Anthropologies

In his remarkable book *Imperium* (subtitled *The philosophy of history and politics* and first published in 1948), the American political thinker Francis Parker Yockey employed insights from Oswald Spengler's philosophy of history in a wide-ranging discussion of Western civilization. He contends that the ideologies of the modern era arose from two political anthropologies that differ fundamentally. From the standpoint of the fundamental ethical quality of human nature, Yockey writes, only two kinds of political theory are possible: "those which posit a 'naturally good' human nature, and those which see human nature as it is." Every rationalistic political theory which regards man as 'good' by nature arose in the eighteenth century, with Rousseau as its most ardent champion. This humanistic anthropology was opposed by Voltaire, who denied this 'essential goodness' of human nature.[55]

---

54. Spengler, *Decline*, 374.
55. Yockey, *Imperium*, 204.

It is therefore not surprising that Voltaire was admired by another realist concerning human nature, Friedrich Nietzsche. In 1878, to celebrate the centenary of Voltaire's death, the German philosopher dedicated the first edition of his book *Human, All-Too-Human* to his French predecessor in anthropological realism. In the same work, Nietzsche took Rousseau to task for superstitiously believing in a wondrous yet repressed goodness of human nature, and for attributing all the blame for that 'repression' on the institutions of culture, in society, state, and education. Yet the optimistic spirit of revolution was not called to awakening by Voltaire's temperate nature, but by "Rousseau's passionate idiocies and half-truths." Because of the latter figure, Nietzsche adds, "the spirit of enlightenment and of progressive development has been scared off for a long time to come."[56]

Yockey illustrates this concept of two contrasting political anthropologies underlying the modern ideologies by means of a conversation reported by Thomas Carlyle. A school inspector named Johann Sulzer explained the new discovery of rationalism, that human nature was essentially good, to Friedrich the Great. The Prussian king (also an accomplished musician and a philosopher-ruler, whom Plato would most likely have admired) wisely replied, *Ach, mein lieber Sulzer, Ihr kennt nicht diese verdammte Rasse*— 'You don't know this damned race.'[57] This rebuttal indicates the most glaring defect of the rationalistic anthropology, namely that it is based on ignorance of human nature.

What do we understand with rationalism? It has been defined by a contemporary philosopher as "any philosophy magnifying the role played by unaided reason, in the acquisition and justification of knowledge."[58] The Traditionalist metaphysician René Guénon has pointed out that philosophical rationalism goes back to Descartes, adding that Protestantism had prepared the way for the rise of rationalism by introducing 'free enquiry' into religion. Rationalism in all its forms involves a belief in the supremacy of reason, which entails a rejection of pure intellectual intuition and thus of all true metaphysical knowledge. Thus, rationalism is closely linked with individualism and its rejection of all spiritual authority.[59]

The opposite political anthropology to that held by rationalism recognizes that man is mostly "disharmonious, problematical, dual, and

56. Nietzsche, *Human*, 209–210.
57. Yockey, *Imperium*, 205.
58. Blackburn, *Oxford Dictionary*, 307.
59. Guénon, *Reign of Quantity*, 110–111.

dangerous." Francis Parker Yockey adds that this way of realistic thinking starts from facts, which are viewed as normative. It is therefore political thinking as opposed to mere thinking about politics, or rationalizing regardless of facts. The Western tradition of realistic political thinking is represented, among others, by Montaigne, Macchiavelli, Hobbes, Leibniz, Fichte, de Maistre, Hegel, and Carlyle. Moreover, whereas rationalism is anti-historical, political thinking is applied history.[60]

Rationalism and Democracy

At the same time as the rise of modern democracy, Oswald Spengler writes, rationalism appears as the enemy of tradition, with criticism as its religion and concepts as its deities. Thenceforth, books and general theories begin to influence politics, as occurred in various Cultures. Examples thereof are Lao Tzu in China, the Sophists in Athens, and Montesquieu in Europe.[61] Francis Parker Yockey also noted that rationalism and democracy arose simultaneously around the middle of the eighteenth century. However, unlike liberalism, the idea of democracy is saturated with will-to-power, using 'the people' as a polemic term to undermine and replace the Estates (i.e., priesthood and nobility). Democracy is actually a cultural illness, Yockey adds, but one through which every High Culture has gone and is thus impelled by organic necessity. It is symbolized *per excellence* by Napoleon, who had spread the Revolution against the Estates but created his own Dynasty and made his own Marshals into Dukes. As a matter of fact, the only 'equality' which democracy admits is equality of opportunity. It does therefore not require an abolition of rank or gradation of rights.[62]

We suggest that the *de facto* non-egalitarian nature of democracy explains the existence of privileged groups in democratic societies committed to 'equal rights' for all. For example, in twenty-first century Britain, as a general rule children have more rights than their parents or teachers (again confirming the relevance of Plato's warning); cyclists have more rights than pedestrians on side-walks and motorists on roads, being allowed to block the traffic flow and menace pedestrians; the savages hunting foxes with packs of dogs have more rights than the animal lovers who try to prevent them, while the police refuse to enforce the ban on such barbaric practices;

---

60. Yockey, *Imperium*, 218–219, 221.
61. Spengler, *Decline*, 365.
62. Yockey, *Imperium*, 224–226.

and the mentally ill (officially, 'persons with learning disabilities') have more rights than their support workers. Moreover, large numbers of these 'mentally ill' persons live comfortable lives in 'supported housing' without ever having to work, while many of them are physically capable of doing undemanding manual labor such as cleaning roads or parks.[63] To those among the latter who refuse to do any kind of work, as well as those non-disabled persons who have found ways and means to live on social benefits for much of their lives, a passage by Friedrich Nietzsche aptly titled 'The parasite' applies: "It shows a complete lack of noble character when someone prefers to live in dependence, at the expense of others [i.e., the taxpayers] in order not to work at any cost, and usually with a secret bitterness towards those on whom he is dependent."[64]

Francis Parker Yockey remarks further that the will-to-power of democracy is manifested in its history of revolution, consolidation, and imperialism. Democracy is not a retreat from reality like liberalism, but strives to make politics a thing of mass—in other words, to make everyone subject to politics and make everyone into a politician. It is a fact that until the end of the eighteenth century, war and politics were mostly conducted by the rulers and small, professional armies. But democracy puts the entire man-power of the nation onto the battle-field, Yockey writes, and forces everyone to have an opinion on matters of government, to be expressed in elections. In addition, since the idea of democracy was born at the same time as the economic age, it has throughout most of its history been a servant of economics in its battle against authority. As explained by Yockey, "Democracy had two poles, ability and mass. It put everyone into politics, and allowed the successful ones an amount of power tenfold that of any absolute monarch."[65]

However, the authoritarian political tendency of democracy was strangled at birth by the power of money in an economic age. Yockey adds that the word 'democracy' then became a slogan in the social battle and the economic battle, always meaning mass and quantity as opposed to quality and tradition. The victory of the mass-spirit was complete in the USA, where the principle of mass was applied even in education. Thus, by the middle of the twentieth century the USA had far more so-called institutions

---

63. All these examples are drawn from the author's personal experience and observation.

64. Nietzsche, *Human*, 177.

65. Yockey, *Imperium*, 226–227.

of higher learning than existed in Europe, its ancestral lands. Not unexpectedly, this victory of quantity over quality in education brought about negative consequences, as Yockey notes: "The practice of giving everyone a diploma meant quite simply that the diploma became meaningless."[66]

Also, during the twentieth century democracy assumed a different meaning from its original poles of ability and mass, since these now merged to serve the purposes of the economic powers. Yockey concludes, "The economic lords of the earth mobilized the masses against the authority of the State, and miscalled it 'democracy.'"[67] It would therefore be apt to describe the form of government in much of the world today as plutocracy instead of democracy, or, even better, plutocracy masquerading as democracy. The term plutocracy is derived from the Greek *ploutos*, meaning 'wealth' and *kratia*, meaning 'rule'—i.e., government by the wealthy.

In the centuries before the rise to power of rationalism, liberalism, and democracy, most (if not all) Western nations harboured the traditional estates of nobility and priesthood, serving as the political and religious authority, respectively. (Interestingly, a similar structure prevailed in classical India, at least from the time of the Aryan settlement during the second millennium B.C. onwards. There the priestly caste of *Brahmins* and the warrior-class of *Kshatriyas* represented the two estates possessing authority). Yockey writes that the nobility and the priesthood represent the two aspects of the Culture-soul with the highest possible symbolic purity: "Nobility represents war, politics, law, race; Priesthood represents religion, knowledge, science, philosophy, the world of thought." The rest of the population, Yockey adds, is just that—the rest.[68]

With this latter remark, Yockey appears to follow Nietzsche's disdain for the human masses. As the German philosopher writes in the Preface to *The Antichrist*, "This book belongs to the very few." Nietzsche then outlines the requirements for understanding him, such as intellectual uprightness to the point of hardness, indifference as to whether truth is profitable or even fatal, and the courage to ask questions that others don't ask. He concludes the Preface as follows: "Very well then! Such men alone are my readers, my proper readers, my preordained readers: of what account are the rest? The rest are simply: humanity. One must be superior to humanity in power, in loftiness of soul—in contempt."

66. Yockey, *Imperium*, 229.
67. Yockey, *Imperium*, 229–230.
68. Yockey, *Imperium*, 355.

Following the victory of the rationalistic ideologies over the traditional estates, which in the Western culture occurred from the eighteenth century onwards, two new orders arose to assume the mantle of authority. These new 'estates' are the intellectuals and the trading class, enamoured by their new-found 'freedom.' In reality, Yockey remarks, they are only the caricature of the old nobility and priesthood.[69] These 'intellectuals' are more correctly termed rationalists, since their thought is limited to the purely 'horizontal' (or immanent) level of reality, without recognition of its 'vertical' (or transcendent) dimensions.

The Financial Servitude of Democracy

In the early life of every Culture an economic life appears, involving mainly peasants in the countryside. In this context, Oswald Spengler adds, human interaction is marked mainly by traffic in goods. Even gold and coins are viewed as goods, albeit highly prized due to their rarity and durability. However, in the towns a different economic life awakens, since the inhabitants are not producers. As a result, goods become wares, and thinking in terms of money replaces thinking in terms of goods. Although this fact is not recognized in modern monetary theories, Spengler continues, money is a category of thought, like number and law. In consequence, "Whereas the earlier mankind *compares* goods, and does so not by means of the reason only, the later *reckons* the values of wares, and does so by rigid unqualitative measures." Thus, the economic picture is reduced to quantities, whereas goods were valued mainly for their quality. And as towns grow into cities, the latter becomes the money-market, in which the trader functions as mediator between producer and consumer. As Spengler points out, "He who commands this mode of thinking is the master of money."[70]

With the rise of democracy, next to the critical spirit appears the power of abstract Money, i.e., money divorced from the prime values of the land. Spengler explains the causal link between democracy and money as follows: "It must be concluded that democracy and plutocracy are the same thing under the two aspects of wish and actuality, theory and practice, knowing and doing. It is the tragic comedy of the world-improvers' and freedom-teachers' desperate fight against money that they are *ipso facto* assisting money to be effective. Respect for the big number—expressed in the

---

69. Yockey, *Imperium*, 363.
70. Spengler, *Decline*, 403–406.

principles of equality for all, natural rights and universal suffrage—is just as much a class-ideal of the unclassed as freedom of public opinion (and more particularly freedom of the press) is so. These are ideals, but in actuality the freedom of public opinion involves the preparation of public opinion, which costs money; and the freedom of the press brings with it the question of possession of the press, which again is a matter of money; and with the franchise comes electioneering, in which he who pays the piper calls the tune."[71] Evidently, democracy cannot be divorced from plutocracy.

It is noteworthy that the domination of politics by money has not been limited to modern democracy. Already in classical Athens and Rome elections were held, providing an arena for the intervention of ever more money. As Spengler comments, "The greater became the wealth which was capable of concentration in the hands of individuals, the more the fight for political power developed into a question of money." In the case of republican Rome, the capital needed to fund election campaigns rose to American dimensions, so that in the elections of 54 B.C. the interest rate doubled from four to eight percent. Even Julius Caesar was heavily indebted to financiers such as Crassus; the future emperor's fortunes only turning around when the conquest of Gaul made him the richest man in the world. Spengler concludes: "Caesar grasped the fact that on the soil of a democracy constitutional rights signify nothing without money and everything with it."[72] Strictly speaking, the Roman republic had been an oligarchy rather than a democracy, but this does not refute the crucial role of money in electioneering.

Economics is understood by Francis Parker Yockey as a form of action, designed to nourish and enrich private life. The reciprocal relation between politics and economics is illustrated by the example of Cecil John Rhodes, the British arch-imperialist who was one of the main instigators of the Anglo-Boer War (1899-1902). In the words of Yockey: "When Cecil Rhodes thought primarily of making himself wealthy, he was thinking economically; when he proceeded to use his wealth for control over the populations of Africa, he was thinking politically."[73] Ironically, Rhodes died shortly before the conclusion of the mentioned war, which gave the British ruling elites control over a continuous African domain from Cape Town to Cairo, the fulfilment of which had been Rhodes' ultimate ambition.

71. Spengler, *Decline*, 366–367.
72. Spengler, *Decline*, 392–393.
73. Yockey, *Imperium*, 239.

The gradual monetarization of economic life in the Western world involved the substitution of the idea of goods with the idea of Money, Yockey writes. This process resulted in the gradual ruination of the material and spiritual life of farmers and laborers in all the Western lands. With the victory of the financiers over the entrepreneurs and the industrialists, came the triumph of the corporate form of business ownership: "This forced every business owner into interest servitude to the Master of Money, for it was the latter who bought the shares and then proceeded to grind the employees of the enterprise by turning the proceeds of the industry entirely into dividends." To the financier, the wages paid to the workers are viewed as merely a cost of production, and by lowering this 'cost' his own profits could be increased, regardless of the social cost thereof, such as starving families.[74]

That the power of money is not limited by ideology has been recognized by Spengler, writing as follows: "The concepts of Liberalism and Socialism are set in motion only by money." For example, English politicians recognized as early as 1700 (the Bank of England having been only recently founded, in 1694) that on the stock exchange they deal with both votes and stocks. And when the news of the French defeat at Waterloo in 1815 reached Paris, the price of French government stock rose: the Jacobins had emancipated money, Spengler notes, and now they stepped forward as lords of the land. Such is the power of Money when it functions in conjunction with popular numbers, that not even supposedly anti-capitalist movements are immune to it: "There is no proletarian, not even a Communist, movement that has not operated in the interest of money, in the directions indicated by money and for the time permitted by money—and that without the idealist amongst its leaders having the slightest suspicion of the fact." Moreover, Spengler writes, whereas intellect has won its victory in its own realm of truths and ideals that are not of this world, "Money wins, through these very concepts, in *its* realm, which is *only* of this world."[75]

It was in England that the rationalistic catch-words sprang up, Spengler continues, with 'liberty' meaning both intellectual and trade freedom. It is no therefore accident that David Hume was the teacher of Adam Smith. It was also in England that money was used most unhesitatingly in politics; not in the bribery of powerful individuals (as was common in parts of Europe), but in 'nursing' the democratic forces themselves. For instance,

74. Yockey, *Imperium*, 429–430.
75. Spengler, *Decline*, 367.

in eighteenth-century England, first the Parliamentary elections and then decisions of the elected members were systematically managed by money. Spengler mentions the example of the Liberal prime minister Henry Pelham paying amounts of £500 to £800 to MPs at the end of each parliamentary session, according to their services rendered to his government.[76]

One of the most pernicious results of rationalism is the rise to political power of the financiers. This could only have occurred in a Western world that had reached a cultural stage by which it was expedient to ignore Christ's injunction against the worship of Money, which in the New Testament is called Mammon: "One cannot serve God and Mammon," Christ taught his disciples (Matt 6:24; Luke 16:13). However, from a survey of the Gospel evidence, it appears that Christ did not condemn property ownership as such—in fact, He did not hesitate to avail himself of the generosity of well-to-do supporters. Among them counted the women Mary Magdalene, Joanna, and Susanna (Luke 8:2–3); the chief tax collector Zacchaeus (Luke 19: 2); and Joseph of Arimathea, a rich man who offered up his own future tomb for Christ's burial (Matt 27:57).

Evidently, Christ's criticism was reserved for the pursuit of riches when it becomes an aim in itself, instead of serving others. In the traditional Christian understanding, ego-serving riches cannot but stand in the way between the owner thereof and the kingdom of God. This is the context in which we should read Christ's saying that it is all but impossible for a rich person to enter heaven: "It is easier for a camel to go through the eye of a needle than for a rich man to enter the kingdom of God" (Matt 19: 24). Arguing along similar lines in his 'Homily on Wealth and Poverty,' the Greek theologian John Chrysostom takes issue with those who are always yearning after the property of others. Such wealthy persons should not even be considered healthy or affluent, he writes, for they are unable to control their own greed.[77]

Although arguing from a different perspective, Nietzsche pointed out the danger in wealth when divorced from intellect, by writing as follows: "Only a man of intellect should hold property; otherwise property is dangerous to the community. For the owner, not knowing how to make use of the leisure which his possessions might secure to him, will continue to strive after more property. So in the end real wealth is produced from the moderate property that would be enough for an intellectual man. Such

---

76. Spengler, *Decline*, 368.
77. Laos, *World Order*, 202.

wealth, then, is the glittering outcrop of intellectual dependence and poverty. Hence it excites envy in the poor and uncultured . . . and gradually paves the way for a social revolution."[78]

Returning to Yockey's assault on rationalism and liberalism, we find him arguing as follows. Having leveled all the political and social powers of earlier cultural stages, rationalism spawned the monster of the absolute power of Money. Yockey vividly depicts the *de facto* omnipotence of the new Western rulers: "The Master of Money desires no limelight, no risk of life, but only money and ever more money. Party politicians exist only to protect him and his operations. The courts are there to enforce his usury. The remnants of the State are there to do him service. Armies march when his trade system is challenged. He is subject to nothing, he is the new Sovereign. He is above nations, and his banking operations transcend national laws."[79] The nineteenth-century British novelist and politician Benjamin Disraeli, a faithful servant of the financial elites, affirmed this reality when he wrote in *Coningsby*: "The world is governed by very different personages from what is imagined by those who are not behind the scenes."[80]

Francis Parker Yockey further describes the take-over of democracy by the power-brokers of money: "In later democratic conditions—in our case from 1850—it was solely the financier whose interest was served by the constitutionalized anarchy called democracy. The word democracy thus passed into the possession of Money, and it was transformed from its historical meaning into its 20th century meaning. To the financier, it means the 'rule of law'—his law, which makes possible his unprecedented usury by means of his monopoly of money." In practice, democracy either proceeded to authoritarian rule like that of Napoleon or Mussolini, or it was a mere cover for unhampered looting by the financier. Ultimately, Yockey notes, democracy is the lowering of everything human to the level of the least valuable human beings.[81]

The subservience of the democratic technique of electioneering to money has also been depicted by Yockey. To begin with, voters have to be organized so that the leaders may perpetuate themselves in office, with the method of organization being the party. Organization, in turn, requires both funds and ideals. The latter are for the voters, while the funds make

78. Nietzsche, *Human*, 362.
79. Yockey, *Imperium*, 362–363.
80. Quoted in Perry, *Treasury*, 462.
81. Yockey, *Imperium*, 227–228.

it possible to spread the ideals. Of these, the funds are more important because they are more difficult to procure. This dependence of party organizations upon a supply of funds enabled rich persons to get party leaders to do their bidding. Yockey concludes: "Even a party leader in office was not independent, for the rich man alone could keep him there. The name given in the books for this type of government is plutocracy, the rule of money."[82]

Ultimately, the monetary servitude of party-political democracy harbours its own downfall. As Oswald Spengler observed, the dictatorship of party leaders supports itself by that of the press (i.e., the mass media). The competing parties strive by means of money to bring readers over *en masse* under their own conditioning, thereby forming the world-view of the readers and voters. In this way, Spengler concludes, "Through money, democracy becomes its own destroyer, after money has destroyed intellect."[83]

Party-political Democracy

During the nineteenth century the democratic politicians devised the dialectic of party-politics, Francis Parker Yockey writes. In terms thereof, the party-politician is expected to assume a 'disinterested' standpoint, whether moral, scientific, or economic. As the opposite side of the coin, the opponent is portrayed as immoral, unscientific, and uneconomic—in other words, 'political,' which is an evil to be combatted. The party-politician also has to feign unwillingness to accept office, until a demonstration of carefully arranged 'popular will' convinces him to 'serve.' Yockey adds, "A book by a party-politician ... praises the entire human race, except certain perverse people, the author's opponents."[84]

The institutionalized farce called party-politics has been picturesquely evoked by Nietzsche in his book *Human, All-Too-Human*: "All political parties today have in common a demagogic character and the intention of influencing the masses; because of this intention, all of them are obliged to transform their principles into great frescoes of stupidity, and paint them that way on the wall." The German philosopher then approvingly quotes Voltaire's remark, 'Once the populace gets involved in reasoning, all is lost.' Yet party-politics often harbours its own nemesis, as Nietzsche argues in an aphorism titled 'The most dangerous partisan': "In every party there is one

82. Yockey, *Imperium*, 458–459.
83. Spengler, *Decline*, 395–396.
84. Yockey, *Imperium*, 221–222.

person who, by his all-too-devout enunciation of party principles, provokes the other members to defect." This reality is a primary cause of political parties (especially those in opposition to the ruling party, its members not enjoying all the benefits of the latter) breaking up, with parts merging with other parties or forming new parties. Moreover, party-politics is not suitable for thinking persons, as Nietzsche writes elsewhere: "He who thinks much is not suited to be a party member: too soon, he thinks himself through and beyond the party."[85]

Later in the same work, Nietzsche expands on this argument by writing that when a party observes that a member has changed from an unqualified to a qualified adherent, it will do everything in its power to drive that member out of the party. "For the party suspects that the intention of finding a relative value in its faith, a value which admits of pro and con, of weighing and discarding, is more dangerous than outright opposition." Due to the same dualistic mentality, "Every party attempts to represent the important elements that have sprung up outside it as unimportant, and if it does not succeed, it attacks those elements the more bitterly, the more excellent they are."[86] In this way political parties confirm their commitment to quantity instead of quality, and to numbers instead of principles.

Interestingly, in his dialogue *Politikos* (translated as Statesman), Plato had remarked that no city-state (*polis*) of his time was ruled by expert statesmen. He therefore suggested that the best alternative is for the government to be directed by an imitator, or a sophist, who does not know the right way but pretends that he does. Elsewhere, in the *Sophist*, the art of sophistry is presented as selling alleged knowledge by speaking persuasively, winning private debates about right and wrong, and refuting false or poorly supported ideas. Although the sophist is aware that he does not know anything, he produces 'copies' of the truth on important subjects; in other words, he speaks words that appear to be true but in fact are false.[87]

Moreover, as Nietzsche has argued, in order for one to become a great man of the masses, the latter should be supplied with something they find very pleasant. However, this should not be given to them immediately, but has to be viewed as gained with great exertion. "The masses must have the impression that a mighty, indeed invincible, strength of will is present. Everyone admires a strong will, because no one has it. Now, if it appears that

---

85. Nietzsche, *Human*, 199, 167, 235.
86. Nietzsche, *Human*, 361, 363.
87. Cooper, *Plato*, 235–236, 294.

this strong will is producing something very pleasant for the masses . . . then everyone admires it all the more."[88] These statements by Plato and Nietzsche are indeed accurate descriptions of the 'successful' party-politician in modern democracies.

The Media as Democratic Means of Control

Given the causal link between the ownership of money and control of the masses through the media, it is not surprising that the ideal of a 'free press' was discovered in Britain. At the same time, it was discovered there that the press serves those who own it. Consequently, Oswald Spengler writes, the press does not spread 'free' opinion, but generates it. Moreover, Anglo-American party-politics have created by means of the press "a force-field of world-wide intellectual and financial tensions in which every individual unconsciously takes up the place allotted to him." Spengler aptly depicts this phenomenon: "Man does not speak to man; the press and its associate, the electrical news-service, keep the waking consciousness of whole peoples and continents under a deafening drum-fire of theses, catchwords, standpoints, scenes, feelings, day by day and year by year, so that every Ego becomes a mere function of a monstrous intellectual Something." In this way, Money is turned into force, and its quantity determines the intensity of its working influence.[89]

As early as 1816, Goethe foresaw the nefarious results of press freedom when it is divorced from the classical virtues. When freedom of the press was introduced into the Duchy of Weimar in that year, the great German writer declared in his *Annalen* that it only gave free rein to authors with a deep contempt of public opinion. Goethe remarked that every right-thinking man of learning foresaw the direct and incalculable consequences of such 'freedom' with regret. "Thus even in his time," Hans Günther comments, "Goethe must have reflected how little the men of the Press were capable of combining freedom with human dignity." This combination of freedom with dignity is found per excellence in the poetry of Homer, as Günther points out: "Homer always represented sensuality without lust and without prudery and never enticingly and seductively or with sensual excitement in mind; he was one of the most innocent poets of all ages and even in describing sexual scenes, he never used a word which exceeded

---

88. Nietzsche, *Human*, 208.
89. Spengler, *Decline*, 393–394.

artistic requirements. This is yet another example of how the Indo-European linked freedom with dignity."[90]

The nefarious role of the mass media was already in the 1880s (when it was limited to the press) observed by Nietzsche, writing as follows: "What significance can we attach to the Press in its present position, with its daily expenditure of lung-power in order to bawl, to deafen, to excite, to terrify? Is it anything more than an everlasting false alarm, which tries to lead our ears and our wits into a false direction?"[91] For his part, Oswald Spengler remarked that for the multitude, truth is that which it continuously reads and hears. Thus, the public truth is produced by the press, so that what the press wills, is true. "Three weeks of press-work, and the 'truth' is acknowledged by everybody."[92] How far this media-created 'truth' is removed from any traditional concept thereof should be abundantly clear in view of our chapter on truth and knowledge.

As far as the mainstream media are concerned, their claims to 'truth' and 'objectivity' are easily shown to be false. For instance, the eminent American linguist, philosopher, and political activist Noam Chomsky has exposed the propagandistic role of the mass media in books such as *Manufacturing Consent: The Political Economy of the Mass Media* (1995) and *Media Control: The Spectacular Achievements of Propaganda* (2008). It is not in the least surprising that Chomsky has since the 1960s, when he correctly depicted the Vietnam War as an act of American imperialism, been viewed as an 'enemy' by the US ruling elites. More recently, we have witnessed the persecution of whistle-blowers such as Julian Assange, Bradley Manning, and Edward Snowden by the 'democratic' Anglo-American elites.

Writing in the early years of the Weimar republic, Oswald Spengler accurately described the relentless stifling of freedom of thought by the mass media, the power of which has in the meantime increased exponentially due to radio and television becoming means of control. In Spengler's words: "No tamer has his animals more under his power. The Press today is an army with carefully organized arms and branches, with journalists as officers, and readers as soldiers. The reader neither knows, nor is allowed to know, the purposes for which he is used, nor even the role that he is to play. A more appalling caricature of freedom of thought cannot be imagined. Formerly a man did not dare to think freely. Now he dares, but cannot; his

90. Günther, *Religious attitudes*, 68, 72.
91. Nietzsche, *Human*, 366.
92. Spengler, *Decline*, 394–395.

will to think is only a willingness to think to order, and this is what he feels as *his* liberty."[93]

The Ideal: Philosopher-rulers

In view of the arguments presented above, we contend that an aristocracy of rigorously trained philosopher-rulers is the best form of government, while the much-vaunted liberal democracy is actually the second worst form, beaten to the lowest position only by tyranny. This preference does not have to exclude the possibility of popular participation in the political process, for example by means of periodic referendums on issues that concern the whole population. Although the outcomes of such polls would be non-binding on the rulers, it would nonetheless be prudent of the rulers to seriously consider the popular vote, and to act on it according to the requirements of wisdom and justice.

Socrates states the case for philosopher-rulers as follows, whilst recognising the difficulty of grasping the necessity thereof: "There will be no end to the troubles of states, or indeed of humanity itself, [until] philosophers become kings in this world, or [until] those we now call kings or rulers really and truly become philosophers, and political power and philosophy thus come into the same hands. This is what I have hesitated to say so long, knowing what a paradox it would sound; for it is not easy to see that there is no other road to happiness, either for society or the individual" (*Pol*, 473d–e). However, it is admitted that the ideal society as described by Socrates will probably never exist on earth, but "perhaps it is laid up as a pattern in heaven, where he who wishes can see it and found it in his own heart" (*Pol*, 592b).

We suggest that the Platonic notion of meritocracy should also apply to the other branches of government than the executive, namely the legislative and judicial bodies. In this regard, Nietzsche made a useful suggestion on the composition of a legislative body (i.e., a parliament). In a section titled 'Of the mastery of them that know,' he writes: "It is easy, ridiculously easy, to set up a model for the choice of a legislative body. First of all the honest and reliable men of the nation, which at the same time are masters and experts in some one branch, have to become prominent by mutual scenting-out and recognition. From these, by a narrower process of selection, the learned and expert of the first rank in each individual branch must

93. Spengler, *Decline*, 395.

again be chosen, also by mutual recognition and guarantee. If the legislative body be composed of these, it will finally be necessary, in each individual case, that only the voices and judgments of the most specialized experts should decide; the honesty of all the rest should have become so great that it is simply a matter of decency to leave the voting also in the hands of these men. The result would be that the law, in the strictest sense, would emanate from the intelligence of the most intelligent."[94]

Clearly, such an elitist model would be the opposite of the party-political chaos of 'democratic' legislation. Nietzsche sketches the latter as follows: "As things now are, voting is done by parties, and at every division there must be hundreds of uneasy consciences among the ill-taught, the incapable of judgment, among those who merely repeat, imitate, and go with the tide. Nothing lowers the dignity of a new law so much as this inherent shamefaced feeling of insincerity that necessarily results in every party division." Nietzsche admits that no power on earth is at present strong enough to realize the mentioned ideal of intelligent legislators (given that we are living in an era of quantity prevailing over quality). He defiantly concludes with a wish that our watchword will be: "More reverence for them that know, and down with all parties!"[95]

It is important to note that Plato's concept of the ideal state flows directly from his Theory of Forms (or Ideas), so that the state as described in the *Politeia* is the Form of a state in its purity. And just as the sensible world is real inasmuch as the Forms take shape or form therein, so the Form of the state may find expression in the concrete world of experience (although it could never be fully realized). Moreover, the ideal state provides us with a yardstick by means of which existing states may be measured and judged.[96]

In his book *The Destiny of Man*, the Russian philosopher Nicolas Berdyaev recognizes that there can be no ideal form of state in this world, and therefore all political utopias are radically false. He adds, "There can only be relative improvements, generally connected with limiting the power of the state. In its demonic will to power the state always strives to exceed its limits and to become an absolute monarchy, an absolute democracy, an absolute communism." This phenomenon was already present in the Hellenic and Roman worlds, in which the city-state and later the *Imperium* were viewed as absolute. However, "limits were fixed by Christianity, which

---

94. Nietzsche, *Human*, 363–364.
95. Nietzsche, *Human*, 364.
96. Dreyer, *Wysbegeerte*, 109–110.

liberates man from the power of the world. The human soul is more precious than the kingdoms of this world, than the state. The state belongs to the world of sin and does not in any way resemble the Kingdom of God." It was therefore an immense mistake to ascribe a sacred or theocratic character to so-called Christian monarchies, whether papist or imperial.[97]

That Plato's dialogue *Politeia* is not a practical political model as such, but rather a methodical study of the metaphysical Idea that should guide an actual, historical republic has been affirmed by Nicolas Laos. Modern scholars who have accused the *Politeia* as being a totalitarian political theory, such as Karl Popper in his book *The Open Society and its Enemies*, have therefore failed to understand Plato's theory of Ideas and its political application in the *Politeia*. Laos explains the difference between Plato's theory and totalitarianism as follows: "The essence of totalitarianism is the thesis that the end of practice (i.e., of historical action) is a necessary practical, historical, and quantifiable goal. On the other hand, if the end of historical action is not a historical goal but a metaphysical one of purely qualitative character, such as Plato's idea of the Good, historical action is based on freedom, for it is a matter of personal choice." Moreover, the classical *polis* rejected absolutism and totalitarianism without lapsing into social disorder.[98] The latter phrase refers to the kind of anarchy that often occurs in democratic societies, since unbridled 'individual freedom' virtually lends itself to anarchy.

The Compromise: Moderate Democracy

If we accept that a true aristocracy, or meritocracy, will never be a practical form of government, given the pervasive presence of error and ignorance among humans, then we have no alternative but to compromise. The second-best choice would then be a moderate democracy in which the interests of state, people, culture, and economics are balanced as much as possible. Such a form of government is the antithesis of the current Western mixture of liberal democracy and plutocracy, in which the interests of the financiers and corporations outweigh all others.

Is there a historical precedent for such a moderate, non-liberal democracy? We answer in the affirmative and hold up the case of the Second German Empire, founded by the statesman Otto von Bismarck in 1871. It

97. Berdyaev, *Destiny of Man*, 195–196.
98. Laos, *Metaphysics*, 17, 57.

is interesting to note that Friedrich Nietzsche, although being highly critical of the Second Empire, nonetheless credited Bismarck's political sensibility in viewing the constitutional form of government as a compromise between government and people.[99] Although it was dissolved at the end of World War One in 1918, this short-lived state serves as a lasting instance of meritocracy and democracy co-existing to the benefit of the bulk of the population. Here are some informative quotes from the Wikipedia entry on the second Reich:

a. "During its 47 years of existence, the German Empire was an industrial, technological, and scientific giant, gaining more Nobel Prizes in science than any other country. By 1900, Germany was the largest economy in Europe, surpassing the United Kingdom, as well as the second-largest in the world, behind only the United States."

b. "Bismarck built on a tradition of welfare programs in Prussia and Saxony that began as early as in the 1840s. In the 1880s he introduced old-age pensions, accident insurance, medical care and unemployment insurance that formed the basis of the modern European welfare state. The social security systems installed by Bismarck (health care in 1883, accident insurance in 1884, invalidity and old-age insurance in 1889) at the time were the largest in the world and, to a degree, still exist in Germany today."

c. "The last legal barriers on Jews in Prussia were lifted by the 1860s, and within 20 years, they were over-represented in the white-collar professions and much of academia. In the popular mind Jews became a symbol of capitalism and wealth. On the other hand, the constitution and legal system protected the rights of Jews as German citizens."[100] It is also noteworthy (given developments from 1933 onwards) that an estimated 100 000 German Jews served in the German Army during World War One, of whom no less than 18 000 received the Iron Cross.[101]

However, when by the late nineteenth century Germany became the dominant economic power in Europe, this unforeseen development jolted the ruling elites in London and Paris into forming a firm political alliance,

---

99. Nietzsche, *Human*, 204.
100. Wikipedia: German Empire.
101. Wikipedia: German Jewish military personnel of World War I.

their centuries-old rivalry notwithstanding. Since economic power naturally leads to geopolitical power in the long run, the Anglo-French imperialists embarked on a relentless campaign to isolate Germany diplomatically, as preparation for an all-out war when the time was ripe. Although Britain and France already ruled over the largest global empires in recorded history, their leaders also desired the small number of German colonies in Africa and the Pacific. Thus, war became inevitable, especially when the Anglo-French elites recruited the Russians into forming the Triple Entente, while the Germans in turn formed an alliance with Austria-Hungary, which together with Ottoman Turkey became known as the Central Powers. By the early twentieth century, the stage was set for the bloodiest and most destructive war up to that point in history, which finally erupted in the late summer of 1914.

Freedom and Liberalism

THE WORDS 'LIBERAL' AND 'liberalism' are derived from the Latin *libertas*, meaning liberty or freedom.[1] Let us first consider the classical Indo-European conception of freedom, as expressed by the Roman historian Tacitus (c. 55–117 A.D.). It has been summarized as follows: "Freedom (*libertas*) in the Indo-European sense is only possible where a people strives to achieve the value of virtue, the dignity of the powerful, upright individual man. If in a people the freedom of the city masses, who desire welfare (bread and circuses) from the state, triumphs then in such a state the freedom of the individual man and that of the minority will be steadily suppressed by the majority, until finally only domination is still possible, that is to say, the equal subjection of all under one tyrant."[2] This description of qualitative freedom being replaced first by quantity and finally by tyranny evokes Plato's schema of mob rule replacing aristocracy, until only tyranny remains.

In the modern era, the concept of 'liberty' became politicized during the French Revolution with its slogan of *liberté, égalité, fraternité*—liberty, equality, fraternity. And ever since, 'freedom' has served as a powerful slogan of revolutionaries and ideologues up to the present. Lincoln and his Unionists waged war on the Confederate states in the name of 'freedom' for all Americans; Lenin and his Bolsheviks waged war on the Tsarist order to bring 'freedom' to the Russians and other nations in the nascent Soviet state; Hitler and his National Socialists overthrew the Weimar republic in order to bring 'freedom' to the Germans and Austrians, which were then dragged into the most destructive war of all time; and since 1945 the American ruling elites have been waging war on numerous nations that have refused to bow the knee before their global hegemony, always described by their servile media and politicians as bringing 'freedom' to those countries.

---

1. Wheeler, *Latin*, 527.
2. Günther, *Religious attitudes*, 43.

Evidently, the concept of freedom is a highly diffuse one, so that it would be serving the truth to further explore its meaning and demonstrate its distortion by liberalism.

Having mentioned Abraham Lincoln and his war against the American South, let us remove another widely held misconception, namely that the Civil War (1861–65) was fought mainly over the issue of slavery. As Francis Parker Yockey has pointed out, most of the richest men in America were found in the Northern states, in which trade and manufacturing were predominant. In contrast, the Southern states mainly had agriculture as economic basis, with half their population consisting of black slaves. Slavery was less efficient than industrialism, for the Southern slaves enjoyed more socio-economic security than the Northern factory workers. From a capitalist viewpoint, the industrialists thus had a lower 'cost of production' than the slave owners. Moreover, the South came to import manufactured goods from Britain, because it was cheaper than buying from the Northern industries with their higher protective tariffs. In order to secure domination over the Southern states, the Northern capitalists fastened on the idea of slavery and made it an issue of war for the Northern masses.[3]

Thus, war became inevitable between the South, with its aristocratic-traditional ethos and economically based on muscle-energy, and the North, with its financial-industrial ethos and economically based on machine-energy. The War of Secession, as Yockey calls it, was a contest between quality and quantity. The North had all the war industries, most of the railroads, and four times the population available for military purposes. On the other hand, the South had a "spiritual superiority on the field of battle, where its heroic spirit gained victory after victory over superior numbers." However, the South could not replace its human losses, which the North could do, for example by drafting German and Irish immigrants in large numbers. With armies numbering in the millions, the war became the largest-scale war in the Western world up to the First World War.[4]

Due to the Civil War and its immediate aftermath, the original American constitution of 1788 became replaced by what legal scholar George Fletcher has called the second American constitution. This 'secret revolution' was prepared through Lincoln's Gettysburg address in 1863, in which

---

3. Yockey, *Imperium*, 459–460.

4. Yockey, *Imperium*, 460–461; however, the total loss of life in the American Civil War amounts to a mere fraction of the millions of fatalities during the Thirty Years War (1618–1648) in Europe.

he employed biblical language from the book of Exodus, and was established through the Thirteenth, Fourteenth, and Fifteenth Reconstruction Amendments issued between 1865 and 1870. It resulted in the following replacements:

i. 'We the people' by 'the nation' (i.e., the national government), as authority;
ii. Freedom by equality, as primary value;
iii. A republican style by democracy, as mode of government; and
iv. The will of the living by the command of history, or a divine mission, as highest power.[5]

In the twentieth century, both the First and the Second World Wars would be fought in the name of 'freedom' and 'democracy' by certain Western nations. In reality, both world wars involved conflicting imperialisms: in the case of the first, between the British, French, and Russian empires on the one hand, and the German, Austro-Hungarian, and Turkish empires on the other; and in the case of the second, between the British, American, and Soviet empires on the one hand, and the German, Italian, and Japanese empires on the other. In addition, the Second World War was a gigantic struggle for power among the three political ideologies of modernism. Initially, from 1939 until 1941, capitalism (as the economic dimension of liberalism) fought fascism while socialism remained neutral. Then, following the Axis attack on the Soviet Union in 1941, socialism and capitalism formed an alliance to fight and ultimately destroy German and Italian fascism by 1945. Ironically, regimes that were more or less fascist survived elsewhere (e.g., in the Iberian Peninsula and South America) for several decades after the war, thus making a mockery of the Anglo-American claim to have destroyed fascism in order to safeguard democracy (as the political dimension of liberalism).

Liberalism

Liberalism, both as word and as ideology, arose around the middle of the eighteenth century, writes Francis Parker Yockey in *Imperium*. Its basic premise is that since human nature is basically good, there is no need to be strict with it, one can be 'liberal.' In contrast to anarchism, which is an

5. Spingola, *Ruling Elite*, 518–519.

idea of genuine political force, liberalism is not a political idea but only an idea about politics, which is why its devotees have to be for or against ideas in order to express their liberalism. Thus, liberalism is essentially non-political, desiring to have politics serve as the handmaid of economics and society.[6]

As rationalism applied to politics, liberalism views the state only as the result of a contract between individuals (e.g., the 'social contract' of Rousseau). The purpose of life is said to be the happiness of the individual. This aim of the state has been coarsely declared by Jeremy Bentham as 'the greatest happiness of the greatest number.' Liberalism is therefore opposed to politics and religion, Yockey contends, which sometimes demands sacrifices for the sake of invisible things, and thus militate against 'happiness.' In contrast, economics and social ethics promote 'happiness,' and are therefore highly regarded.[7]

The ethical theory called utilitarianism, as advocated by Bentham and other British thinkers, answers all questions about how to live, in terms of the maximization of utility, or happiness. Moreover, utilitarianism underlies most modern political and economic planning, based on the assumption that happiness is measurable in economic terms.[8] This emphasis on 'happiness' as the highest aim in life disregards the utter subjectivity of the word, since what gives happiness to one person, or a group of persons, might well have the opposite effect on others. For example, drug addicts strive to maximize their 'happiness' by the frequent intake of drugs, with disastrous results for themselves and those who have to deal with them.

As could be expected from one of the greatest psychologists among philosophers, Friedrich Nietzsche attacked the 'happiness' doctrine, writing: "If a man knows the wherefore of his existence, then the manner of it can take care of itself. Man does not aspire to happiness; only the Englishman does that." At best, Nietzsche argues elsewhere, "the destiny of men is designed for *happy moments* (every life has those), but not for happy eras." The latter is a false conclusion drawn from the relaxation that followed upon powerful exertion in hunting or war, imagining that such a state of happiness could endure in intensity and duration.[9]

---

6. Yockey, *Imperium*, 205, 207.
7. Yockey, *Imperium*, 210.
8. Blackburn, *Oxford Dictionary*, 375.
9. Nietzsche, *Twilight*, 6; Nietzsche, *Human*, 211.

The rationalistic assumption of the inherent goodness of human nature developed two main branches of political theory, Yockey writes. These are (a) liberalism, which uses the assumption to make the state subservient to society; and (b) anarchism, which results from radical acceptance of this assumption. Furthermore, liberalism wants to subject the state to economics by means of the technique called 'balance of power.' Liberalism opposes the state as center of gravity of the political organism, instead preferring 'society' as a loose grouping of free groups and individuals, with their freedom only limited by criminal law. Accordingly, "Liberalism has no objection to individuals being more powerful than the State, being above the law. What Liberalism dislikes is authority. The State, as the grandest symbol of authority, is hated. The two noble orders [i.e., priesthood and aristocracy], as the symbols of authority, are likewise hated."[10] What is understood by authority in this context? Oswald Spengler explains that for States that exist in reality and not merely in intellectual schemes, the most vital question is that of their inner authority, which cannot be maintained in the long run by material means, but only through a belief (by both friend and foe) in their effectiveness.[11]

Yockey continues his literary assault on liberalism by remarking that it is an entirely negative and destructive force, not a living idea. Liberalism wishes to replace the twin authorities of Church and State with economic freedom and social ethics. Even this undermining of proper authority is not enough, for in in its final stages, liberalism produced social atomism. By this stage of socio-cultural decay not only State authority is fought, but even those of society and the family. As a result, divorce takes equal value with marriage, and children assume equality with parents. We have earlier noted Plato's description of the final stage of democratic excess, which applies *ipso facto* to liberalism as well. Ironically, in order to remain politically relevant, the adherents of liberalism have during the nineteenth and twentieth centuries supported 'unfree' ideologies such as anarchism, socialism, and Communism.[12]

An interesting distinction has been made by Yockey between Marxism and Socialism, namely that the former is a religion, whereas the latter is "an instinctive organizatory-political principle." Accordingly, "Marxism had its bible [*Das Kapital*], its saints [Marx and Engels], its apostles [e.g.,

10. Yockey, *Imperium*, 205–206.
11. Spengler, *Decline*, 360.
12. Yockey, *Imperium*, 212–213.

Lenin, Luxemburg, Liebknecht, Stalin, Castro, and Guevara], its heresy-tribunals [of Trotsky and his followers], orthodoxy and heterodoxy [the latter including Mao and Tito], its dogmas and exegesis, sacred writings and schisms."[13] The same observation could be applied to National Socialism in Germany, which also functioned as a secularized version of religion and with the same range of features.

There is a saying that liberals are the most tolerant of people, provided one agrees with them. This well-attested intolerance is attributed by John Gray to liberalism (as is the case with all the modern political ideologies) being a lineal descendant of Christianity and sharing the militancy of its parent faith. The British philosopher remarks further: "The ferocity with which liberal societies have treated their enemies cannot be accounted for in terms of self-defence alone." Gray is of the opinion that liberal societies are worth defending, to the extent that they embody a kind of civilized life in which rival beliefs can peacefully co-exist. However, "when they become missionary regimes this achievement is put at risk. In waging war to promote their values . . . existing liberal societies are corrupted." And this is what happened, Gray notes, when the use of torture was legalized by the US military early in the twenty-first century.[14]

The arch-enemy of liberalism is authority, Yockey remarks, which has two aspects: power and responsibility. Authority is thus the opposite of individualism, which is psychologically speaking nothing but egoism. Therefore, individual 'happiness' (as conceived in liberalism) is actually selfishness. This correlation is exemplified by Rousseau, the grandfather of liberalism, who sent his five children to the foundling hospital in Paris. Yockey further illustrates the relation between power and responsibility with the case of the modern financier, who has only power, but no responsibility: "his very existence is the apotheosis of egoism"; and "he is eminently corruptible by base means, as his ruling desire is for money and ever more money."[15]

These financier-liberals have evolved the theory that power corrupts due its very nature. The classic formulation thereof was by the British historian Lord Acton: "Power tends to corrupt, and absolute power corrupts absolutely." As a matter of fact, Yockey counters, it is vast anonymous wealth (such as that of the financiers) that corrupts, since there are no

13. Yockey, *Imperium*, 88.
14. Gray, *Black Mass*, 271.
15. Yockey, *Imperium*, 215–216.

super-personal restraints on it. It was in the fields of economics and law that liberalism had its most destructive effects on the health of Western civilization. In the words of Yockey: "The criminal law reflected finance-Liberalism by punishing crimes of violence and passion, but not classifying such things as destroying national resources, throwing millions into want, or usury on a national scale." Moreover, liberalism developed an abstraction named 'economic man,' spurred by greed alone. This economic entity serves as the unit of the liberal world-view, and thus for liberalism 'Humanity' is the sum-total of these economic grains of sand.[16]

In his book *Twilight of the Idols*, in a section titled 'My concept of freedom,' the German philosopher Friedrich Nietzsche contrasts true freedom from that 'freedom' proclaimed by liberalism. He writes: "Sometimes the value of a thing does not lie in that which it helps us to achieve, but in the amount we have to pay for it—what it *costs* us. For instance, liberal institutions straightway cease from being liberal the moment they are soundly established: once this is attained no more grievous and more thorough enemies of freedom exist than liberal institutions."[17] Does this reasoning not remind one of the phenomenon called political correctness in the 'liberal democracies' of our time, with its relentless hostility towards freedom of speech?

Nietzsche continues his assault on liberalism as follows: "Liberalism, or in plain English, the *transformation of mankind into cattle*. The same institutions, so long as they are fought for, produce quite other results; then indeed they promote the cause of freedom quite powerfully. What in sooth is freedom? Freedom is the will to be responsible for ourselves. It is to preserve the distance which separates us from other men. To grow more indifferent to hardship, to severity, to privation, and even to life itself. To be ready to sacrifice men for one's cause, one's self included. The man who has won his freedom, and how much more so, therefore, the spirit that has won its freedom, tramples ruthlessly upon that contemptible kind of comfort which tea-grocers, Christians, cows, women, Englishmen and other democrats worship in their dreams. The free man is a *warrior*."[18]

This notion of freedom as something acquired through struggle and sacrifice pertains not only to individuals but also to nations, Nietzsche writes. "The nations which were worth anything, which *got to be* worth

16. Yockey, *Imperium*, 217–218.
17. Nietzsche, *Twilight*, 71.
18. Nietzsche, *Twilight*, 71.

anything, never attained to that condition under liberal institutions: *great danger* made out of them something which deserves reverence, that danger which alone can make us aware of our resources, our virtues, our means of defence, our weapons, our *genius*—which *compels* us to be strong. *First* principle: a man must need to be strong, otherwise he will never attain it."[19] The German philosopher here echoes the same Indo-European spirit as did Goethe (whom he much admired), when the great writer criticized the false idea of freedom as liberation from all traditional values. As Goethe wrote, "Everything which liberates our spirit, without increasing our mastery of ourselves, is pernicious."[20]

In a further section of the same work titled 'A criticism of modernity,' Nietzsche writes that modern democracy is a decaying form of the state. He then contrasts democracy with something more vigorous: "For institutions to be possible there must exist a sort of will, instinct, imperative, which cannot be otherwise than anti-liberal to the point of wickedness: the will to tradition, to authority, to responsibility for centuries to come, to *solidarity* in long family lines forwards and backwards *ad infinitum*. If this will is present, something is founded which resembles the *Imperium Romanum*: or Russia, the *only* great nation today that has some lasting power and grit in her, that can bide her time, that can still promise something. The whole of the Occident no longer possesses those instincts from which institutions spring, out of which a *future* grows: maybe nothing is more opposed to its 'modern spirit' than these things. People live for the present, they live at top speed—they certainly live without any sense of responsibility; and this is precisely what they call 'freedom'. Everything in institutions which makes them institutions, is scorned, loathed and repudiated: everybody is in mortal fear of a new slavery, wherever the word 'authority' is so much as whispered."[21]

In 1848 much of Europe was swept by waves of revolutionary activities, beginning in France (perhaps not surprisingly, given the 1789 revolution and its aftermath). These revolutions have been described as essentially democratic and liberal in nature, with the aim of removing the old monarchical structures and creating independent nation states. The countries most affected by these revolutions were France, the Netherlands, the German states that would make up the Second Empire, Italy, and the Austrian

---

19. Nietzsche, *Twilight*, 71–72.
20. Quoted in Günther, *Religious attitudes*, 71.
21. Nietzsche, *Twilight*, 72–73.

Empire.²² The resulting loss of individual freedom due to the rise of liberalism has been described as follows: "After every constitutional alteration and every upheaval since the middle of the nineteenth century, the peoples of the west have lost more of the freedom of the individual originally peculiar to their nature, and have to bear instead more subjection. Since this process took place gradually, the loss of the freedom which was inherent in the spirit of Indo-European yeomen [freeholders], the loss of that freedom which although weakened and distorted, was still effective in the political liberalism of the nineteenth century, has proceeded unnoticed, while calculating opportunists have readily learned how to exploit officialdom or have themselves obtained high appointment in government offices. As a result there has been a gradual but powerful growth of authoritarianism in both the state and political parties, and in the influence, exercised either openly or in secret of moneyed people behind them."²³

In order of their historical appearance, the three main ideologies of the twentieth century were liberalism, socialism (including Communism), and fascism (including National Socialism and the regimes of Franco, Perón, and Salazar). The violent conflict between these ideologies led to the bloody political history of the twentieth century. As further remarked by Alexander Dugin, liberalism turned out to be the most successful among them, having by the end of the century prevailed over its rivals, of which the most convincing challenge came from Communism. Although fascism emerged later than the others, it vanished before them, due to the alliance between liberalism and socialism during World War Two, combined with Hitler's "suicidal geopolitical miscalculations."²⁴ With the defeat of National Socialism in 1945, the ensuing conflict between liberalism and socialism took the form of the Cold War and generated the strategic geometry of the bipolar world, the latter lasting for nearly half a century. By 1991, liberalism had defeated socialism, as symbolized above all by the break-up of the Soviet Union.²⁵

---

22. Wikipedia: Revolutions of 1848.

23. Günther, *Religious attitudes*, 81–82.

24. Of which we adduce the following examples: (i) invading the USSR in the summer of 1941, while the British Empire remained undefeated in the West; and (ii) declaring war on the USA towards the end of the same year, by which time the Wehrmacht had already become locked into a brutal war of attrition on the Eastern Front, which it had no realistic chance of winning.

25. Dugin, *Theory*, 15–16.

In his perspicacious book *The Metaphysics of World Order*, Nicolas Laos has remarked on the parallels between the former ideological adversaries of liberalism. Both socialism and fascism are totalitarian types of achieving social unity, albeit in variant ways. On the one hand, the biological way of achieving social unity is founded on material processes of adaptation, and it is politically manifested through the total adjustment of all forms of social life to geopolitical and geo-economic conditions, thus leading to fascism/National Socialism. On the other hand, the state-centric way of achieving social unity is founded on what bureaucrats and the Politburo define as a historical necessity, thus leading to Bolshevism or Maoism. And just as Bolshevism is a rationalist interpretation of the Russian people's communal traditions and eschatological visions, so is Maoism a rationalist interpretation of the Chinese people's metaphysical tradition. Both ways attempt to achieve a metaphysical goal by means of legal institutions, and they are therefore unjust.[26]

Paradoxically, the ostensible triumph of liberalism also marked its end, Alexander Dugin contends. How did this come about? While the other competing ideologies were in existence, liberalism continued to grow stronger as an ideology. Each of the three modern ideologies had its own historical subject: for Communism it was class, for fascism it was the state (or race in the case of National Socialism), and for liberalism it was the individual, freed from any collective identity. With the apparent victory of liberalism, the phenomenon of globalization appears, together with the postmodern era and its post-industrial society. As a result, the Russian philosopher adds, "Humanity under liberalism, comprised entirely of individuals, is naturally drawn toward universality and seeks to become global and uniform. Thus, the projects of 'world government' or globalism are born."[27]

That the dehumanizing nature of such a global system of control was foreseen by Nietzsche is evident from these prophetic words penned by him: "Once the earth is brought under all-embracing economic control, then mankind will find it has been reduced to machinery in its service, as a monstrous clockwork system of ever smaller, more finely adjusted wheels."[28] This prophetic view of Nietzsche on the de-humanization of humankind functioning as machinery was shared by twentieth-century

---

26. Laos, *World Order*, 196–197.
27. Dugin, *Theory*, 17–18.
28. Quoted in Günther, *Religious attitudes*, 79.

thinkers such as Albert Schweitzer and Ernst Niekisch. In his autobiography, *My Life and Thought*, Schweitzer writes about the threat of global trade and industrialization to civilization, the latter being founded on agriculture and handicraft. He adds that the machine age (in which we live) has created conditions of existence which made the possession of civilization problematic. In his turn, Niekisch writes of the human reliance on machines, having rejected faith in God, until eventually humans are themselves transformed into machines.[29]

The Greek philosopher Nicolas Laos notes that the origins of modern liberalism can be traced to the English Revolution of 1688, being ideologically based on British empiricism (i.e., the work of the philosophers Locke, Berkeley, and Hume) and constitutionalism. Over the past few centuries, liberalism has undergone the following stages:

i. Original or primitive liberalism, which is characterized by individualism, scepticism, and social-contract theory, and with *laissez-faire* capitalism as its economic component. The Scottish political economist Adam Smith provided the latter system with an ideological foundation in his book *The Wealth of Nations* (1776), arguing that the market mechanism is a self-regulating 'natural' order through which social behaviour is regulated.[30]

ii. Social liberalism, which includes (a) liberal nationalism, derived from the philosophy of Hegel; (b) liberal humanism/cosmopolitanism, derived from the philosophy of Kant; and (c) liberal social democracy, derived from a synthesis of Kantianism, Marxism, phenomenology, and existentialism. In our time, Laos remarks, the latter two aspects of social liberalism have been emphasized by the Hungarian-born American financial speculator George Soros, who has been using his personal wealth and political influence to promote 'progressive' causes in various parts of the world, including the well-established American practice of 'regime change,' aimed at the establishment of a liberal humanist global order.

iii. Conservative liberalism, which involves a synthesis of free-market economics, Hegel's ethnocentric communitarianism, the importance of religious and social traditions, and Heidegger's philosophy of

---

29. Coomaraswamy, *Civilization*, 7, 11.

30. This book has ever since its appearance functioned as the political and economic Bible of the capitalist world, as Alexander Dugin has noted; *Theory*, 141.

Dasein. A prominent representative hereof is the American political scientist Leo Strauss.[31]

As explained by Alexander Dugin, liberalism is a political and economic philosophy and ideology with the following salient characteristics:

i. The understanding of the individual as the measure of all things (thus confirming that liberalism is conceptually based on the world-view of humanism, according to which mankind is the measure of all things);

ii. Belief in the sacred character of private property;

iii. The assertion of the equality of opportunity as the moral law of society;

iv. Belief in the 'contractual' basis of all socio-political institutions, including governmental;

v. The abolition of any governmental, religious, and social authorities who lay claim to 'the common truth';

vi. The separation of powers and the making of social systems of control over any government institution whatsoever;

vii. The creation of a civil society without races, peoples, and religions in place of traditional governments;

viii. The dominance of market relations over other forms of politics, according to the thesis that economics is fate;

ix. Certainty that the historical path of Western peoples and countries is a universal model of development and progress for the entire world, which must, in an imperative order, be taken as the standard and pattern.[32]

It is important to note that the 'freedom' espoused by liberalism is not 'freedom to,' but only 'freedom from.' In other words, it is a purely negative freedom, as was advocated by liberal philosophers such as John Stuart Mill. In this conception, liberty implies freedom from something, from where the word 'liberalism' is derived. Dugin further remarks that on the meaning and goal of freedom, which is 'freedom to,' liberals are silent, thinking that it is up to each individual to apply his/her freedom or to neglect it altogether. In contrast, the 'freedom from' of liberals is precisely defined, namely to be free from governmental control over the economy, politics and civil

---

31. Laos, *Metaphysics*, 107, 110–111.
32. Dugin, *Theory*, 140–141.

society; churches and their dogmas;[33] class systems; any common areas of common responsibility for the economy; any attempt at redistribution of wealth, since social justice is viewed as 'immoral'; ethnic attachments; and any kind of collective identity.[34]

Oswald Spengler had earlier observed that liberalism is constituted by two main kinds of freedom from restrictions, namely freedom of the intellect for every kind of criticism, and freedom of money for every kind of business. Moreover, in the democratic context, freedom is a purely negative thing, involving the repudiation of tradition. However, this results in the transfer of executive power from the former institutions to the new forces of party leaders, dictators, presidents, and their adherents.[35]

Some of the practical implications of the liberal insistence on 'freedom from' are pointed out by Alexander Dugin. Government should sooner or later die out, opening the way for the establishment of a world government and a world civil society. All socio-political institutions should be repudiated, including the family and sexual differentiation. This explains the liberals' support for the freedom of abortion and the rights of homosexuals and transsexuals. The organic institution of the family becomes a purely contractual matter, conditioned by legal agreements. The 'freedom from' of liberals pertain not only to any sense of tradition and the sacred, but also to socialization and redistribution; the latter distinguishing liberalism from other leftist ideologies such as Communism and socialism.[36]

Neo-conservatism

With the ostensible victory of liberalism over rival ideologies at the beginning of the 1990s, symbolized above all by the breakup of the Soviet Union and the transition of Russia and most of Eastern Europe from socialism to capitalism, liberalism obtained a monopoly on the direction of historical development. Alexander Dugin adds that in this situation the USA, as the citadel of world liberalism, became the only remaining superpower. As a result, "the USA received a concrete confirmation of its messianism, which,

---

33. It is significant that the anti-religious stance which is so popular among Western liberals is mainly aimed at Christianity, since they usually support 'religious freedom' for adherents of any of the non-Christian religions or cults, in the name of 'equal rights.'
34. Dugin, *Theory*, 141–142.
35. Spengler, *Decline*, 368–369, 392.
36. Dugin, *Theory*, 142–143.

in the ideology of Manifest Destiny, was, since the Nineteenth century, an article of faith for the American political elite. American neo-conservatives recognized this arrangement of matters more clearly than anyone else. In the words of one of their most important ideologues, William Kristol, 'The Twentieth century was the century of America's rise, but the Twenty-first century will be the American century.'" According to the neo-conservatives, Dugin continues, "The entire planet must henceforth become a 'World America', 'World Government' or 'World State'. This is not simply colonisation or a new form of imperialism, this is a programme of the total implementation of the one and only ideological system, copied from American liberal ideology."[37] And since the beginning of the new millennium, nations in different parts of the world have been paying a heavy price in blood and destruction for this permutation of liberalism into neo-conservatism, as expressed in the slogan of 'American exceptionalism.'

However, the reciprocity between neo-liberalism and neo-conservatism has by no means been limited to the United States. In his well-argued book *Black Mass: Apocalyptic Religion and the Death of Utopia*, the British philosopher John Gray depicts the take-over of British politics by adherents of utopian ideologies. This process began during the premiership of Margaret Thatcher, who came to power in 1979 as a conservative and during the 1980s transformed into a neo-liberal. By the time Thatcher was ousted from power in 1990, she had come to view neo-liberal policies as a model for a global programme. Rather ironically, although Thatcher rejected the celebrated statement by Francis Fukuyama that history had come to an end (referring to the apparent capitalist victory over socialism at the end of the Cold War), she became convinced that the United States had become at the end of the twentieth century what she believed Britain had been a century earlier—the final guarantor of world-wide progress, by means of American 'democratic capitalism.'[38]

Thatcher's mantle would be assumed by Tony Blair, the Labour leader who also came to accept neo-liberal policies. However, after the 2001 attacks in New York, Blair shifted decisively to neo-conservatism. In a passage aptly titled 'An American Neo-Conservative in 10 Downing Street,' Gray proceeds to describe Blair's ideological commitment to the global enforcement of neo-liberalism/neo-conservatism. This includes military attacks on Iraq in 1998 and Serbia in 1999, and invading Afghanistan in

---

37. Dugin, *Theory*, 147–148.
38. Gray, *Black Mass*, 106, 116.

2002 and Iraq in 2003. In the context of Blair's flagrant use of deception and disinformation to instigate war against Iraq, Gray also remarks that "whereas in the past lies were an intermittent feature of government, under his leadership they became integral to its functioning."[39]

The ideological kinship (based on utopianism) between Blair and his fellow warmonger, the American president George Bush, has been accurately stated by John Gray. Both 'leaders' combined "a shallow but intense religiosity with a militant faith in human progress." Both interpreted recent history, the only history they knew, as showing that humankind had entered a completely new era. Both conceived "the challenges of the early twenty-first century in terms of the triumphal illusions of the post-Cold War era." Finally, both "practised a missionary style of politics, whose goal was nothing less than the salvation of mankind."[40]

The American ideology of messianism had earlier been accurately described by Francis Parker Yockey. During the twentieth century, the American universalizing of ideology turned into messianism—the idea that America must save the world. "The vehicle of the salvation is to be a materialistic religion with 'democracy' taking the place of God, 'Constitution' the place of the Church, 'principles of government' the place of religious dogmas, and the idea of economic freedom the place of God's grace. The technic of salvation is to embrace the dollar, or failing that, to submit to American high-explosives and bayonets."[41] These words ring as true today as when they were written in the late 1940s, except that the enforcement is now also done by means of 'regime change' and drone attacks.

Post-liberalism

The ideological monopoly enjoyed by liberalism in the twenty-first century, Alexander Dugin writes, has resulted in its content changing from classical liberalism to post-liberalism, corresponding to the epochal switch-over from modernity to post-modernity. The current ideology of post-liberalism displays the following grotesque characteristics:

---

39. Gray, *Black Mass*, 119, 131, 137, 147.
40. Gray, *Black Mass*, 148–149.
41. Yockey, *Imperium*, 456.

i. The measure of all things becomes not the individual, but the post-individual or 'dividual', being little more than an ironic combination of parts such as organs, clones, and simulacra;[42]

ii. The idolization of private property, which ends up owning its owner;

iii. Equality of opportunity becomes equality of the contemplation of opportunities, as manifested in the 'society of the spectacle';

iv. Belief in the contractual character of all socio-political institutions grows into a merging of the real and the virtual, so that the world becomes a technical model;

v. All forms of non-individual authority disappear completely, so that common rationality is replaced by unfettered subjective individualism;

vi. The principle of the separation of powers (i.e., legislative, executive, and judicial) transforms into the notion of a constant electronic referendum, where each internet user constantly 'votes' by giving his/her opinion in any number of forums, so that each individual effectively becomes his/her own branch of government;

vii. So-called 'civil society' completely displaces government and degenerates into a global, cosmopolitan melting pot;

viii. The thesis 'economics is destiny' is replaced by 'the numerical code is destiny', with all economic activity becoming virtual.[43]

The socio-political concept of gender has naturally also changed under the conditions of postmodernity, Dugin remarks. He writes that all three political theories of modernity (liberalism, socialism, and fascism) project their own gender archetypes into postmodernity. The resulting postmodern gender is a maximization of 'the liberal man', the archetype of which applies to all of its antitheses, such as the stupid, the poor, and the non-white. It is also the gender of globalization, in which the properties of liberalism are universalized as social standards. The Russian philosopher adds: "Hence the idea that the proletarians are only the bourgeoisie who have not grown rich yet, blacks are unmodernised whites, and women are not yet fully liberated men. That is, we see that this all-consuming archetype becomes meaningless." Dugin then predicts that the postmodern

---

42. Hence the fascination with cyborgs and androids in science-fiction films since the 1980s, such as the *Terminator*, *Alien*, and *Blade Runner* sagas.

43. Dugin, *Theory*, 150–151.

re-extension of existing gender models will explode (or perhaps implode) into a final breaking of gender. This break with the reality of gender includes the phenomena of feminism, homosexuality, sex-change operations, and trans-humanity.[44]

Against those liberal ideologues who have vainly been attempting to preserve classical liberalism, including the market, the nation-state, and scientific rationalism, Dugin points out that this transformation from 'normal' liberalism to the liberalism of post-modernity is neither arbitrary nor voluntary. Instead, it is contained in the very structure of the liberal ideology, for in the course of the gradual liberation of humankind from all supra-individual values and ideals, sooner or later such a person is freed from his or her own self.[45] Clearly, post-modern liberalism has to be condemned as a satanic parody of true freedom.

How did humankind arrive at this metaphysical abyss? Dugin explains: "The path that humanity entered upon in the modern era led precisely to liberalism and to the repudiation of God, tradition, community, ethnicity, empires and kingdoms. Such a path is tread entirely logically: having decided to liberate itself from everything that keeps man in check, the man of the modern era reached his logical apogee: before our eyes he is liberated from himself. The logic of world liberalism and globalisation pulls into the abyss of postmodern dissolution and virtuality. The usual phenomenon now is the loss of identity, and already not simply only national or cultural identity, but even sexual, and soon enough even human identity."[46]

Considering these facts and arguments, those who value truth and justice have to agree with Alexander Dugin that liberalism is an absolute evil, not only in its practice but also in its theoretical presuppositions. He adds: "'Freedom from' is the most disgusting form of slavery, inasmuch as it tempts man into an insurrection against God, against traditional values, against the moral and spiritual foundations of his people and his culture." Therefore, this evil can only be defeated by tearing it out from its roots; the latter being precisely the heresy of humanism, according to which man is the measure of all things.[47] Rather ironically, this modernist version of

---

44. Dugin, *Theory*, 190–191.
45. Dugin, *Theory*, 151.
46. Dugin, *Theory*, 154–155.
47. Dugin, *Theory*, 155.

humanism is actually less and less a true humanism since it de-humanizes, while its vaunted individualism is ever more infra-individual.[48]

The conceptual link between liberalism and humanism, as well as its globalist aspirations, has also been remarked on by John Gray. In his thought-provoking book *Straw Dogs*, the British philosopher observes that liberal humanism today holds the pervasive power that in times past belonged to revealed religion. In addition, the humanists' belief in 'progress' is a superstition which is further from the truth about humankind than any of the world's religions. Rather ironically, the idea of free will, which is so important in the secular humanist world-view, has its origins not in science, but in the Christian faith which the humanists view as their arch-rival.[49]

However, Gray continues, it is a matter of pride among contemporary philosophers to be ignorant of theology. Consequently, the Christian origins of secular humanism are rarely understood, although it was clear to the French Positivists Henri Saint-Simon and August Comte, who founded the so-called Religion of Humanity early in the nineteenth century. This was a vision of a universal civilization based on science, which became the prototype for the political religions of the twentieth century (i.e., liberalism, socialism, and fascism). The mentioned Positivists shaped both the secular creed of liberalism through their influence on John Stuart Mill, and that of 'scientific socialism' through their influence on Karl Marx. Ultimately, Gray points out, humanism is not science, but religion—namely, "the post-Christian faith that humans can make a world better than any in which they have so far lived." Moreover, humanism is the transformation of the Christian doctrine of salvation into a project of universal emancipation; and the idea of progress is a secular version of the Christian belief in providence.[50] We could therefore say that liberalism, humanism, and globalism are secularized residues, if not caricatures, of the Christian religion.

It has been pointed out by Nicolas Laos that from the viewpoint of Hellenic and Byzantine philosophy, both Western humanism and its ostensible opposite, theocracy, are based on erroneous ontological views. Whereas theocracy conceives the purpose (Greek, *telos*) of being as a petrified institution, Western humanism subordinates the significance of beings and things to historical becoming. Laos contrasts these views with the theocentric character of Hellenic and Byzantine thought, according to

---

48. Schuon, *Ancient Worlds*, 71.
49. Gray, *Straw Dogs*, xi–xii.
50. Gray, *Straw Dogs*, xii–xiii.

which existence is not a value in itself and time is not a self-moving dimension of existence. Moreover, the meaning of being cannot be completely determined by logic, and it is therefore not a closed system.[51]

Alexander Dugin writes that in our time liberalism appears to be inevitable according to the logic of fate, as was the case with National Socialism in Germany in the 1930s. And like those patriotic Germans who resisted the rise of Hitler (such as the 'National Bolsheviks' Ernst Niekisch and Harro Schulze-Boysen), knowing that they were facing a fate-driven force that appeared to be invincible, so those in our time who value truth and justice are called to arms by Dugin: "Liberalism is the evil fate of human civilization. The battle with it, opposition to it, and refutation of its poisonous dogmas—this is the moral imperative of all honest people on the planet. At all costs, we must, argumentatively and thoroughly, again and again, repeat that truth, even when to do so seems useless, untimely, politically incorrect, and sometimes even dangerous."[52] Or, as Nietzsche argued, if one holds a positive view of freedom, which is 'freedom to,' one has to be relentlessly anti-liberal.

Unipolarity and Multipolarity

The postmodern world that we are now living in is unipolar, with the global West as its center and the United States as its core. This situation holds certain geopolitical and ideological implications, Alexander Dugin adds. Geopolitically, unipolarity is the strategic dominance of the Earth by the North American hyperpower and its relentless project to organize the planetary balance of forces in such a manner that it can rule the whole world according to its own national and imperialist interests. Ideologically, unipolarity is based on modernist and postmodernist values that are openly anti-traditional in nature. Dugin expresses his agreement with Traditionalist authors such as René Guénon and Julius Evola, who viewed modernity and its expressions in individualism, liberal democracy, capitalism, and consumerism to be the cause of the future catastrophe of humanity.[53] Such a world-wide catastrophe will most likely be the outcome if the ongoing process of socio-cultural decay and degradation brought about by the postmodern West can't be reversed.

51. Laos, *World Order*, 195–196.
52. Dugin, *Theory*, 139–140.
53. Dugin, *Theory*, 193.

Alexander Dugin continues his assault on the evil of unipolarity, as he calls it: "Spiritually, globalisation is the creation of a grand parody, the kingdom of the Antichrist. And the United States is the centre of its expansion. American values pretend to be 'universal' ones. In reality, it is a new form of ideological aggression against the multiplicity of cultures and traditions still existing in the rest of the world." While calling for opposition by all those who support traditional principles and values against Western globalization, Dugin admits that there are exceptions. For example, there are people in the West, including the United States, who are opposed to modernity and postmodernity. As Dugin writes, "They are the defenders of the spiritual traditions of the pre-modern West. They should be with us [traditionalists] in our common struggle." The common enemy is Western globalization and American imperialism, and therefore our allies include those Muslims, Christians, Hindus, Jews, Russians, Chinese, both of the Left and the Right, who reject the present social reality. Employing Aristotelian terminology (in Latin), Dugin writes: "Our ideals that differ are potential ones (*in potentia*). But the challenge we are dealing with is actual (*in actu*). That is the basis for a new alliance." And this includes those Americans who choose the path of tradition over the present decadence.[54]

In the current unipolar world, liberals and neo-conservatives (which in practice amount to the same thing, both being anti-traditional and therefore anti-civilization) strive to enforce their hegemony over the whole world. This ongoing project of global dominance has been opposed by recent thinkers who have posited a multipolar world order. In such a world, Alexander Dugin notes, the poles will be as many as the various civilizations, such as those listed by Samuel Huntington.[55] In his 1996 book titled *The Clash of Civilizations and the Remaking of World Order*, the American political scientist divides the world into the following major civilizations:

i. Western: North America and Europe to the west of Belarus, Ukraine, and Romania;
ii. Chinese: China, Korea, and Vietnam;
iii. Japanese: Japan;
iv. Buddhist: Mongolia, Tibet, and Indochina minus Vietnam;
v. Islamic: North Africa, South-western Asia, Indonesia, and Malaysia;

---

54. Dugin, *Theory*, 193–194.
55. Dugin, *Theory*, 117.

vi. Hindu: India and Nepal;

vii. Slavic-Orthodox: Russia, Kazakhstan, Georgia, Armenia, and Eastern Europe from Belarus southwards to Greece and Cyprus;

viii. Latin America: South and Central America;

ix. Africa: south of the Sahara.[56]

It is significant, we suggest, that at least four of these civilizations have been determined by their respective religious traditions (i.e., Buddhist, Islamic, Hindu, and Orthodox), thereby confirming the essential link between spirituality and culture, as traditionally understood but rejected by modernism. In this regard, we also mention the concept of cosmogenetic systems underlying civilizations, as postulated by Nicolas Laos. Each cosmogenetic system comprises a historical and spiritual entity, summarized as follows:

i. Occidentalism, i.e., the civilizations that constitute 'the West.' This system is based on a thesis that arose in Western Christianity, namely that truth is inseparable from the individual. It is expressed in individualism, of which liberalism is the dominant form in Anglo-American political thought. In partial contrast, German individualism is counter-balanced by holism in social organization.

ii. Orientalism, i.e., the civilizations that constitute 'the East,' of which the major constituent parts are the Indian, the Chinese, and the Islamic civilization zones. In this system, society imposes tightly interdependent relations among its members on the one hand (i.e., holism), while allowing mystics to pursue their independence from the social environment through renunciation of the world. Oriental mystics could therefore be viewed as 'otherworldly' individuals, as opposed to Western 'worldly' individuals. Prominent mystical ways in the East are Taoism and Sufism, which have also attained some popularity in the West.

iii. Hellenism, i.e., the spiritual tradition founded by Plato and further developed in Orthodox theology. This system differs fundamentally from both individualism and holism, for it conceives the act of being as participation in the Logos. Moreover, since the Logos is the

56. Wikipedia: Clash of Civilizations.

metaphysical foundation of society, 'to be' and 'to be social' are identical.[57]

Stated in terms of international politics, Laos continues, Western Europe is the cradle of Occidentalism. It finds itself in the dilemma of being unable to create a true society, due to its commitment to individualism. And since the members of this system are 'individuals' and not 'persons' (the latter, in the classical understanding, meaning an existential otherness in social relationships, characterized by freedom of will), social unity can only be attained by suppressing individualism through authoritarianism and totalitarianism. In its turn, Asia is the cradle of Orientalism. In so far as it adheres to the tradition of holism, it gives rise to traditionalist conservatism. However, this does not prevent rich systems of spirituality coexisting with material poverty and exploitative relations. In contrast to these Western European and Asian systems, Hellenism offers the prospect of a sustainable international order through its assimilation and transcending of both individualism and holism, being based on the metaphysics of personhood. Geopolitically, this conception leads to a multipolar system, since multipolarity is philosophically founded on the concept of personhood.[58]

Of further relevance is the observation by Alexander Dugin that Europe has two identities: the 'Atlantic,' comprising Britain and the countries of Eastern Europe, all being motivated by Russophobia; and the 'Continental,' centred on Germany, France, Spain, and Italy. In contrast to the former group, the latter is more inclined to a degree of independence from American domination.[59] And as far as contemporary Greece is concerned, Nicolas Laos points out, it should not in any way be identified with Hellenism. The modern Greek state was founded in 1830 on the basis of Western political principles obtained from Germany, France, and Britain. Thus, both the Greek state and the Church of Greece became subservient to Western interests.[60] The same observation applies to the Greek Orthodox patriarchate based in Istanbul, which views itself as the Orthodox version of the Catholic papacy by claiming supremacy over the whole Orthodox church family. It has also since the early twentieth century been engaged in an ongoing campaign against the largest member of this church family, the

57. Laos, *World Order*, 204–208.
58. Laos, *World Order*, 209–212.
59. Dugin, *Theory*, 118.
60. Laos, *World Order*, 159, 210; for a detailed discussion, see Sherrard, *Greek East*, 165-195.

Russian Orthodox, thereby serving the interests of the Western ruling elites with their ingrained Russophobia.

The list of civilizations mentioned above gives us an idea of the composition of a multipolar world order, in which humanity will enjoy a broad choice of cultural, social, and spiritual alternatives. In such a multipolar world, Alexander Dugin adds, "Reason and the philosophical, social, political, and economic systems created by it will be able to develop according to its own lines, while the collective unconscious will freely preserve its archetypes, its basis and inviolability." Thus, "There will be no universal standard, neither in the material nor in the spiritual aspect. Each civilization will at last receive the right to freely proclaim that which is, according to its own wishes, the measure of things."[61]

It is our contention that the geopolitical models mentioned above correspond to various cosmological models. First, there existed the bipolar world order of the Cold War era (1945–91), which was dominated by the American and Soviet blocs, and in which each side was powerful enough to deter the other from an all-out attack. This corresponds to a dualist cosmology in which there is no common principle above the two realms. Next, there exists the unipolar world order which the Anglo-American elites and their European followers have been striving to enforce onto the rest of the world since the end of the Soviet era. That this situation is far more dangerous than the previous bipolar order has been experienced since the 1990s by several countries in different parts of the world (e.g., Serbia, Iraq, Libya, Syria, and Ukraine). This model corresponds to a monist cosmology in which ontological differentiation is not recognized. In contrast to both of these models, we propose a multipolar world order, which is based on various civilizational centers characterized by different spiritual and cultural traditions. This model corresponds with the cosmology of a differentiated unity, in which the many receive their reality from a single Principle.

Undoubtedly, the world-wide cultural freedom within a multipolar world order will approximate true freedom, or 'freedom to,' much more so than the negative freedom, or 'freedom from,' of liberalism. A multipolar world order would also correlate with the metaphysical reality of the transcendent One manifesting in the many of the here and now, thereby remaining true to the nature of the cosmic order.

---

61. Dugin, *Theory*, 119–120.

Bibliography

Unless otherwise indicated, quotations from the Bible are from the New King James Version, with Greek text obtained from the Greek-English New Testament; quotations from the Pre-Socratic fragments are from the translation by Richard McKirahan; quotations from the *Bhagavad Gita* are from the translation by Mohandas Gandhi; quotations from the Neoplatonic writings are from the translations by John Dillon and Lloyd Gerson; and quotations from the Dionysian writings are from the translation by Colm Luibheid.

Alfeyev, Hilarion. "*Music and Faith in My Life and Vision.*" American Orthodox Institute (2011). http://www.aoiusa.org/met-hilarion-alfeyev-music-and-faith-in-my-life-and-vision/

———. *The Mystery of Faith. An Introduction to the Teaching and Spirituality of the Orthodox Church.* Edited by Jessica Rose. London: Darton, Longman & Todd, 2002.

———. "*Western secular civilization leads to extinction*" (2013). http://www.pravmir.com/church-and-state-an-international-forum-on-coexistence/

Aquinas, Thomas. *Selected Philosophical Writings.* Translated by Timothy McDermott. Oxford & New York: Oxford University Press, 1993.

Aristotle. *Categories.* Translated by E.M. Edghill. In *The Basic Works of Aristotle*, edited by Richard McKeon. New York: The Modern Library, 2001.

———. *Metaphysics.* Translated by W.D. Ross. In *The Basic Works of Aristotle*, edited by Richard McKeon. New York: The Modern Library, 2001.

———. *Nicomachean Ethics.* Translated by W.D. Ross. In *The Basic Works of Aristotle*, edited by Richard McKeon. New York: The Modern Library, 2001.

———. *On the Soul.* Translated by J.A. Smith. In *The Basic Works of Aristotle*, edited by Richard McKeon. New York: The Modern Library, 2001.

———. *Physics.* Translated by R.P. Hardie and R.K. Gaye. In *The Basic Works of Aristotle*, edited by Richard McKeon. New York: The Modern Library, 2001.

———. *Politics.* Translated by Benjamin Jowett. In *The Basic Works of Aristotle*, edited by Richard McKeon. New York: The Modern Library, 2001.

Augustine. *The City of God against the Pagans.* Edited and translated by R.W. Dyson. Cambridge: Cambridge University Press, 1998.

———. *The Confessions.* Translator unknown; edited by Patricia Klein. Peabody, Massachusetts: Hendrickson, 2004.

Basil of Caesarea. "Homilies on the Hexaemeron." In *The Patristic Understanding of Creation. An Anthology of Writings from the Church Fathers on Creation and Design*, edited by William A. Dembski et al., 284-339. Riesel, Texas: Erasmus, 2008.

BIBLIOGRAPHY

Berdyaev, Nicolas. *The Destiny of Man*. Translated by Natalie Duddington. London: Geoffrey Bless, 1954 (Fourth edition).

———. "The Problem of Being and Existence." In *The Existentialist Tradition. Selected Writings*, edited by Nino Langiulli. New Jersey: Humanities, 1981.

Bhagavad-Gítá. The Song of God. Translated, with a Commentary, by Mahatma Gandhi. Stepney, South Australia: Axiom, 2002.

Black, Jonathan. *The Sacred History. How Angels, Mystics and Higher Intelligence Made our World*. London: Quercus, 2013.

———. *The Secret History of the World*. London: Quercus, 2010 (Second, revised edition).

Blackburn, Simon. *The Oxford Dictionary of Philosophy*. Oxford: Oxford University Press, 2008.

Bloom, Anthony. "Death and Bereavement." In *Living Orthodoxy in the Modern World*, edited by Costa Carras and Andrew Walker. London: SPCK, 1996.

Bolton, Robert. *The Order of the Ages. The Hidden Laws of World History*. Kettering, OH: Angelico Press/Sophia Perennis, 2015 (Third, revised edition).

Bucke, Richard Morris. *Cosmic Consciousness* (1901). http://www.sacred-texts.com/eso/cc/index.htm

Campbell, C.G. *Race and Religion*. Westport, Connecticut: Greenwood, 1970.

Camus, Albert. *Christian Metaphysics and Neoplatonism*. Translated by Ronald D. Srigley. Columbia, Missouri: University of Missouri Press, 2007.

———. *The Myth of Sisyphus*. Translated by Justin O'Brien. Middlesex: Penguin, 1975.

Carabine, Deirdre. *John Scottus Eriugena*. New York and Oxford: Oxford University Press, 2000.

Cohen, S. Marc. "*Plato's Cosmology: The Timaeus*" (2006). http://faculty.washington.edu/smcohen/320/timaeus.htm

Coomaraswamy, Ananda. *The Bugbear of Literacy*. Bedfont, Middlesex: Perennial, 1979.

———. *What is Civilization? And other essays*. Ipswich: Golgonooza, 1989.

Cooper, John M., editor. *Plato. Collected Works*. Indianapolis, Indiana: Hackett, 1997.

Cornford, Francis. *Plato's Cosmology. The Timaeus of Plato*. Indianapolis, Indiana: Hackett, 1997.

Curd, Patricia. "Presocratic Philosophy." Stanford Encyclopedia of Philosophy (2011). http://plato.stanford.edu/entries/presocratics/

Dillon, John and Lloyd P. Gerson, eds. *Neoplatonic Philosophy. Introductory Readings*. Indianapolis, Indiana: Hackett, 2004.

Dionysius the Areopagite. *Pseudo-Dionysius. The complete works*. Translated by Colm Luibheid. Mahwah, New Jersey: Paulist, 1987.

Dreyer, P.S. *Die Wysbegeerte van die Grieke* [The Philosophy of the Greeks]. Kaapstad & Pretoria: HAUM, 1975.

Dugin, Alexander. *The Fourth Political Theory*. Translated by Mark Sleboda and Michael Millerman. London: Arktos, 2012.

Ferguson, Kitty. *Pythagoras. His Lives and the Legacy of a Rational Universe*. London: Icon, 2011.

Flannery, Michael A. *Alfred Russell Wallace's Theory of Intelligent Evolution*. Riesel, Texas: Erasmus, 2011.

Geldard, Richard. *Anaxagoras and Universal Mind. The Birth of Philosophy in Classical Greece*. New York: The Ralph Walso Emerson Institute, 2007.

Gerson, Lloyd P. *Aristotle and Other Platonists*. Ithaca, New York: Cornell University Press, 2005.

Goosen, Danie. *Die Nihilisme. Notas oor ons tyd* [Nihilism. Notes on our time]. Pretoria: Praag, 2007.

———. *Oor Gemeenskap en Plek. Anderkant die onbehae* [On Community and Place. Beyond Unease]. Pretoria: FAK, 2015.

Gray, John. *Black Mass. Apocalyptic Religion and the Death of Utopia.* London: Penguin, 2008.

———. *Straw Dogs. Thoughts on Humans and Other Animals.* London: Granta, 2003.

Greek-English New Testament. Greek text Novum Testamentum Graece, in the tradition of Eberhard and Erwin Nestle, edited by Barbara and Kurt Aland. Stuttgart, Deutsche Bibelgesellschaft, 2001 (Ninth, revised edition).

Guénon, René. *Man and his Becoming according to the Vedanta.* Translated by Richard Nicholson. London: Luzac, 1945.

———. *The Reign of Quantity and the Signs of the Times.* Translated by Lord Northbourne. Ghent, New York: Sophia Perennis et Universalis, 1995.

———. "Spirit and Intellect." *Studies in Comparative Religion*, Vol. 15, No. 3 & 4 (1983). www.studiesincomparativereligion.com

Günther, Hans F. K. *The religious attitudes of the Indo-Europeans.* CreateSpace, 2013 (Third edition).

Haudry, Jean. *The Indo-Europeans.* Translated by Ian Allan. Lyon: Institut d'Études Indo-Européenes, 1994.

Heidegger, Martin. *Introduction to metaphysics.* Translated by Gregory Fried and Richard Polt. New Haven: Yale University Press, 2000.

The Holy Bible. New King James Version. Nashville, Tennessee: Thomas Nelson, 1982.

Hughes, David G. *A History of European Music. The Art Music Tradition of Western Culture.* New York: McGraw-Hill, 1974.

Iamblichus (attributed to). *The Theology of Arithmetic. On the Mystical, Mathematical and Cosmological Symbolism of the First Ten Numbers.* Translated by Robin Waterfield. Grand Rapids, Michigan: Phanes, 1988.

Kalachanis, Konstantinos, et al. "The Theory of the Big Bang and the early Christian Teaching about the 'ex nihilo' Creation of the Universe." *European Journal of Science and Theology* Vol 15, No 2 (2019) 31-37.

King, Russell, ed. *Origins. An atlas of human migration.* London: Marshall, 2007.

Knuuttila, Simo. "Time and creation in Augustine." In *The Cambridge Companion to Augustine*, edited by Eleonore Stump and Norman Kretzmann. Cambridge: Cambridge University Press, 2001, 103-115.

Laos, Nicolas. *The Metaphysics of World Order. A Synthesis of Philosophy, Theology, and Politics.* Eugene, Oregon: Pickwick, 2015.

Liddell and Scott Greek-English Lexicon (Abridged edition). Oxford: Oxford University Press, 2004.

Lossky, Vladimir. *The Mystical Theology of the Eastern Church.* Translated by the Fellowship of St Alban and St Sergius. Cambridge: James Clarke., 1991.

———. *Orthodox Theology. An Introduction.* Translated by Ian and Ihita Kesarcodi-Watson. Crestwood, New York. St Vladimir's Seminary, 1978.

Lundy, Miranda. "Sacred Number" and "Sacred Geometry." In *Quadrivium. The four classical liberal arts of number, geometry, music & cosmology*, edited by John Martineau. Glastonbury: Wooden, 2010.

Marlow, A.N. "Hinduism and Buddhism in Greek Philosophy." *Philosophy East and West* Vol 4, no 1 (1954) 35-45. http://ccbs.ntu.edu.tw/fulltext/jr-phil/marlow.htm

Martijn, Marije. Review of *Physics and Philosophy of Nature in Greek Neoplatonism*, edited by Riccardo Chiaradonna and Franco Trabattoni. *Aestimatio : Critical Reviews in the History of Science* 9 (2012) 25-52.

McKeon, Richard, editor. *The Basic Works of Aristotle*. New York: The Modern Library, 2001.

McKirahan, Richard. *Philosophy before Socrates. An Introduction with Texts and Commentary*. Indianapolis, Indiana: Hackett, 1994.

Mendl, R.W.S. *The Divine Quest in Music*. London: Rockliff, 1957.

Moore, Edward. "Neoplatonism." Internet Encyclopaedia of Philosophy (2005). http://iep.utm.edu/neoplato/

———. "Plotinus." Internet Encyclopedia of Philosophy (2001). http://www.iep.utm.edu/plotinus/

Moran, Dermot. *The Philosophy of John Scottus Eriugena. A Study of Idealism in the Middle Ages*. Cambridge: Cambridge University Press, 1989.

Myers, Ken. "Music in a Meaningful World: The Church's Witness." Philip Edgcumbe Hughes Lecture Series. Dallas, Texas: The Chapel of the Cross, 2016.

Nietzsche, Friedrich Wilhelm. *The Antichrist. An Attempted Criticism of Christianity*. Translated by Antony M. Ludovici. London: Wordsworth, 2007.

———. *Beyond Good and Evil*. Translated by Helen Zimmern and Paul V. Cohn. London: Wordsworth, 2008.

———. *Human, All-Too-Human. A Book for Free Spirits*. Translated by Helen Zimmern and Paul V. Cohn. London: Wordsworth, 2008.

———. *Thus Spoke Zarathustra*. Translated by R.J. Hollingdale. Harmondsworth: Penguin, 1969.

———. *Twilight of the Idols, or How to Philosophize with the Hammer*. Translated by Antony M. Ludovici. London: Wordsworth, 2007.

Northbourne, Lord. *Looking back on progress*. Ghent, New York: Sophia Perennis et Universalis, 1995.

Oosthuizen, J.S. *Van Plotinus tot Teilhard de Chardin. 'n Studie oor die metamorfose van die Westerse werklikheidsbeeld* [From Plotinus to Teilhard de Chardin. A study on the metamorphosis of the Western world-view]. Amsterdam: Rodopi, 1974.

The Oxford Study Bible. Revised English Bible with the Apocrypha. Edited by M. Jack Suggs, Katharine Doob Sakenfeld and James R. Mueller. New York: Oxford University Press, 1992.

Perl, Eric D. *Theophany. The Neoplatonic Philosophy of Dionysius the Areopagite*. Albany, New York: State University of New York Press, 2007.

Perry, Whitall N., ed. *A Treasury of Traditional Wisdom*. Cambridge, Quinta Essentia, 1991.

Plato. *Cratylus*. Translated by C.D.C. Reeve. In *Collected Works*, edited by John M. Cooper. Indianapolis, Indiana: Hackett, 1997.

———. *Laws*. Translated by Trevor J. Saunders. In *Collected Works*, edited by John M. Cooper. Indianapolis, Indiana: Hackett, 1997.

———. *Letter VII*. Translated by Glenn R. Morrow. In *Collected Works*, edited by John M. Cooper. Indianapolis, Indiana: Hackett, 1997.

———. *Parmenides*. Translated by Mary Louise Gill and Paul Ryan. In *Collected Works*, edited by John M. Cooper. Indianapolis, Indiana: Hackett, 1997.

———. *Phaedo*. Translated by G.M.A Grube. In *Collected Works*, edited by John M. Cooper. Indianapolis, Indiana: Hackett, 1997.

———. *Phaedrus*. Translated by Alexander Nehamas and Paul Woodruff. In *Collected Works*, edited by John M. Cooper. Indianapolis, Indiana: Hackett, 1997.
———. *The Republic*. Translated by Desmond Lee. London: Penguin, 1987.
———. *Second Alcibiades*. Translated by Anthony Kenny. In *Collected Works*, edited by John M. Cooper. Indianapolis, Indiana: Hackett, 1997.
———. *Sophist*. Translated by Nicholas P. White. In *Collected Works*, edited by John M. Cooper. Indianapolis, Indiana: Hackett, 1997.
———. *Symposium*. Translated by Alexander Nehamas and Paul Woodruff. In *Collected Works*, edited by John M. Cooper. Indianapolis, Indiana: Hackett, 1997.
———. *Theaetetus*. Translated by M.J. Levett, revised by Myles Burnyeat. In *Collected Works*, edited by John M. Cooper. Indianapolis, Indiana: Hackett, 1997.
———. *Timaeus*. Translated by Donald J. Zeyl. In *Collected Works*, edited by John M. Cooper. Indianapolis, Indiana: Hackett, 1997.
Pythagoras. *The Golden Verses*. Translated by Nicholas Rowe (1904). https://www.sacred-texts.com/cla/gvp/index.htm
Quiles, Carlos and López-Menchero, Fernando. *A Grammar of Modern Indo-European* (Third edition). Badajoz, Spain: Indo-European Language Association, 2012.
Ross, David. *Aristotle*. London and New York: Routledge, 1995 (Sixth edition).
Schuon, Frithjof. *Castes and Races*. Translated by Marco Pallis and Macleod Matheson. Pates Manor, Middlesex: Perennial, 1982.
———. *From the Divine to the Human. Survey of Metaphysics and Epistemology*. Translated by Gustavo Polit and Deborah Lambert. Bloomington, Indiana: World Wisdom, 1982.
———. *Light on the Ancient Worlds*. Translated by Deborah Casey. Bloomington, Indiana: World Wisdom, 1984.
———. *The Transcendent Unity of Religions*. Translator unknown. Wheaton, Illinois: Quest, 1993.
Sheldon-Williams, I.P. "The Greek Christian Platonist tradition from the Cappadocians to Maximus and Eriugena." In *The Cambridge History of later Greek and early Christian Philosophy*, edited by A.H. Armstrong, 421–533. Cambridge: Cambridge University Press, 1967.
Sherrard, Philip. *The Greek East and the Latin West. A Study in the Christian Tradition*. Limni, Greece: Denise Harvey, 2002.
Smith, Wolfgang. *Christian Gnosis from Saint Paul to Meister Eckhart*. Kettering, OH: Angelico Press/Sophia Perennis, 2011.
Spengler, Oswald. *The Decline of the West* (Abridged edition). Translated by Charles Atkinson. Edited by Helmut Werner. Oxford: Oxford University Press, 2007.
Spingola, Deanna. *The Ruling Elite. A Study in Imperialism, Genocide and Emancipation*. Bloomington, Indiana: Trafford, 2011.
Taha, Abir. *Twelve Resolutions for a Happy Life. A Manual of Happiness*. Colac, Victoria: Numen, 2015.
Taylor, Thomas. *Introduction to the Philosophy & Writings of Plato*. Seaside, Oregon: Watchmaker, 2010.
Uzdavinys, Algis, ed. *The Golden Chain. An Anthology of Pythagorean and Platonic Philosophy*. Bloomington, Indiana: World Wisdom, 2004.
———. *Orpheus and the Roots of Platonism*. London: The Matheson Trust, 2011.
Watts, Alan W. *Myth and Ritual in Christianity*. New York: Evergreen, 1960.

BIBLIOGRAPHY

Weithman, Paul. "Augustine's political philosophy." In *The Cambridge Companion to Augustine*, edited by Eleonore Stump & Norman Kretzmann. Cambridge: Cambridge University Press, 2001, 59-70.

Wheelock, Frederic M. *Wheelock's Latin*. Revised by Richard A. LeFleur. New York: Harper Collins, 2011 (Seventh edition).

Wilson-Dickson, Andrew. *A Brief History of Christian Music. From Biblical Times to the Present*. Oxford: Lion, 1992.

Yockey, Francis Parker. *Imperium. The Philosophy of History and Politics*. Torrance, California: Noontide, 1962.

Zeyl, Donald. "*Plato's Timaeus*." Stanford Encyclopedia of Philosophy (2009). http://plato.stanford.edu/entries/plato-timaeus/

Index

Abraham, 79
Achilles, 10–11
Acton, Lord, 222
Adam, 86–87, 118
Aesop, 108
Akhenaten, Pharaoh, 79
Alfeyev, Hilarion, 45–46, 56, 60, 69–70, 84, 86, 88, 90, 103–4, 113, 141–43, 154, 160–61, 164, 169, 174
Ambrose of Milan, 158
Anaxagoras, 33–40, 43–44, 93
Anaximander, 10, 113
Anaximenes, 146
Andronicus of Rhodes, 25
Aquinas, Thomas, 28, 50, 70, 144
Arius, 141n14
Aristotle, x, 11, 14, 24–25, 30, 32, 39–40, 48–50, 52, 57–59, 66–67, 73–74, 77, 82, 96–98, 109–11, 127–28, 137, 144–46, 189–94, 236
Arjuna, 12, 78, 131
Atticus, 128
Augustine of Hippo, x, 15, 44, 66, 68, 85–87, 91, 101–2, 112–13, 120–21, 128, 130, 132, 142, 155–56, 193–95

Bach, Johann S., 154–55, 161
Bachofen, Johann, 166–67
Basil of Caesarea, 15, 45, 84, 111, 175
Beethoven, Ludwig van, 154–55, 159, 161
Bentham, Jeremy, 220
Berdyaev, Nicolas, 17–19, 76–77, 87, 104–6, 119–20, 167, 213–14
Bernard of Clairvaux, 156
Bismarck, Otto von, 214–15

Black, Jonathan, 41–42, 62–63
Black Sabbath, 90
Blackburn, Simon, 13, 93, 132, 135, 146, 199, 220
Blair, Tony, 89, 230–31
Blake, William, 131, 137
Bloom, Anthony, 119–20
Boethius, 144, 157
Böhme, Jakob, 19, 122, 137
Bolton, Robert, 114–16
Brahms, Johannes, 122, 154–55, 162
Bucke, Richard M., 135–37
Bush, George, 89, 194, 231

Campbell, C.G., 2, 5, 79, 92, 137–38, 169
Camus, Albert, 12, 44, 61, 85–87, 98–99, 102, 119
Carabine, Deirdre, 19, 28, 70, 105
Carlyle, Thomas, 199–200
Cecilia, Saint, 157–58
Chaboseau, Augustin, 140
Chomsky, Noam, 211
Clement of Alexandria, 45, 101, 156
Cohen, S. Marc, 47, 108, 147
Constantine, Emperor, 158, 175
Coomaraswamy, Ananda, 20, 53, 65, 76, 108–9, 121–22, 131–33, 138–39, 142, 151, 178, 180–81, 227
Cooper, John M., 74–75, 93–94, 124, 148, 187–88, 209
Cornford, Francis, 47–49, 51, 54–56, 61, 73, 99, 109, 125, 147
Curd, Patricia, 34, 93

Daniel, 114, 143
Dante, 137, 142

INDEX

Darwin, Charles, 43, 140
Descartes, René, 199
Dillon, John, 12, 21, 25, 29, 60–62, 68, 98, 100, 128
Diogenes of Apollonia, 38–40
Dionysius the Areopagite, 13, 15–16, 28, 68–70, 76, 84–86, 103–5, 112, 179
Diotima, 17, 75
Disraeli, Benjamin, 207
Dostoyevsky, Fyodor, 81, 119, 123, 160
Dreyer, Petrus, 10, 25, 27, 39–40, 52, 54, 58–59, 66–67, 82, 94, 123, 125, 146, 179–80, 182–83, 188–89, 191, 213
Dugin, Alexander, x, 166, 168, 170–71, 225–26, 227n30, 228–33, 235–36, 238–39

Eckhart, Meister, 13, 18, 24, 28, 37, 109, 142
Eddington, Arthur, 30, 35
Einstein, Albert, 59
Empedocles, 10, 100, 113, 131–32
Engels, Friedrich, 167, 221
Eriugena, John S., 16–17, 28, 70, 105, 142
Euripides, 4, 33
Evola, Julius, 235

Ferguson, Kitty, 45, 145, 147
Flannery, Michael A., 43, 71–72
Fletcher, George, 218
Florovsky, Georges, 86
Friedrich the Great, 199
Fukuyama, Francis, 230

Geldard, Richard, 30, 33–34, 36–38
Gersenshon, Daniel, 38
Gerson, Lloyd P., 12, 21, 25, 27, 29, 35, 47, 50, 58, 60–62, 68, 98, 110, 128
Gilson, Etienne, 102
Gimbutas, Marija, 1
Gödel, Kurt, 150
Goethe, Johann W. von, 210, 224
Goosen, Danie, 21–22, 27, 59, 61, 74, 167–68
Goswami, Amit, 30

Gray, John, 89, 91, 113, 143, 194, 222, 230–31, 234
Greenberg, Daniel, 38
Greene, Brian, 30
Gregory of Nyssa, 84, 129–30, 157, 175
Gregory of Rome, 4, 158
Gregory Palamas, 105–6
Guénon, René, 41, 53, 55, 57, 99, 199, 235
Günther, Hans F.K., 6–8, 78, 114, 132, 168, 210–11, 224, 226

Haeckel, Ernst, 72
Hart, David B., 81
Haudry, Jean, 1–5, 7, 91, 180, 186–87, 191
Hegel, Georg, 140, 200, 227
Heidegger, Martin, 20–21, 24–25, 92, 227–28
Heisenberg, Werner, 42
Heraclitus, 6, 10, 24, 34, 36, 57, 92, 109, 113
Hesiod, 15, 114, 187
Hippolytus, 33
Hitler, Adolf, 113, 186, 217, 225
Homer, 4, 127, 133, 210
Hughes, David G., 158
Hume, David, 205, 227
Huntington, Samuel, 236–37
Hussein, Saddam, 89

Iamblichus, 14, 22, 61, 99, 128, 145, 148, 152
Isaiah, 169

James, Saint, 79
Jeans, James, 35
John Chrysostom, 119, 163, 173n23, 206
John of Damascus, 18, 46
John Philoponus, 111
Joseph, 175
Julius Caesar, 204

Kafka, Franz, 134
Kalachanis, Konstantinos, 15, 31, 111
Kant, Immanuel, 30, 227
Kepler, Johannes, 150
King, Russell, 2

INDEX

Kristol, William, 230
Knuuttila, Simo, 87, 112, 121

Laos, Nicolas, x, 17, 60, 83, 92, 94–96, 101, 105, 108, 110–11, 150, 161, 177, 206, 214, 226–28, 234–35, 237–38
Lazarus, 79
Le Bon, Gustave, 196–97
Lee, Desmond, 26, 51, 95, 126, 152, 178, 180–85
Leibniz, Gottfried, 149–50, 200
Lenin, Vladimir, 217, 222
Lincoln, Abraham, 217–19
López-Menchero, Fernando, 2
Lossky, Vladimir, 13, 16, 18, 20, 63, 84, 102–3, 105–6, 112, 118–19, 175n26
Lucretius, 113
Lundy, Miranda, 148–49
Lyell, Charles, 43

Mahler, Gustav, 133–34, 155, 162
Mandela, Nelson, 89
Marcus Aurelius, 157
Marlow, A.N., 6, 10
Marx, Karl, 143, 221, 234
Martijn, Marije, 41, 99
Mary Magdalene, 170, 175, 206
Maximus the Confessor, 16, 25–26, 112, 175
McKirahan, Richard, 33–34, 37–39, 48, 92, 123, 132, 146–47
Mendl, Robert W.S., 142, 152–58, 163
Mill, John S., 228, 234
Moore, Edward, 12, 44, 59–60, 83
Moran, Dermot, 16–17, 86
Mozart, Wolfgang, 155, 159, 161
Myers, Ken, 81, 155–57

Napoleon, 197, 200, 207
Nasr, S.H., 162n74
Nebuchadnezzar, 114
Newton, Isaac, 150
Nicholas of Cusa, 103, 150
Niekisch, Ernst, 227, 235

Nietzsche, Friedrich W., x, 26, 59, 76, 78, 80, 100, 106, 133, 139, 151, 159, 163n75, 165, 172–73, 176, 181–82, 185–86, 189–90, 196, 199, 201–2, 206–13, 215, 220, 223–24, 226, 235
Northbourne, Lord, 35

Odysseus, 127, 133
Oosthuizen, J.S., 14, 60, 82
Orwell, George, 88
Ovid, 131

Parmenides, 6, 9–11, 16, 24, 36, 48, 57, 92–93
Paul, Saint, 18, 53, 79, 90, 101, 103, 119, 137, 155, 173–74
Pelham, Henry, 206
Penrose, Roger, 30
Pericles, 33
Perl, Eric D., 12, 28, 62, 69, 76, 85, 96, 98, 104, 179
Perry, Whitall N., 11, 15, 19, 46, 75, 88, 103–4, 116, 140, 152, 157, 180, 207
Philaret of Moscow, 19–20, 56
Philo of Alexandria, 103, 109, 121, 151, 163
Pindar, 78
Plato, x, 5–6, 8, 10–11, 13–15, 17, 23–24, 26–28, 32, 36, 39–40, 44–52, 54–58, 60–61, 63, 66, 73–76, 78, 82–83, 91, 93–98, 100, 108–11, 113, 122–29, 132, 137, 146–52, 154, 156, 162, 178–89, 192–94, 199–200, 209–10, 213–14, 217, 221, 237
Plotinus, 12–14, 21, 32, 44, 59–62, 82, 98–99, 106, 110, 112, 132, 137, 156, 163
Plutarch, 138
Popper, Karl, 214
Porphyry, 14, 26, 44, 123, 128, 132, 145, 163
Proclus, 14, 22, 25, 27, 40–41, 46, 55, 61–62, 67, 69, 74, 83, 99–100, 110, 146

249

INDEX

Protagoras, 37, 78, 93
Pythagoras, 6, 32, 42, 77, 123, 132, 145–46, 150–52, 188

Quiles, Carlos, 2

Rhodes, Cecil J., 204
Robespierre, Maximilien, 89
Rose, Eugene, 81n1
Ross, David, 49–50, 67, 74, 77, 82, 97–98, 144, 190, 193
Rousseau, Jean-Jacques, 198–99, 220, 222
Rumi, 131, 142

Schrödinger, Erwin, 38, 42
Schuon, Frithjof, 6–7, 13, 37, 41, 107, 138, 166, 170, 180–81, 234
Schweitzer, Albert, 151, 227
Scupoli, Lorenzo, 104
Sextus Empiricus, 92
Shakespeare, William, 88
Shankara, 131, 142
Sheldon-Williams, I.P., 26, 105
Sherrard, Philip, 27, 29, 56–57, 66–67, 93, 95–96, 102, 106, 238n60
Smith, Adam, 205, 227
Smith, Wolfgang, 24, 28, 101
Socrates, 5, 17, 26, 37–38, 74–75, 81, 93–94, 96, 107, 122–27, 129, 152, 178, 182–86, 212
Soros, George, 227
Spengler, Oswald, x, 141–42, 149–50, 152n47, 164–65, 196–98, 200, 203–6, 208, 210–12, 221, 229

Spingola, Deanna, 218–19
Steiner, Rudolf, 42
Strauss, Leo, 228

Tacitus, 4, 170, 217
Taha, Abir, 140
Taylor, Thomas, 37, 99–100
Thales, 10, 146
Thatcher, Margaret, 230

Uzdavinys, Algis, 14, 100, 107, 124, 127

Vaughan Williams, Ralph, 154
Vernant, Jean-Pierre, 187
Vidal, Gore, 89
Voegelin, Eric, 167
Voltaire, 198–99, 208

Wagner, Richard, 77, 159, 162
Wallace, Alfred R., 42–43, 71–72
Waterfield, Robin, 148
Watts, Alan W., 19, 56, 88
Weithman, Paul, 193–96
Whitehead, Alfred N., 11–12n5
Wilde, Oscar, 177
Wilson-Dickson, Andrew, 148, 154–59

Yockey, Francis P., x, 2, 4–5, 31–32, 63, 135, 142, 171–72, 178, 197–205, 207–8, 218–23, 231

Zarathustra, Prophet, 78–79, 91
Zeno, 10–11
Zeyl, Donald J., 49, 55, 147

www.ingramcontent.com/pod-product-compliance
Lightning Source LLC
Chambersburg PA
CBHW060559230426
43670CB00011B/1885